# THE SUPERNATURAL

# The Supernatural

*Making Room
for the
Power of God*

## A.B. Simpson

CHRISTIAN PUBLICATIONS
CAMP HILL, PENNSYLVANIA

Christian Publications
3825 Hartzdale Drive, Camp Hill, PA 17011

*Faithful, biblical publishing since 1883*

ISBN: 0-87509-565-8
LOC Catalog Card Number: 94-71704
© 1994 by Christian Publications
All rights reserved
Printed in the United States of America

94 95 96 97 98   5   4   3   2   1

# Contents

# *The Present Truth*

*So I will always remind you of these things, even though you know them and are firmly established in the truth you now have. (2 Peter 1:12)*

While all inspired truth is necessary and important yet there are certain truths which God emphasizes at certain times. He is ever speaking to the age and generation, and He never speaks at random but always to the point and to the times.

When the thought of the age was being drawn to the supremacy of one man and taught to recognize the Sovereign Pontiff as the viceroy of heaven and the direct representative of Christ on earth, God raised up John Calvin to emphasize the doctrine of God's sovereignty and to teach the age that He alone had a right to dominate the hearts of men.

When Formalism had spread its soporific influence over the heart of Christendom, God raised up the Wesleys, George Whitefield, Fletcher and the evangelical leaders of that generation to teach the necessity of the new birth and to emphasize the work of the Holy Spirit.

Later an evangelical movement brought into clear and bold relief the doctrine of justification by faith and the premillennial coming of Christ as against the nominal church teachings of the times.

A generation ago God used the ministry of Charles Finney and the testimony of his followers to bring into prominence the doctrine of a deeper Christian life as an antidote to the worldliness and compromising spirit of the times.

And so from age to age God speaks the special message most needed, so that there is always some portion of divine truth which might properly be called *present truth*, God's message to the times. God is always wanting messengers that understand Him and that preach the preaching He bids, and when He can find such instruments He will always use them and bless their ministry.

There is one line of truth which seems to be preeminently present truth and that is the truth about the *supernatural*.

Man has become so much in love with man that he is in danger of overlooking God. The boasted progress of our times has so dazzled us with its secondary light that we cannot see the glorious Sun that is shining in the firmament of God's heaven. The devil is trying to get the supernatural out of the Bible, out of the church and out of our individual Christian lives. He wants to reduce religion to a human science, obliterating everything that cannot be explained on a rational principle and from natural causes, so that even our blessed hope of the coming kingdom is laughed down and man thinks himself all-sufficient to achieve his own destinies and bring about the highest development of the race.

Over against this stands God's revelation of the supernatural. Let us look at it until it dwarfs our human pride into its true insignificance and give us adequate views of ourselves and our times in the light of the infinite God "from whom . . . and . . . through whom all things came" (1 Corinthians 8:6).

# CHAPTER 1

# *The Supernatural God*

*In the beginning God created the heavens and the earth. (Genesis 1:1)*

The first sentence in the Bible brings us face to face not with men, not even with nature, but with God—"In the beginning God." True, there is a verb "created" that follows; but long before we reach that there is an emphatic pause, and the infinite deity stands before us filling immensity and enfolding within His own being the whole creation and the myriad beings that are afterwards to come forth from His almighty hand. The Bible begins with God, and it would be a good thing if every book and every chapter in every life had the same safe and sublime beginning.

The Bible also ends with God. We turn to the last message and we read in the Apocalypse, "I am the Alpha and the Omega, the First and the Last, the Beginning and the End" (Revelation 22:13). He that began as Alpha is ending as Omega, and between these two extremes lies the whole story of redemption.

If we turn to the last verse of the Apocalypse, leaving out the benediction, we find that the Bible ends with Jesus Christ. It begins with God and ends with Jesus Christ—and between these two divine names lies the whole story of revelation.

In beautiful similarity the apostle's great draft upon the bank of heaven, "And my God will meet all your needs according to his glorious riches in Christ Jesus" (Philippians 4:19), begins with "My God" and ends with "Christ Jesus," while between lies all our need and its infinite supply. What a safe and blessed place to be!

In accordance with this majestic beginning God is always projecting His personality and presence upon the scene of the story of revelation and redemption. There is a sublime egotism in the Bible; that which in others would be unbecoming is in Him absolutely right. Over and over again He asserts Himself, and every instinct of our being recognizes His preeminence, His sovereignty and His right to be supreme. It contains just what man needs to know and recognize, the presence and the glory of his God. It shows what our lives need above all other needs, to know Him, to realize His presence and to live under the shadow of the Almighty.

We sometimes meet men who impress us not so much with their own personality as with the presence of God which they carry with them.

This was the characteristic of Enoch. The only thing remarkable said about him was that he walked in the divine Presence. We read of Samuel and Elijah that each was recognized as "the man of God."

This is what we want in our lives, to know God, to walk with God, to be men and women of God and then to minister God to other men and women.

Whenever God called men into a closer relation or sent them on some higher commission, the call was always accompanied with some marked revelation of Himself.

We find Him coming to Abraham at the crisis of his life as *El Shaddai* and then commanding Abraham to rise to a higher place in conformity to the new revelation that He had given.

"I am God Almighty [*El Shaddai*]; walk before me and be blameless" (Genesis 17:1). I am the Almighty, the Absolute, the Infinite, the All-sufficient God. Now live up to the vision you have had, the revelation I have given. Stand straight up to the standard God has given. Live as if you had a God that is all-sufficient.

God told Abraham, "You have not been living thus. You have not been walking before Me. You have been walking before Sarah, before Hagar, before circumstances, before your difficulties and limitations and infirmities. Now lift your vision above all these, look at Me alone and see in Me the God who is enough, and stand upright in uncompromising faith."

And so henceforth Abraham "did not waver through unbelief regarding the promise of God, but was strengthened in his faith and gave glory to God, being fully persuaded that God had power to do what he had promised" (Romans 4:20-21).

The secret of Abraham's faith was his realization of the supernatural God. And so in describing him in the fourth chapter of Romans the apostle says that he measured up to God, "in whom he believed—the God who . . . calls things that are not as though they were" (Romans 4:17).

When God came to Moses to send him forth on his stupendous undertaking, the only thing He sought to impress upon his mind was the supernatural Presence that was to go with him. His one answer to all the fears and doubts of Moses was, "I AM WHO I AM" (Exodus 3:14). He just drew a great check upon Himself and signed it, leaving a blank line for Moses to fill in anything he pleased. He seemed to say, "I am courage in your difficulties; I am power in your weakness; I am victory over Pharaoh; I am sovereignty over the Red Sea; I am bread for the wilderness and water from the rock; I am the guide for the desert and the conqueror for the Midianites and the Canaanites; I am mercy and forgiveness for the gainsaying people that you lead." And oh, that Moses had also added one thing more, "I am grace and strength to keep even you from missing the Promised Land."

And when Moses still parleyed and procrastinated, God answered with that one final word, "I will be with you" (3:12). Later in the story of the wilderness we find Moses falling back on this great promise and crying, "If your Presence does not go with us, do not send us up from here" (33:15), and the answer came, "I will do the very thing you have asked" (33:17). It was God and God alone that made Moses what he was and Israel what it became.

## A New Leader, the Same Presence

This was all the equipment of Joshua for his victorious succession to Moses. "Be strong and courageous. Do not be terrified; do not be discouraged, for the LORD your God will be with you wherever you go" (Joshua 1:9) was the divine assurance. "I will be with you; I will never leave you nor forsake you" (1:5). When a little later Joshua was in danger of looming up too large in his own leadership, God met him and laid him in the dust and took command Himself of Israel's victorious armies of faith. Going forth to reconnoiter the ramparts of Jericho he met a man with a drawn sword, and, true to his soldierly instinct, he challenged him and cried, "Are you for us or for our enemies?" (5:13). The answer that came laid him prostrate on his face. " 'Neither,' he replied, 'but as commander of the army of the LORD I have now come. . . . Take off your sandals, for the place where you are standing is holy' " (5:14-15). I am the Leader and you have but to do My bidding and let Me triumph through you.

It was the vision of God that called Isaiah to his ministry and strengthened him to bear the rejection of his countrymen and to stand alone with God in the midst of a gainsaying people.

## Something out of Nothing

There is nothing finer in the Scriptures than His majestic promise to Jeremiah: "This is what the LORD says, he who made the earth, the LORD who formed it and established it—the LORD is his name: 'Call to me and I will answer you and tell you great and unsearchable things you do not know' " (Jeremiah 33:2-3).

This is a very glorious and inspiring promise but the most glorious part of it is the preface and the name by which God introduces Himself to the prophet: "Thus saith the LORD [Jehovah], the maker thereof" (33:2, KJV)—not the Creator of the universe but the Creator of the thing which Jeremiah is about to ask for. It is something which does not now exist and for which the very materials do not yet appear. It is something which, naturally speaking, is impossible. It is something which God has to cut, not out of whole cloth, but out of no cloth. It is something which must be created in order to become a reality and of which He says, "I am the maker thereof; I will create it at the call of your faith; I will form it and then I will establish it."

This is the faith of which the apostle speaks in the epistle to the Hebrews: "By faith we understand that the universe was formed at God's command, so that what is seen was not made out of what was visible" (11:3). That is to say, it is a faith that believes in the unseen and in the creation of things that are not yet real. It is a faith that can take Him for a gentleness you do not have in your temper, for courage when you are like a trembling reed shaken of the wind, for a steadfast will when you are as irresolute as the drifting sand, for righteousness and holiness when every instinct of your nature and every tendency of your training leads you in the downward road, for health and strength when your body is a wreck and the very elements of health are gone, for souls that seem as hard as adamant, and for service where every door appears to be closed and every effort vain. This is the God with whom we are dealing, the God of the supernatural, "the maker thereof . . . Jehovah is His name." Let us recognize Him. Let us trust Him; let us use Him in His infinite all-sufficiency.

## "My Spirit Remains"

In the book of Haggai there is a beautiful collection of promises in which God tells His struggling little flock, as they are seeking to accomplish the great work of the restoration in troublesome times and with feeble resources, that His presence is with them: "My Spirit remains among you. Do not fear" (2:5). He says this so they may be strong and work with the confidence of success. In this beautiful paragraph it is striking to notice how often the prophet repeats the lofty name. "This is what the LORD Almighty says" (1:2). It is as though God were ever bidding His trembling children to look up in His face to reassure themselves that He was speaking, that He was there and that He was equal to even this emergency.

It is paralleled by that beautiful promise of Christ to Paul in the midst of his infirmities. "He said to me," or to better translate the Greek, "He *kept saying* to me, 'My grace is sufficient for you' " (2 Corinthians 12:9). Over and over again He repeats to us the assurance of His presence and His all-sufficiency.

When Christ was about to give the commission to His apostles to go forth and evangelize the nations, He emphasized to them that mighty assurance of His Almightiness and Omnipresence. "All authority in heaven and on earth has been given to me. . . . And surely I am with you always, to the very end of the age" (Matthew 28:18, 20).

This is the warrant for our missionary enterprise, for our boldest faith, for our loftiest endeavor, for our most difficult undertaking. We have the supernatural Christ to lead us as we go forth against principalities and powers and the forces of earth and hell.

## We Must Recognize His Supremacy

The reason God emphasizes His supremacy is because of man's ignorant and foolish pride. We live in an age of human self-sufficiency when boasting man is saying, "Come, let us build ourselves a city, with a tower that reaches to the heavens" (Genesis 11:4), and God is saying in divine pity and scorn, "Come, let us go down and confuse their language" (11:7).

But it is not in the spirit of our petty egotism that God is ever asserting Himself. It is because His sovereignty is as necessary for the universe as for His own glory. As He repeats the personal pronoun and stands before us in sublime self-consciousness we feel that what would be presumption in any man is right in the case of God, and that it is essential to the order and well-being of the universe that He should be recognized as All in all.

His sovereignty and supremacy are the supply of all our need. The more we become less and let Him become greater (John 3:30) the more our happiness and blessing will increase. Our own self-importance is the greatest hindrance to the revelation of God in our hearts and lives. In order that He may come in, self must go out. The more we die to ourselves the more room we have to receive Him in His fullness.

There is much wholesome instruction in the incident of the lad whose father was reprimanding him because of his poor progress in his studies. The little fellow was complaining that he did his best and that he was not able to remember the things he read. The father had noticed in the boy's room a good many yellow-covered books, and he said, "Charlie, I want you to empty out that basket of apples, on the sideboard."

Charlie emptied out the apples, and then his father said, "Go out to the carpenter shop next door and bring me a basketful of chips and shavings." He did as he was told and when the basket came back it was half full of chips. "Now," said his father, "put in the apples." Charlie put in a few of the apples and they began to tumble off.

"Put them in," said his father, "put them all in."

"I can't," said Charlie, "they won't go."

"Why won't they go?" asked his father.

"Why," said Charlie, "because the basket is half full of chips and it won't hold all the apples now."

"Ah," said his father, "that is the trouble with you. You have been trying to fill your head with wholesome knowledge when it is already crammed with foolish story books."

Carry the story a little higher and we will find the secret of our spiritual failures. We have been trying to fill with the Holy Spirit hearts that are already filled with a thousand things. We have been trying to make Christ King while all the time the old rebel self was in His way and usurping His throne.

## A Foretaste of the Future

Finally, the revelation of God in our hearts and lives is but the overlapping of that glorious revealing of God for which the age is waiting. We are looking for "the blessed hope—the glorious appearing of our great God and Savior, Jesus Christ" (Titus 2:13), and He comes first in the inner vision and then in the outward revelation.

He is projecting His personality upon the heart of His waiting Bride. He is making Himself intensely real to those who will let Him, and for them some day He will burst through the veil of sense and they will cry as they behold Him, "Surely this is our God; we trusted in him" (Isaiah 25:9).

In the old days of New England a company of our Pilgrim fathers was in great destitution, waiting for a ship from England with supplies which was long overdue. One good woman in the company had been praying in strong faith and telling the people that the ship would come in due time. Sure enough, one evening they looked out over Boston Bay and the ship was in full view and their hearts were filled with joy and hope. But when the morning dawned the ship had disappeared. Some of them said it was a mirage, or perhaps a refraction of the coming ship projected by indirect rays of light before the ship itself came into full view, but they felt sure that as they had seen the vision they would surely see the ship. And they did. Before the week was over she was docked in the harbor and was dealing out her stores of bread to the starving colonists.

And so God gives us first the vision of the living, personal, glorious Christ and soon our eyes will see Him and we will be with Him forever. Let us understand Him in all His glory and some day "we shall be like him, for we shall see him as he is" (1 John 3:2).

# CHAPTER 2

# The Supernatural Book

*For you have been born again, not of perishable seed, but of imperishable, through the living and enduring word of God. For,*

> *"All men are like grass,*
> *and all their glory is like the flowers*
> *of the field;*
> *the grass withers and the flowers fall,*
> *but the word of the Lord stands forever."*
> *(1 Peter 1:23-25)*

There is no testimony that needs to be more emphatically pressed upon the hearts of men today than the inspiration and supreme authority of the Word of God. The malignity of Satan and the pride of human culture are striving as never before to eliminate the supernatural from the Holy Scriptures and change the Book of God into a mere collection of ancient writings, saved out of the wreck of the world's literature.

The Bible stands apart from all other books, and has survived and will survive all the attacks of its enemies. It is like the electric torch that shines over the water of New York Harbor, struck by the wing of many a seabird that dashes against it in its reckless flight, but still shining on unmoved while the foolish and reckless assailant falls bleeding and wounded at its feet.

It is an anvil which has worn out many a hammer of hostile criticism, while the anvil still remains unshaken amid the wreck of all that have assailed it.

It stands above all other books in a supreme and sublime isolation. "Bring me the Book," said Sir Walter Scott to his son-in-law, when he was dying. As Lockhart asked him, "What book, Sir Walter," his simple answer was, "There is but one—the Bible."

When Alexander Duff was on his voyage to India with a large quantity of excellent baggage, including a splendid library of more than 800 volumes, the ship on which he was sailing was wrecked off the Cape of Good Hope, and when the rescued passengers reached the shore the only thing of all his baggage that was saved was a Bible that the waves had washed upon the sands. As he picked it up and removed the wrapping he found it was perfectly uninjured, and he was so deeply touched with the incident that he opened it and read some of its precious promises to the little company that stood around him on the shore. All his splendid books had perished, but the Bible remained as the only salvage from the wreck. To him it was a beautiful figure of that which afterward became the object of his life, that the Bible was the only book that would remain out of the world's literature, and the only book which was worth giving to India, the land for which he was going forth to live and die.

## *The Bible Survives*

All the literature of the ages must perish in the flight of time, but, like Duff's rescued Bible, God's Word will live and survive the wreck of ages, and also give to those that embraced it an immortality as glorious as its own.

It is very sad and humbling to see the tendency among so many of those who ought to be the defenders and the teachers of this holy volume to win a little cheap popularity and wear the reputation of higher culture by joining in the ranks of those who, if they do not reject it altogether, will compromise its supremacy and question its infallible authority.

The Bible is either everything or nothing. Like a chain which depends upon its weakest link, if God's Word is not absolutely and completely true, it is too weak a cable to fix our anchorage and guarantee our eternal peace. Thank God, we have reason to accept it as the supernatural revelation of the supernatural God, the word not of man, but the Word of God that lives and abides forever.

It has survived the assaults of its critics as the

ages have gone by. And while not claiming to teach philosophy and science, yet even philosophy and science with all their progress have not been able to establish a single argument against its credibility. While the so-called science of one generation has challenged it, the advanced knowledge of the next generation has but confirmed it.

The time was when the first chapter of Genesis was supposed to contradict the established facts of science by teaching that light was created in the beginning, while the sun and the other heavenly bodies were not created until the fourth day. But a few years later God led science to discover the spectroscope, and with it the fact that light did exist before the sun, and that Moses was in perfect accord with the real facts of nature.

Reverent scholarship is finding out every day that even in the very allusions of God's Word to the sublime facts of nature there are hidden harmonies with the great truths which science is only now discovering, and when Job spoke of the sweet influence of the Pleiades and David sang in the 19th Psalm of the light speaking, they were really teaching some of the deepest facts and latest discoveries of the majestic sciences of optics and astronomy. Out of every conflict this divine Book will come forth vindicated and victorious.

> Like some tall cliff that lifts
>     its awful form,
>         Swells from the vale and midway

> leaves the storm,
> Though round its breast the rolling
>    clouds are spread,
> Eternal sunshine settles
>    on its head.

Let it suffice to bring five witnesses to the supernatural character and supreme authority of the Word of God.

## 1. Miracles

This Book appeals to us by a supernatural test. It claims as its credentials the superhuman power of its witnesses. It appeals to the infinite Creator to certify to its message by the works which are known to be beyond the power of any created agent. The stock objection to miracles which has become famous through the writings of David Hume is that a miracle is contrary to the uniformity of nature and therefore cannot be true, because we are bound to believe the uniform testimony of nature against any single testimony that seems to contradict it. This argument is absolutely as weak and foolish as our experience of nature is limited and partial.

An explorer told a chief from the Upper Congo about the ice of our northern climates, and assured him that he had seen rivers completely frozen over and water become as solid as stone. "Such a thing is contrary to all the experience of nature," replied the chief, and he laughed him to scorn. Such a thing had never been heard of by him or his fathers, or any of the neighboring chiefs, or, in fact, anybody in Central Africa. But his little world was but a segment of a vaster circle.

So David Hume's experience and the experience of the world as he had traced it and observed it was by no means conclusive as to the complete facts even of nature itself. There was a larger circle that he had not compassed, and within that circle the facts of miracles are as real as the facts of the ordinary operations of nature on the lower plane. In fact, some day we will probably find that even miracles are but the operation of the higher laws on a divine plan which we have not understood, that it is the letting down for a moment of the forces of that spiritual realm which some day will be our natural sphere.

But the facts themselves when demonstrated by satisfactory evidences are conclusive seals and attestations of the truth of the testimony which appeals to God through these credentials. Christ distinctly appealed to the works that He did as the evidences of His divine character and the truth of His teachings, and we cannot imagine God, if He be a holy God, answering this appeal and bearing witness to His testimony if it were not true.

The maker and custodian of the great clock in Strasburg Cathedral had a grave misunderstanding with the authorities of the cathedral. Finding them unwilling to yield he quietly touched a spring in the tower and the clock stopped moving. The people wondered, questioned, complained and protested. The authorities employed mechanics and experts and skilled artisans in vain. Nobody could understand the works or make the clock go until at last they were obliged to appeal to the maker and yield to his terms. Then he quietly touched the spring again and the whole mechanism began to move. Because he was the maker he could arrest it and he could restore its operations.

And so there is but one Hand that can suspend the mighty wheels of nature's complicated mechanism, and there is but one Hand that can restore the power when interrupted. And when we see that Hand put forth to close the heavens at the word of Elijah, and then to open the brazen skies and send forth the copious showers at the same prophetic word, we know that He is bearing witness to the word of His servant. When we see the waves stilled, the sick healed, the dead raised, the very Son of God Himself come forth from the sealed tomb, with the distinct affirmation that these are the very credentials claimed by the witnesses who have given to us this Word, what but obstinate and inveterate blindness can doubt that this is indeed the authorized message of heaven, the Word of the living God?

## 2. Prophecy

The shrewdness of the human intellect may succeed in guessing with some degree of probability about the future. But there is an infinite distance between the boldest and wisest guesses of heathen oracles or human sages and the clear, decided predictions of the Holy Scriptures.

The criteria of prophecy are exceedingly simple and obvious:

First, the event predicted must be at a sufficient distance in the future.

Second, the predictions must be explicit and marked by points of identification about which there can be no mistake, such as locality, circumstances, names and so forth.

Third, there must be no apparent cause or train of circumstances that might bring about the event in question which could be known to the author of the prediction.

Fourth, the fulfillment must be open, public and sufficiently witnessed to render all deception impossible.

These are but a few of the tests of prophecy which distinguish them from the guesses of human wisdom, and in these respects the Scriptural prophecies shine in the meridian sunlight of truth.

Let us look for a moment at three classes of prophecies. First, there are the prophecies concerning the nations and political systems of the world. Centuries before the time of their fulfillment a number of prophetic witnesses, including such men as Isaiah, Jeremiah and Daniel, foretold the actual order of the world's great empires, the rise and fall of Babylon, Medo-Persia, Greece, Rome, and the political and ecclesiastical systems that were to come out of Rome. A perfect panorama of the political future of the world was laid out, and all the centuries since have been literally fulfilling it. Now, how could any human guess have ever foreshadowed these stupendous results? The events were too far in the distance to render them probable, and the fulfillment has been open in the face of the universe.

The same conclusion would be reached if we had time to take up in detail special prophecies concerning the fall of Nineveh, the capture of Babylon, the career of Cyrus, the history of nations like Edom, Egypt and Tyre, in the light of which we see a divine presence and exact fulfillment.

The second class of prophecies is concerning the Jews. As long ago as the time of Moses and down through the whole Old Testament, there is a clear line of prophecy pointing out the great facts of their national history, their supremacy among the nations, their fall under the power of the Gentile conquerors, their captivity on account of their sins, their rejection of the Messiah, their dispersion among all nations, their preservation distinct from all other peoples, their restoration ultimately to their own land.

How manifestly all this meets the test already given. There was nothing likely to lead up to that. The fulfillment has been open as the day, and so marked has been their providential history that when the great statesman was asked by one of the sovereigns of Europe what argument he could give for the truth of Christianity his simple answer was, "The Jews, your majesty, the Jews."

The third great class of prophecies are those respecting the Lord Jesus Christ. How explicitly, how exactly the ancient prophecies point out all the circumstances attending His first and second advent, His name, His birth of a virgin mother, the very place of His birth—Bethlehem, His rejection by His countrymen, His life of humility and suffering, His betrayal for 30 pieces of silver, His crucifixion and all the attending circumstances of His death, His resurrection, His coming again. So complete was the chain of Messianic prophecy that the evangelist stops to note at every stage of the last sad drama of His agony how each incident that happened was "that the scripture . . . be fulfilled" (John 19:24, 28, 36). So perfect is the picture that we could construct a biography of Christ from the Old Testament prophecies alone. Who can answer this mighty weight of prophetic testimony? Who can challenge this divine vindication of God's supernatural Book? Who can hesitate to say with holy veneration and humble faith, "Your word, O LORD, is eternal; it stands firm in the heavens" (Psalm 119:89).

## 3. The Life and Character of the Lord Jesus Christ

The story of Jesus is the mightiest proof of the truth of the Gospels. Such a story is absolutely without any explanation unless it is literally true.

Such a character is to us a miracle, and for any human mind to conceive it, invent it, to unfold it in these records would be a literary achievement so stupendous that the author would deserve to be immortalized as himself divine.

Who conceived this marvelous ideal? Whose brain originated this stupendous Book, if it was but a book? As Rousseau has well said, the creation of such a fiction would have been a greater miracle than to believe the fact itself to be true.

Dr. Fisher has forcibly said that this character is original. The world had nothing like it before. It is a blending of all the elements at once of gentleness and strength, of intellectual force and moral perfection, of self-surrender and yet sublime dignity and self-respect. There is no weakness about it, and yet there is no hardness, no selfishness, no pride, no despotic ambition to aggrandize Himself at the expense of others, like all the heroes of human history. It is evidently a sinless and spotless and perfect character. There is not a single failure anywhere. The ideal is sustained throughout consistently with itself, and even in the very tragedy of His death there is a moral sublimity and a triumph of character greater even than earthly success.

Then it is to be noticed that this character is not a study of literary skill, wrought up with any preconceived plan to create an ideal, but it is developed incidentally out of a thousand common occurrences in actual life, unfolding day by day and evidently as unforeseen by the writers as by us. It all grows up naturally out of facts as they develop and it bears upon its very surface the impression of simplicity, genuineness and absolute reality. No man can candidly read these Gospel narratives and not feel that he is standing in the presence of a life that is supernatural and divine, and the book that records it must be the Word of God.

Even the great Napoleon remarked, "I think I understand somewhat of human nature, and I tell you all these were men, and I am a man, but not one is like Him. Jesus Christ was more than a man. Alexander, Caesar, Charlemagne and myself founded great empires, but upon what did the creation of our genius depend but on force? Jesus alone founded His empire upon love, and to this day millions would die for Him. The gospel is no mere book, but a living creature, with a power which conquers all that possess it. Here lies the Book of books upon this table."

## 4. The Influence of This Book

It has revolutionized human society. It has civilized the nations that have accepted it. It is the secret of the greatness and power of the Protestant nations. It goes into the heathen populations, and lo, a cannibal of the South Sea islands is transformed into a gentle Christian, a warring Indian anarchist becomes a peaceful disciple of Christ, a selfish Asian merchant develops into a heroic martyr, and a downtrodden African villager rises to the noblest type of manhood. The polygamist gives up his wives, the sorcerer gives up his superstitions, thousands of men and women become outcasts from their homes and often martyrs for their faith, and the whole phase of human society is stamped with the uplifting impress and the heavenly influence of the Book of God.

Skepticism is well enough to laugh and talk about, but, as Voltaire once said when his infidel friends were discussing their theories at his dining table, "Hush gentlemen, till the servants are gone. If they believed as we do none of our lives would be safe."

## 5. Experiential Evidence

The experience of the child of God, and the internal evidence which it brings to every heart that receives it on its own terms with obedience and trust is the final evidence of the supernatural nature of this Book. Like the Jewish tabernacle which was very coarse and common looking on the outside, but whose beauties could only be seen from within, this blessed Book must be loved to be understood and appreciated. It speaks to the spirit of the child of God with an assurance that awakens the spontaneous sensibilities of his renewed being, and answers like the people of Samaria, "We have heard for ourselves, and we know that this man really is the Savior of the world" (John 4:42).

If you want to know that this Book is true, meet it on its own terms. Take it to your heart, read it with simplicity and candor, test it by obedience, and you will find it is all it claims to be.

In a city where I once was a pastor there was a brilliant lawyer who, with his young wife, attended my ministry. She was a devoted Christian. He was a notorious skeptic, and was recognized as the leading free thinker of the community. I knew it was vain to argue with him, but many hearts were praying for him. At last this lovely girl died. A few days after her death he sent for me to his office, and in a very frank way immediately began to tell me that he had just become a Christian. I was quite surprised, and asked him how it happened.

"Well," he said, "I have read everything on the subject for years, and I never could reach a conclusion. As I read one side of the argument I was partly convinced, but when I read the other the balance turned, and I never seemed quite able to decide between the two. The brain was not strong enough to balance these weights, and so I have been all my life in a state of honest indecision. But while my wife lived with me I saw in her something which I did not possess, and something that I knew to be real; and when she died I saw that it was worth all that I possessed and in the agony of my bereavement I suddenly found myself one day praying to her God. Instantly my reason came to me and protested, and I said to myself, why are you praying to somebody you don't believe in; but before I could stop it the prayer had got into heaven and God had answered it, and something came to my heart that I had never felt before. It was the touch of the supernatural Presence, and it was so exquisite and comforting that I just kept on praying; God kept on answering until this very moment. Although I cannot explain it, I cannot justify it by my reason, yet I know that it is true. I know that it is God and I am a Christian, not through my head, but through my heart."

That is the secret of faith. That is the supreme test. Dare to test it.

> Oh, make but trial of His word,
>   Experience will decide
> How happy they and only they
>   Who in His truth confide.

When you cannot understand the Bible through your brain, take it in your soul, press it to your heart, bring to it your sorrow, your sin, your need; and you will know it is true because it has searched you, it has converted you, and it has satisfied you.

A blind girl lay dying and her paralyzed fingers had ceased to be able to read by touch the raised letters of her precious Bible. With a sad cry she dropped it, and she said, "My precious Bible, I cannot feel any more the touch of your precious promises." Then in an impulse of passionate love she pressed it to her lips to say goodbye, when suddenly she gave a great cry of joy, and she said, "I can read it still; I can feel it with my lips." She pressed it again and again, page after page, to her sensitive lips as she drank in its consolations, and went to sleep with her head pillowed upon its heavenly promises.

Beloved, when all other senses fail, you can read and understand the Bible with your love. It is not a Book for intellectual discussions or brilliant exhibitions of our exegetical acuteness. It is a Book to love! It is a Book to translate into living copies and holy example.

"Each of us is either a Bible or a libel." Let us reverence it. Let us believe it. Let us love it. Let us live it. Let us give it to a perishing world.

> Eternal are Thy mercies, Lord;
>   Eternal truth attends Thy Word;
> Thy praise shall sound from shore to shore.
>   Till suns shall rise and set no more.

# CHAPTER 3

# The Supernatural Life

*I no longer live, but Christ lives in me.*
*(Galatians 2:20)*

The best edition of the Holy Scriptures is a holy life. God wants to translate His supernatural Book into the living experience of all His children.

When someone said to Sir Walter Scott that he was going to write a book, he answered, "Be a book."

When the enemies of the apostles saw the man who had been healed standing in their midst they could say nothing against it. A living, consistent Bible Christian is an unanswerable witness for God and evidence for Christianity in every age. Christ Himself was the greatest miracle of the Gospels and so every Christian should be greater than all his works.

The radical distinction between Christianity and all other religions is in the characters that it produces. "By their fruit you will recognize them" (Matthew 7:16) is Christ's own test. Judged by this test, Christianity is unanswerable. The Christian character is not the product of moral culture. The holiest men are the readiest to acknowledge that in them dwells no good thing, and that every virtue and grace is due alone to the power of the divine Presence as it dwells within them and strengthens them against their temptations and weaknesses.

## *The Fact of Justification*

The first supernatural fact in the Christian life is a divine righteousness or what is termed in the language of theology, justification. The Apostle Paul uses a very fine phrase in unfolding this fundamental principle of the gospel by which man becomes right with God. He calls it the righteousness of God. It is not merely the mercy of God overlooking our fall but it is the righteousness of God settling our account and putting us right with Him. God wants us to stand approved in His presence—not by our own works, but by the imputed righteousness of the Lord Jesus Christ. God meets us at the very threshold when we come guilty, condemned, unworthy and excluded from His favor and His presence. He clothes us in the very merits of His own Son, enabling us thus to look in the face of the very throne and even of the victims and witnesses of our crimes and know that we are without blame, justified and counted righteous in His sight and standing in the same attitude as if we had never sinned. This is the free gift of God—holy, supernatural and divine. We are clothed in God's own righteousness and while we have nothing of our own to boast, yet we can look up in the blessed light of the throne and say,

> Jesus, Thy blood and righteousness
>    My beauty are, my glorious dress.
> Sinless with these garments on
>    I'll face the splendors of Thy throne.

## The Fact of Regeneration

The second supernatural fact of a Christian life is regeneration. This is quite different from justification. The latter makes our relations right with God. The former makes our nature right. It is the divine impartation to the human being of a new life communicated directly from God—pure and holy as His own very being. This is not moral elevation, self-improvement, doing or being better, but a miracle of grace, a new creation, a wonder so stupendous that Nicodemus, a Jewish professor of ethics and religion, could not comprehend it but looked with wonder in the face of Christ and asked how these things could be.

There is nothing parallel to it in nature. Perhaps the nearest analogy to it is the little ichneumon that deposits its tiny eggs through the coarse skin of the caterpillar in its body and leaves them there to hatch in the warm temperature of its victim until they germinate and, feeding upon the flesh of the caterpillar, grow to maturity and then burst the shell and spring into life.

But the ichneumon is a natural progenitor of this germ of life. In regeneration there is no human power that can propagate this life. No man can give it to his brother. No parent can communicate it to his child. "Children born not of natural descent, nor of human decision or a husband's will, but born of God" (John 1:13). The feeblest saint is a new order of being, in the eyes of the angels as marvelous as when Adam stepped out upon the theater of Eden, "while the morning stars sang together and all the angels shouted for joy" (Job 38:7).

## *The Fact of Sonship*

The next supernatural fact in the Christian life is sonship. We enter at once into the heavenly family. This, too, is a surpassing wonder and quite contrary to the precedents of the divine government. Angels were very high in the scale of being, but they dared not enter the family of God; yet sinful man stepped across the threshold of the palace and the prodigal came home to his Father's bosom and claimed a place no archangel can ever know. "How great is the love the Father has lavished on us, that we should be called children of God!" (1 John 3:1) was the cry of John, the man who stood nearest to the very center of the throne.

We are the sons of God by virtue of our being

born of God. We are not only "called" but we "are" the sons of God. Not only are we sons by a decree of adoption but every intuition of the new heart leaps to meet the Father and knows its own delightful place of filial recognition, for we have "received the Spirit of sonship. And by him we cry, '*Abba*, Father' " (Romans 8:15).

We have a still higher claim to sonship by virtue of our union with Christ, the only begotten Son of God. Wedded to Him, we come into His peculiar sonship. And so we are called the firstborn ones, the very name that He holds. As a bride inherits her husband's home and is accepted as a child, so we go in with Him to the innermost chambers of the palace of the King while we hear Him say, "My Father and your Father, . . . my God and your God" (John 20:17).

## *The Fact of Christ's Indwelling*

The indwelling of Christ is the next supernatural fact into which we are brought. This is a transition as stupendous as regeneration itself. "If anyone loves me," Christ says, "he will obey my teaching. My Father will love him, and we will come to him and make our home with him" (14:23). This is not a figure but a fact so glorious and real that the Apostle Paul declared it to be the very secret which had been hid from ages and from generations but which at last had been made known to the saints and which was committed to him to give as a talisman of the victory and the secret of heaven's own life to the children of God.

## *The Fact of the Baptism of the Holy Spirit*

The baptism of the Holy Spirit is the fifth supernatural fact of our life. While the same in its effects substantially as the indwelling of Christ and while it is through the Holy Spirit that we come into union with Him, yet it is a distinct privilege and experience of the Christian life. The prophet Ezekiel, in describing the experience of a converted soul, after telling of the new heart and the new spirit that He would put within them adds this higher promise, "And I will put my Spirit in you and move you to follow my decrees and be careful to keep my laws" (Ezekiel 36:27). God's own Spirit comes into the new spirit. It is not only that we have a new heart but we have the Almighty God residing in that new heart. So stupendous was the change which this brought to the apostles after the day of Pentecost that all men took knowledge of them that they had been with Jesus. They were clothed with a new power. They were invested with a divine authority and efficiency by which their words brought conviction to the consciences of men, and the works of the risen Christ were wrought through their hands, and all men felt a supernatural presence and power around them and upon them.

A supernatural holiness becomes a fact of our lives, for sanctification is not our personal virtues, graces or attainments, but it is the life of Christ manifested in us. The finest definition of it is given by Paul in First Corinthians 1:30-31: "It is because of him that you are in Christ Jesus, who has become for us wisdom from God—that is, our righteousness, holiness and redemption. Therefore, as it is written: 'Let him who boasts boast in the Lord.' "

Sanctification is here distinctly recognized not as our character but as the inworking and the outworking of Christ's own life in us. He is made unto us of God our righteousness, our sanctification just in order that we may not glory in our own goodness but may recognize everything we are and do as the grace of Christ.

This is the same thought expressed by John in his Gospel where he says, "From the fullness of his grace we have all received one blessing after another [grace for grace, KJV]" (John 1:16). That is, His grace gives to us the supply which constitutes the different graces in us. Do we want humility? We take Christ's Spirit within us to be the spirit of humility. Do we want patience and love? We put on Christ as our patience and love and He works out in us and relives through us His own longsuffering, unselfish life. Out of His fullness we thus receive even "grace for grace" and when the work is accomplished we do not stand before our fellow men as paragons and patterns of superiority, but examples of the free and sovereign grace which they may have as well as we.

Not only does Christ give us a supernatural supply but a supernatural standard of holiness. In this respect Christianity differs from all human ethics. Chinese morality had crystallized itself in a proverb not unlike our golden rule though not nearly so clear and strong. But even the golden rule does not express the highest standard of New Testament holiness. "Love your neighbor as yourself" (Leviticus 19:18) is the Old Testament morality; "A new command I give you: Love one another. As I have loved you, so you must love one another" (John 13:34). This is the supernatural standard of Christianity. "Be perfect, therefore, as your heavenly Father is perfect" (Matthew 5:48). This is an aim transcending the highest dream of the world's teachers. "Love your enemies, do good to those who hate you, bless those who curse you, pray for those who mistreat you" (Luke 6:27-28).

This, when exemplified in living obedience, awes the human heart and convicts it of a power superhuman and divine.

Divine guidance is one of the supernatural privileges of the Christian life. For every consecrated soul God has a distinct plan and a divine program lifting it above all common lives and making it marked and sublime. It may be a very simple life and exercised in a very humble sphere but the fact that God is shaping, molding and using it gives to it a dignity unspeakably high. The life of a Joseph, the life of an Esther, the life of a Paul is a romance of providence, and every one of us may possess such a charmed life and know that God has made of us a pattern of our earthly temple and is building better than we know.

When the great Hildebrand was dying, he told

some of his friends that the secret of his life was that he had taken St. Peter as the patron saint of his whole career and that all along the way he felt that the influence of this mighty spirit was directing all his ways. How much better for us to take Peter's Master as the pattern of our life and let Him so possess it that He will have a loving pride in making out of us the very best possible for a trusting soul and a human career.

Along with this it may be added that divine providence enters directly into the life of the child of God. Especially is this true when our whole life is dedicated to God and conformed to His high calling. Then for us the promise becomes true, "in all things God works for the good of those who love him, who have been called according to his purpose" (Romans 8:28). This is not true in the same sense of every Christian but only of those who are living according to His purpose, as stated in the context, "to be conformed to the likeness of his Son" (8:29).

If that is the character of our life and if we thus truly love and live for God with the singleness and strength of an undivided heart, we will find that all the wheels of providence move at the touch of the Hand that is leading us.

How wonderful is the story of providence in God's Word and especially in the lives of those who truly belonged to God. He ruled and overruled in the stories of Joseph, Moses, Nehemiah, Daniel, Philip in his meeting with the eunuch in the desert and Peter in his marvelous deliverance from prison while his pursuer was stricken in the same hour by the hand of God. How inadequately we realize and claim that overshadowing promise that covers all our way, "All authority in heaven and on earth has been given to me. . . . And surely I am with you always, to the very end of the age" (Matthew 28:18, 20). How often we forget that the affairs of nations and even the business of the world moves simply for the sake of Christ and His people. He is Head over all things for His body, the Church. Our vast political systems and commercial activities are but the agencies through which He is preparing the way for the witnessing of the gospel and the evangelization of the world. Oh, to ride forth with Him in His chariot and see Him triumph over all our enemies and His! This is the supernatural privilege of the sons of God and the service of Christ.

There is no wonder more supernatural and divine in the life of the believer than the mystery and the ministry of prayer. The mighty statesman Daniel turned away from his official task and the courtly visitors that awaited him, and for three whole weeks was prostrate on his face in prayer before the throne of a greater king than Cyrus. As he prayed, the earth's mightiest conqueror was unable to sleep. He called for the archives of his kingdom and the records respecting the Jews, and when the morning dawned, sent for his scribe and dictated this decree: "The LORD, the God of heaven, has given me all the kingdoms of the earth and he has appointed me to build a temple for him at Jerusalem in Judah. Anyone of his people among you—may the LORD his God be with him, and let him go up" (2 Chronicles 36:23).

How did this heathen conqueror know about the Lord Jehovah? What did he care for Israel's God? What cared he for fear or favor respecting the little captive bands of Israel in his land? What but a touch from the throne could put such a thought in his heart or such language on his lips? Ah, it was the answer to Daniel's prayer. It was the moving of a scepter which is touched in the silent closet. Those captive bands arose and started forth on their homeward way with Zerubbabel, Ezra and Nehemiah; the temple was raised from its ruins; the city walls were restored; the ages rolled on until the Son of God Himself preached the gospel of the kingdom. The vision given Daniel in answer to his prayer does not close until the latest ages have all rolled by and the course of empires is finished and the vision of prophecy fulfilled and the times of the Gentiles ended and the Lord Himself has come.

Wonder of wonders! Mystery of mysteries! Miracle of miracles! The hand of the child touching the arm of the Father moves the wheels of the universe. Beloved, this is your supernatural place and mine, and over its gates we read this inspiring invitation, "Call to me and I will answer you and tell you great and unsearchable things you do not know" (Jeremiah 33:3).

# CHAPTER 4

# *The Supernatural Church*

*Christ loved the church and gave himself up
for her to make her holy, cleansing her by the
washing with water through the word, and to
present her to himself as a radiant church,
without stain or wrinkle or any other blemish,
but holy and blameless. (Ephesians 5:25-27)*

There is a social and collective element in our
human life, and therefore, Christianity involves not only a supernatural man but a divine
society. Adam represented the race as a whole
and Christ also has a people who are bound
together by certain ties of life and fellowship and
united under certain common characteristics as
an organic whole.

Early in the story of the human race we find
humanity divided into two great societies. One is
called the sons and daughters of men, developing
in the family of Cain, the other the sons of God,
connected with the family of Seth.

Immediately after these two lines separate we

find this remarkable statement in Genesis 4:26: "At that time men began to call on the name of the LORD." More correctly this passage may be translated, "At that time men began to call themselves by the name of the LORD." This was the organization of a divine society and it was organized with a divine name. They called themselves by the very name of the Lord as God's own special people.

In beautiful harmony with this we find in the early chapters of the New Testament that the society of believers also took a special name. This was the name of Christ. "The disciples were called Christians first at Antioch" (Acts 11:26) and it has been happily suggested by one that this name was probably given not merely by the world around them but assumed by themselves as linking them more closely and directly with Christ. They were a divine society—Christ ones, literally.

Now, the Church of Jesus Christ is a divine society and there is no truth that has more need of emphasis in these days of compromise than the supernatural character and destiny of the Church of the Lord Jesus. Christ Himself announced its heavenly character before He left the world, as, referring to His own divinity, He declared, "On this rock I will build my church, and the gates of Hades will not overcome it" (Matthew 16:18).

In the later teachings of the Holy Spirit through the inspired apostles the doctrine of the Church is unfolded with great fullness and the fundamental principles of this divine society are brought out with great clearness under the three striking figures of the building, the body and the bride.

## Called by His Name

The Church has a divine Head. "For no one can lay any foundation other than the one already laid, which is Jesus Christ" (1 Corinthians 3:11). So intimately is He connected with it that in the 12th chapter of First Corinthians, the great chapter of the Church, it is even called by His very name, not the Church of Christ, but Christ: "The body is a unit, though it is made up of many parts; and though all its parts are many, they form one body. So it is with Christ" (12:12). He identifies Himself here with the Church just as a man is identified with his own body.

No human name is big enough to dominate the Church. No single doctrine is important enough to give name and character to the Church of Christ. Methods have their place, but that place is not important enough to constitute a Methodist church. Baptism is very dear to every believer in the Bible, but baptism is not near enough the center to justify the establishment of the Baptist church. Presbyterianism recognizes the equality of the ministry but even this is not of sufficient consequence to substitute for the name of Jesus the name of Presbyterian. Episcopacy recognizes the dignity of the bishop and the sacredness of the government of the Church but an Episcopal church is a lower name than the dignity of

Christ's Church demands.

It is well for us to recognize in the life and fellowship of Christ all these sections of the circle, but it would be much more to the honor of Christ if all were lost in His all-glorious name. He is the Head of the Church. He alone should govern and control it. He alone should be its end and aim, its all in all.

The Church has a divine constitution. "See to it that you make everything according to the pattern shown you on the mountain" (Hebrews 8:5) was the law of the ancient tabernacle and it applies to the Church of which that tabernacle was the type.

Man cannot construct a church according to his theories and preferences. God has settled the question of its worship, ordinances and membership, and any society which claims to be a church and is not founded upon a regenerated membership, the inspiration of the Word and that supernatural presence, power and authority of the Lord Jesus Christ, may be a Sunday club or a literary Lyceum—but it is not the Church of the Lord Jesus Christ.

The Church has a supernatural life. We must be born into the Church. We cannot be added to it. We are added to Him, as the passage in Acts (2:41) literally should be translated, and that adds us to the Church.

"For we were all baptized by one Spirit"—or rather, *in* one Spirit—"into one body—whether Jews or Greeks, slave or free—and we were all given the one Spirit to drink" (1 Corinthians 12:13). It is not only *by* the Holy Spirit, but *in* the Holy Spirit that we are united to the Church. A simple figure will illustrate the difference between the two prepositions.

That ship in the sea is connected with the sea, but not part of it. They are distinct substances. But it is very different with the mighty river, the Hudson, which this moment is flowing into the sea and is now merged in the sea. The Hudson is part of the sea. It is blended with it; they are one.

That is the way we become members of the Church. We partake of the common life of the body through the Holy Spirit.

This was brought out in the typical story of Eve's birth and marriage. She was made out of Adam with a common life, and then she was given back to Adam to be his bride.

So the Church is born out of Christ's life, and then put back into Christ's arms as His beloved.

Nothing less than this supernatural life can ever constitute true membership in Christ's Church. Sacraments will not do it. Subscriptions to the Church funds will not do it. Official position will not do it. The laying on of hands and rites of ordination or confirmation will not do it. It is a heaven-born oneness—a unity of life.

In the Church of Ephesus there was a fine organization; there was a great deal of work. There was a great zeal for orthodoxy and a deliberate hunting down of heretics; but, notwithstanding all this, Christ was so grieved and even disgusted that He was about to remove the candlestick of Ephesus out of its place simply because they had left their first love and their life, as He literally expressed it respecting another of these churches, was "about to die" (Revelation 3:2).

## Not of This World

The Church has a supernatural object. She is not an earthly kingdom, but a heavenly people. As truly as her Master can she say, "My kingdom is not of this world" (John 18:36). What has she to do with vast endowments, social preeminence, parliaments of religion, mayoralty contests, political campaigns and royal patronage? It is hers to go "up from the desert, leaning on her lover" (Song of Songs 8:5). It is the mark of the false, earthly, apostate church that she is seen sitting on the beast of earthly power, allied to the arm of flesh, and bearing as her seal the boastful legend, "She sits supreme over all the world" (see Revelation 17).

The beginning of the great apostasy was the ambition of the first prelates and bishops of the early Church to have the foremost place in the banquets of the Emperor. And that little strife about who should go in first to dinner or stand in the Church was the beginning of the very papacy itself.

Alas, even in our democratic age the bribe of the world's favor and the popular applause of the multitude has proved as fatal to the Church's purity and left her with Laodicea, which means to "please the people," basking in the smiles of the world, but standing on the very verge of the awful and impending judgment of her indignant and insulted Lord.

What are the great objects of the Church of Christ? First, she must worship God and glorify her Father in heaven. Second, she must bear witness to the truth. She is called the pillar and crown of truth—that is, as the pillar supports the archway with its inscription, so the Church is called to uphold the great archway of revelation and hold before the world the testimony of God. And therefore her heavenly object is propagation, evangelization, to gather to her bosom the sinful world, to instruct and build them up in the life of Jesus, to be the training school for heaven and to give the gospel to all mankind. This is her heavenly calling. She is the only divine society on earth, the only institution that is essential and eternal, the only one that will survive the wreck of time and the dissolution of the present age. Let us understand her high calling and oh, let her be true to it!

## The Church's Source of Power

The Church is endowed with supernatural powers. To her is given the baptism of the Holy Spirit. In her abides the living heart of Christ while the Head sits upon the mediatorial throne controlling all things for her good.

Christianity differs in this from all other systems. Each of them had a head, but the heart is cold to death. The heart of Christianity is the

Holy Spirit living still in all the omnipotence of God in the bosom of the Church and quickening her with her Master's risen life. It is He that uses her testimony to "convict the world of . . . sin and righteousness and judgment" (John 16:8). It is He who clothes her messages with "the power of God for the salvation of everyone who believes" (Romans 1:16). It is He who gives wisdom to her leaders and efficiency to her plans. It is His presence that separates her from all other societies, and makes this her distinguishing glory, as Moses said of Israel of old. Her object is not to lean on mighty intellects or large wealthy, powerful organizations, but upon the living God.

And He has clothed her with supernatural powers in the physical realm. When John sent to Jesus for the credentials of His ministry the answer given was, "Go back and report to John what you hear and see: The blind receive sight, the lame walk, those who have leprosy are cured, the deaf hear, the dead are raised, and the good news is preached to the poor" (Matthew 11:4-5). These are still Christ's confirmatory signs for His true Church. God forgive her for having so long surrendered them! God help her to reclaim them in these last days, to keep them in their true place and yet never to ignore them. They are like the jewels on Rebekah's robes, the earthly insignia of Isaac's love. Her robe is holiness; her jewels are the gifts of power.

Christ intended that His Church should embrace all forms of ministry for all classes of need—the sick, the orphan, the stranger, the poor, the ignorant, the lost. Oh, for the revival of apostolic and primitive Church life! Oh, for the vision of the woman clothed with the sun, crowned with stars and the moon, the lower light of earth's midnight, under her feet (Revelation 12:1)!

The Church has a supernatural support. The ascended Christ with all the resources of His providential government is her Head and Light. As He sends her forth her all-sufficient guarantee is this: "All authority in heaven and on earth has been given to me. . . . And surely I am with you always" (Matthew 28:18, 20).

As the bride of the Lamb and the co-heir of all His boundless wealth, what business has she to go about with her hat in her hand begging the petty pittance of their gifts from the brewers, distillers, gamblers and speculators of the earth, selling tickets for strawberry festivals, broom drills and indescribable follies of every kind and vainly competing with the literary lecture bureau or with the cheap theater for platform entertainments to draw the masses, and sometimes stoop even to the promiscuous dance to attract visitors to her Sunday school picnic or help out the deficiency in the preacher's salary? God convict her and God deliver her!

## A Calling from God

The Church has a supernatural destiny. Her calling is to be the glorious Church, and some day when He presents her to Himself "without stain or wrinkle or any other blemish" (Ephesians 5:27), bright with all the glory of the apocalyptic vision of the New Jerusalem, brightest of all with the reflected light and beauty of her Bridegroom and her Head, she will be the wonder of the universe; and they will come from every star to gaze upon her while the attendant angels will say, "Come, I will show you the bride, the wife of the Lamb" (Revelation 21:9).

A beautiful old legend intimates that in the very center of man's first paradise was a temple of gems, where Adam worshiped God in the days of his unfallen innocence. Its floor was of shining gold and its walls were of carbuncles, jaspers, rubies, emeralds and amethysts; its dome was a blazing diamond. But in the ruin of the fall that temple was torn to fragments and all the pieces scattered over the earth, and today we find them in little broken gems in the hearts of the mountains and in the depths of oceans. By and by, the legend tells us, in the age to come they are to be crystallized again into a yet more glorious temple, the vision of John, the New Jerusalem.

Well, whatever the legend amounts to, at least, we know that the children of God today are scattered, like jeweled fragments, in every race and clime, but they are gems of unparalleled preciousness and value. Next to Christ, the most precious thing on earth is Christ's people.

All our work here is but imperfect. Builders are like Solomon's workmen in the mountains, sending off one by one the stones and timbers but not seeing the building yet. The Church will rise in silent majesty as Solomon's temple rose, and as we look upon its stately splendor, its external foundations, its celestial towers, its glorious brightness, its supernal light, we will not be sorry for the toils and tears we gladly gave and the song we often sang:

I love Thy kingdom, Lord,
 The house of Thine abode,
The Church our blessed Redeemer bought
 With His own precious blood.

In conclusion, let us never dwarf the glorious conception of the Church of Jesus by identifying it only with our little sectarian conceptions. Let us love and cherish every branch of the true Church of God, but let us rise above them all to the divine conception, and in all our fellowships, associations and alliances let us steadily hold that great communion of saints which is part of the Apostle's Creed and the eternal hope. It has been said: "We are not come-outers. We are come-uppers and go-outers." Stripped of its colloquialism it just means, lift the Church higher and carry the gospel further to a dying world, and so hasten the day when He will come to the general assembly and Church of the firstborn ones who are written in heaven, to the New Jerusalem and innumerable company of angels, to God, the Judge of all, and "the spirits of righteous men made perfect" (Hebrews 12:23).

# CHAPTER 5

# The Supernatural Body

*And if the Spirit of him who raised Jesus from the dead is living in you, he who raised Christ from the dead will also give life to your mortal bodies through his Spirit, who lives in you. (Romans 8:11)*

The redemption of the body is an accepted truth of Christianity. The chief difference among Christians is with respect to the extent of its application. Many believe that this part of our redemption is only to be realized at the close of the present age in the translation and resurrection at the coming of our Lord. Others of us have been led to believe that we anticipate in the present life to a certain extent the power of our future resurrection, and that we have a foretaste of heaven.

This, we believe, is what is meant by the use of the word "earnest" (2 Corinthians 1:22, 5:5, Ephesians 1:14, KJV) or "firstfruits" (Romans 8:23) applied in several instances in relation to the work of the Holy Spirit in our bodies. An earnest is a first installment, a pledge in kind of the thing which is afterward to be given in full. As the earnest of our spiritual future, He gives us in our spirit the foretaste of the heavenly glory; as the earnest of the resurrection of the body, He gives us the physical life of Christ in our mortal body. He anticipates in our material form now, as far as we are able to receive it, that which we will enjoy in boundless fullness in the body of glory in the ages to come.

An earnest is the very same in kind but less in degree than that of which it is the pledge. Therefore, if the Holy Spirit is to be the earnest of our physical resurrection, it must be through some physical operation in our being now.

We believe that we will have a supernatural body in the heavenly world, but we also believe that we begin to receive the elements of that body now, if not its form at least its vital element and the hidden power which is to animate it then.

## The Blessing Is for Today

We are always putting forward God's blessings to some future time instead of accepting them now, if not its form at least its vital element and the hidden power which is to animate it then. We are like poor Martha who, when our Lord had said to her, "Your brother will rise again," timidly pushed it forward to the distant future and answered, "I know he will rise again . . . at the last day." Jesus gently reproved her error and answered quickly, "I am the resurrection and the life" (John 11:23-25). It was as if He had said, "Martha, do not postpone the blessing your faith would claim but take Me for it now. The resurrection when it comes will come through Me and where I am there is the power of the resurrection. I am speaking to you in the present tense; I have for you a present blessing." Then He proceeded to expand the thought in every direction that we have been explaining. "He who believes in me will live, even though he dies; and whoever lives and believes in me will never die" (11:25-26).

He seems clearly to teach us that believing in Him we receive the life which passes through death to us, or rather rises above it and lives on forever, tunneling through the dark of the tomb and passing on in unbroken, uninterrupted being into the larger life beyond.

This then is the truth which we desire to unfold from the Holy Scriptures, that we may possess even now, through the Lord Jesus Christ, a measure of supernatural life and strength in our mortal frame sufficient to enable us for all the pressures and duties of this life and sustain us until our life's work is done.

We see some foreshadowings of this great truth in the story of the fall. In consequence of sin man was instantly debarred from the tree of life, which was the symbol and source of his physical immortality. But while this supply of perpetual physical life was withdrawn it was not forever precluded, for God erected at the gate of Eden a glorious medium of approach to His presence described as the cherubim and the flaming sword "which turned every way, to keep the way of the tree of life" (Genesis 3:24, KJV).

This symbolic figure of the cherubim and the sword we do not believe are emblems of divine judgment so much as of divine mercy. The Hebrew verb here is *Shekinah*; literally, He "shekinahed" the cherubim and flaming sword. We know that the Shekinah and the cherubim as they reappear in the later symbols of the tabernacle were tokens of the divine mercy and Jehovah's covenant with Israel, and we cannot but think that the fiery sword was some supernatural light, perhaps the Shekinah itself, which indicated the presence of God and the blessing on the worship.

That which we have associated with terror and repulsion was the first gate of mercy open for fallen man and the sense in which it was to "keep the way of the tree of life" might more properly be expressed by using the word "guard." It was to guard the way and to guide the way to the tree of life. From that tree sinful man was debarred on the natural plane, but he could now approach it on the higher plane of grace. His physical life was forfeited by his fall, but it could be won back again by the great redemption of which that cherubic sign was the glorious symbol.

We get back our lost strength now, not through nature but through the supernatural, not through the toil of Eden or the efforts of the flesh but through the Lord Jesus Christ, our redeeming Lord and our living Head.

Coming down the line of divine revelation we next meet with a distinct recognition of the supernatural life of God in our bodies in the story of Abraham, Sarah and Isaac. Here the strength of nature was allowed to fail before the seed of promise could be born. It was something like a foreshadowing of the birth of the Son of God which was not in a natural but in a supernatural way. Isaac, the seed of promise and the first type of the coming One, could not come into life until the natural life of his parents had withered and by a directly supernatural touch God had given new life even to their bodies.

## Believing God for Your Body

This is what Paul meant in his description of Abraham's faith. We are told that he considered his body "as good as dead" (Romans 4:19) without being discouraged, for he was strong in faith, giving glory to God and looking directly to Him, by supernatural means, to make good that for which nature had no resources. Could there be a more signal and emphatic object lesson of the fact that God would lift the hearts of His people to a divine source even for the strength of our mortal frame? Could there be a more striking foreshadowing of the supernatural body which Christ has been preparing for the members of His mystical body?

The story of Israel was a significant illustration

of the supernatural physical life which God can give His children. All through the wilderness they were physically sustained by directly divine agencies. The very symbol of their life was a burning bush that burned and was not consumed (Exodus 3). This great sign which preceded Israel's call out of Egypt embodied in itself the idea of tremendous pressure overcome by infinite strength and divine protection. This was the story of the chosen people all the way through.

Indeed, Moses himself in reviewing it tells us that the very object of God in leading them as He did along the pilgrim way was to show them and teach them that "man does not live on bread alone but on every word that comes from the mouth of the LORD" (Deuteronomy 8:3). It was an illustration of a supernatural physical life while walking with God and drawing life directly from Him.

As this was true of the nation as a whole so it was also true of the most prominent individuals in the nation. Therefore we see that Moses' own life was distinctly supernatural. He began his great work at the age of 80 when most men would be writing their will and preparing for their funeral, and at the age of 120 we are told that his eye was not dimmed nor his natural force abated, but he calmly climbed a lofty mountain and in his full maturity stepped into the chariot of God and passed in victorious strength and voluntary surrender into the glory.

The life of Caleb was also supernatural. Surely

he had enough to break his heart and wear out his life in the strivings of a gainsaying people who kept him nearly half a century out of the promised land. But, when an old man of 85, we behold him standing before Joshua and asking as the choicest privilege of his life the opportunity of leading an assault upon the stronghold of the Canaanites, the old citadel of Hebron, and declaring, "I, however, followed the LORD my God wholeheartedly. . . . Now then, just as the LORD promised, he has kept me alive. . . . So here I am today, eight-five years old! I am still as strong today as the day Moses sent me out; I'm just as vigorous to go out to battle now as I was then" (Joshua 14:8, 10-11). He attributed his whole physical strength to the blessing of God and the blessed results of obedience and fidelity.

## *Physical Strength and Righteousness*

But God has given us a still more distinct object lesson of this great principle of the supernatural body in the wonderful story of Samson. The one purpose of his life seems to have been to illustrate the connection between physical strength and rightness with God. When true to his Nazirite vow of separation and filled with the Spirit of God, he was a giant of unequaled muscular might. But when he broke his sacred vow of separation and lost the Holy Spirit he became as weak as unspun flax and sank helpless in the hands of his foes. Probably he did not lose an ounce of weight but he lost the secret of his strength, the life of the Holy Spirit. It is not the size of a wire that constitutes its strength. A little hair wire filled with an electric current is mightier than one of the cedars of Lebanon. It is the fluid that sweeps through it that makes it strong.

And so the supernatural life in which God is leading those who are willing to learn and to follow is not the result of physical culture but is the unfolding of the divine life and the anticipation of the unseen forces of the world to come.

The same great principle is illustrated in the story of David, who constantly recognized his military prowess, his courage and the strength of his victorious arm as due to the touch of God. He was clothed with a supernatural body and he could say of Jehovah, "He trains my hands for battle; my arms can bend a bow of bronze" (Psalm 18:34); "who . . . heals all your diseases, who redeems your life from the pit . . . who satisfies your desires with good things so that your youth is renewed like the eagle's" (Psalm 103:3-5).

But as we turn to the New Testament the very first view we obtain of the Lord Jesus Christ, our great Teacher and Example, is in this very connection. We see Him standing in the wilderness going through His first conflict with Satan and living out for us that great object lesson of our own life. The first of these temptations was a physical one, the temptation to secure His bodily strength from human sources. And how did He meet it? By the very passage we have already quoted from Deuteronomy, by the very lesson He had learned from the story of Israel in the wilderness. The devil was trying to persuade Him that He must get out of this strait by some means and that He must resort to earthly measures of relief. He replied by telling Satan, "Man does not live on bread alone, but on every word that comes from the mouth of God" (Matthew 4:4). He did not deny the place of the human and the earthly in supporting the life of man, but He did protest against being dependent upon the human and the earthly.

Bread has its true place but it is not "bread alone." There is something more for a man to say than "I must live." The true thing to say is, "I must meet God in my trial, I must learn my lesson, I must accomplish the purpose for which He has brought me here, and the purpose for which He has brought me here is to show that He is all-sufficient even for my body. I must stand there until this purpose is fulfilled. I must throw myself upon Him until He gives me relief and deliverance."

It is very significant that in this quotation Christ does not say the Son of Man but He says "man." It is very plain that He means the lesson for all His disciples. It is for us as well as Him.

## Avoid the Extremes

It is true there is danger of extremes. All truth has its possibility of extravagance. There is a reckless disregard of the natural. God does not mean to teach us that. There is a place for food and sleep but we have not learned to enjoy that rightly until we have also learned that, if necessary, God can strengthen us even without them.

Beloved, is not our trouble this, that in the hour of testing we are more anxious to be delivered than to meet God's thought and glorify God's grace? What Christ was concerned for in that conflict was not so much to get bread as to show the all-sufficiency of God and stand obedient to His Father's will, trusting implicitly His Father's love.

Our blessed Lord has taught us this deep spiritual truth in one of His most profound discourses and left for our guidance through the Christian age the great principle on which He Himself built His own life and overcame the assault of the enemy in His body. That discourse was so marked in its teachings, so deep and heart-searching in its scope that most of His disciples were unable to accept it and, indeed, with the exception of the Twelve the whole of His Galilean flock grew tired of such deep teaching and utterly deserted Him on account of it. "This is a hard teaching," they replied. "Who can accept it?" (John 6:60).

That sermon was the wonderful discourse given about the living Bread in the sixth chapter of the Gospel of John. The one thought that pervades it is that we are to draw our lives both spiritually and physically directly from the Lord Jesus even as He draws His strength from the Father. Its one keynote is the profound verse, "Just as the living Father sent me and I live because of the

Father, so the one who feeds on me will live because of me" (6:57).

By eating Him, He explains explicitly that He means taking His flesh and blood as the source of life and strength. He tells us that this will give us an eternal life, life that will flow on even until the resurrection, for He adds in connection with it, that He will raise us up at the last day. As the babe lives upon its mother's life, the believer lives on Jesus' and the profound words become more true than any language can express, "in him we live and move and have our being" (Acts 17:28).

But this profound truth receives its deepest, largest unfolding in the later teachings of the Holy Spirit through the ministry and example of the Apostle Paul. It runs like a golden principle from the heavenly fountain through all his teachings and experience.

## *The Lord for the Body*

With great vividness Paul unfolds the doctrine of our union with Jesus Christ, our living Head. "We are members," he says, "of his body" (Ephesians 5:30)—of His flesh and bones. The Lord is for our body and the body is for the Lord. Our bodies are the members of Christ and the temples of the Holy Spirit. The Spirit that dwells within us "give[s] life to [our] mortal bodies" (Romans 8:11). This certainly cannot mean our future body as it shall be raised from the tomb. It is the "death-doomed" body, as Rotherham happily translates it—the body in which the Spirit is now dwelling, liable to death, but not yet dead; and divinely equipped, exhilarated, renewed by the indwelling life of the Holy Spirit.

In the fourth chapter of Second Corinthians he unfolds this doctrine of the supernatural body more fully than anywhere else. There he tells us that his natural life is constantly exposed to death "so that the life of Jesus may also be revealed" in his mortal flesh (4:10).

This life of Jesus is something more distinct from and far transcending his own natural life. When they dragged him through the streets of Lystra and hurled him on the pavements as one dead the life of Paul was about gone, but it was then that the "life of Jesus" came to his relief and as the disciples stood around him in prayer and his own sinking heart was lifted up to heaven, there came a touch of divine quickening and he rose upon his feet and went forth again to his work on the borrowed strength of heaven.

So he went through life, not strong in himself, but saying that "we have this treasure in jars of clay to show that this all-surpassing power is from God and not from us" (4:7). And so, quoting from the fine translation of Rotherham, he adds, "On every side we are pressed hard but not hemmed in; without a way but not without a by-way; pursued but not abandoned; thrown down but not destroyed, at all times the putting to death of Jesus in the body bearing about; that the life also of Jesus in our body might be made manifest" (4:8-10).

Space and time will not permit us to follow at greater length this sublime thought. We will only add one other illustration of it in his reference to the thorn in the flesh which is perplexing so many inquirers and expounders.

Now the principle we have been unfolding supplies the very solution of this difficult case. Supposing for the time that Paul's thorn was not literally removed in answer to his prayer, still the fact would remain that something was given to Paul in exchange which was better for him than if it had been removed, something in kind which really supplied the place of its removal. He calls it the power of Christ. It was not the comfort and consolation of Christ's love. It was not patience to bear it, but it was actually power through which he was enabled to do more than if the thorn had been taken away, so that he could say a little later, "The things that mark an apostle— signs, wonders and miracles—were done among you with great perseverance" (12:12). He actually affirmed while this thorn was still remaining, "when I am weak, then I am strong" (12:10).

Assuming then that it was a physical infirmity and that it was not taken away, yet it was perfectly certain that something was given to him that constituted real strength, ample strength, superior strength to even his own perfect soundness and health.

This is the very thing of which we have been speaking. It was an invisible life. It was a supernatural source of vitality. It was not a bigger wire, but a stronger current through the wire. It was the life of Jesus instead of the life of Paul.

## Inner, Not Outer, Strength

This will explain many a perplexing experience with divine healing. Your actual physical condition is not always taken away, but if you would only keep looking to Jesus you would find an inner strength given to you, a supernatural spring in the depths of your being, a vigor and vitality that made you superior to the drain upon you of that depressing symptom and that carried you in spite of it with winged feet through all the pressures of your physical life.

God is thus trying to teach us to live in the unseen realm, to walk upon the waters of the spiritual sphere, to tread the seeming void by faith and find a rock beneath.

And so he sums up his sublime argument for the supernatural body in the fourth chapter of Second Corinthians by that passage which apart from this principle would be obscure: "Therefore we do not lose heart. Though outwardly we are wasting away, yet inwardly we are being renewed day by day" (4:16). As this whole discussion is about the physical life he must mean that the natural and material sources of our spiritual strength are failing, but the hidden and divine source within our being is renewed and strengthened. But he tells us that this is only while we look not at the things which are seen but at the things which are not seen. It is only while we dwell on the experience of faith in the immaterial realm, in the unseen region where God lives and we live with Him, having food to eat that the world knows nothing about (John 4:32), appropriating our very life from the heart of the risen Son of God.

In conclusion this great truth of the supernatural body is an intensely practical and present truth for answering unbelief. It is an answer to the unbelief of the age. Professor Tyndale challenged the disciples of Christ to produce an actual physical miracle. No wise man was rash enough to take up that challenge so presumptuously made, but God took it up. From that day there have been literally thousands of cases of divine healing as remarkable in many respects as those of the apostolic records.

God wants us today to show the unbelieving world that His presence and power are real on every plane of human life and experience, and although He will not give us signs when we tempt Him by asking for them, yet He will make us signs to the unbelieving world and confirm His Word with signs following if we are faithful to the testimony and claim by faith the fulfillment of His own promise.

## Spiritual and Physical Intertwined

The experience of a supernatural body is a blessed auxiliary to the deeper life of the soul. The body is a conducting or a non-conducting medium of the Holy Spirit in His communications to the spirit, according as it is in harmony with God or out of actual touch with Him. Someone has used the phrase "a converted body." There are bodies that are divinely touched and there are others that are as cold and gross as the clods of clay beneath our feet. When God has to pass through the medium of a course physical organism to get into the heart there is obviously a distinct hindrance. There is a great difference between taking your dinner on a hot plate or a cold plate; a cold plate chills the best dinner ever served. And so the Holy Spirit wants the medium through which He ministers to our spirit to be itself spiritual. When our whole physical being is permeated with the presence of God and the baptism of the Holy Spirit, we are in more distinct touch with God's thoughts, influence and suggestions. Our very environment is holy and heavenly and the walls of the city are protected from the incursions of the enemy as well as the citadel itself.

Merely natural health and material and organs have about them an inborn tendency to selfish and even sensual gratification, but when Christ fills our hearts the very desire for unholy things is removed and we are saved from innumerable suggestions of evil that spring from the strong sensuous life of those who have never felt the touch of God in their mortal frame.

Divine healing in its deepest and highest sense saves from a thousand liabilities to self-indulgence and earthliness of thought, feeling and act. Our whole being becomes a well-tuned instrument on which God can play, and we learn to glorify Him in our body which is His, while the spirit sympathizes with the divine touch in all the lower realms of nature and every avenue of our being is thrown open to the unfolding presence of God, so that we cannot tell where the body ends and the spirit begins, but "HOLY TO THE LORD" (Exodus 28:36, Zechariah 14:20) is written on every fiber of our being.

## Preparation for Service

The experience of this supernatural life greatly enhances our efficiency for service. Not only does it save us from innumerable physical hindrances and sources of selfish misery, murmuring and depression, not merely does it give us increased vigor and ability for arduous service and long endurance, but the quality of the service given by a body that is divinely touched is much higher. The voice that speaks and sings for God has more power in its tone and ministers grace more directly than if we were merely using an instrument of clay. The feet that are divinely touched not only go faster to bear the messages of God, but they accomplish more directly spiritual results. The grip of the hand is different. The grip of the hand communicates something which could never be expressed without this added touch of heaven.

It is not only the divine message and a divine

messenger but the very medium through which it goes has been spiritualized and made sacred by being itself steeped in the fountains of heavenly life and power.

Finally the Church of God needs especially today a new touch of supernatural power in the confirmation of her testimony to the world and especially to the heathen world.

While, as we have said in a former chapter, this truth is liable to extravagance, yet there is even a greater danger of overlooking it and sinking to the low plane of naturalism and rationalism in giving our testimony to mankind. In every age it ought still to be true: "God also testified to [the gospel] by signs, wonders and various miracles, and gifts of the Holy Spirit distributed according to his will" (Hebrews 2:4). If the Christ of Christianity is "the same yesterday and today and forever" (13:8), the Christianity of Christ ought also to be the same yesterday, today and forever.

# CHAPTER 6

# The Supernatural Hope

*While we wait for the blessed hope—the glorious appearing of our great God and Savior, Jesus Christ. (Titus 2:13)*

*As you look forward to the day of God and speed its coming. (2 Peter 3:12)*

In the opening verses of the chapter in Second Peter from which the last of these two texts is taken, the apostle speaks of a school of thinkers who would arise in the last days and should say, "Where is this 'coming' he promised? Ever since our fathers died, everything goes on as it has since the beginning of creation" (2 Peter 3:4). This is but another form of expressing the very doctrine which a certain school of philosophers and scientists are promulgating in this very day.

It is substantially the principle of the doctrine of evolution. Its vital principle is this: the things that are have been evolved out of similar things in the past and they will go on developing into similar unfoldings in the future. There has been no real crisis suspending the natural order of things and there will be none. Therefore, such a harsh, strained doctrine as that of the interposition of the supreme Being directly in the future history of this planet, and His advent on the stage of earth in personal form, does violence to all the finest instincts of culture and all the established principles of science.

It is the devil's own trick of trying to reduce everything in the universe to a rational basis and eliminate the supernatural not only from the past but from the future history of the human race, and making man and nature all sufficient and all in all.

Now, nature itself bears witness against this false assumption. The profoundest scientists themselves tell us that this world carries within its bosom the elements of destruction, and that in the very nature of things there are causes at work leading up to a great final catastrophe in the very orbits of the heavenly bodies. Humboldt himself, the prince of scientists, predicted a great terrestrial collapse at some future period in the lapse of ages. As Peter tells us in this passage, even the recent past of our planet's history bears witness to a tremendous convulsion when the flood of waters swept the whole human race away, foreshadowing the greater fact yet to come, when the flood of flame will wrap the world in final conflagration. The story of the past has not been evolution but revolution and a still greater catastrophe looms before us in the vision both of nature and of prophecy.

Then besides, the whole framework of our human life bears witness that the present is but an imperfect foreshadowing of something greater and more abiding. All we feel and see and know today is but the embryo of a boundless future. The deepest instincts of our nature tell us of a larger sphere, a loftier life and a more abiding home. Here we have scarcely learned to love when the grave closes over the objects of our affections. Our plans are only made when the rude hand of death or change dissolves the vision and defeats the project. Life is full of broken columns and new-made graves. The very creation groans for some better day and some great Deliverer. Every voice within us seems to cry,

> Beyond the flight of time,
>   Beyond the reign of death,
> There surely is some brighter clime
>   Where life is not a breath,
> Nor life's affections transient fires
> Whose spark flies upward and expires.
>
> There is a world above
>   Where parting is unknown,
> A long eternity of love
>   Formed for the good alone;
> And faith beholds our lost one's here
> Translated to that glorious sphere.

Thank God the light of revelation is clear and cloudless respecting this blessed hope. Undimmed and increasing it shines from the dawn of revelation to the glorious consummation.

## Biblical Figures

Away back at the gate of Eden the mystic figure of the cherubim was a type of redeemed humanity, first in its glorious Head and ultimately in all its members. The face of the lion spoke of its kingliness; the face of the ox its strength; the face of the man its perfect humanness; the face of the soaring eagle its loftiness and union with the divine. All this was to be accomplished first in Christ and then in His redeemed ones. It was like a photograph placed at the gate of Eden showing the future glory of his race to poor broken-hearted Adam as he went forth a fugitive from the paradise that he had lost.

That is the vision God gives to every man who will accept restoration through the Lord Jesus Christ. Lost and sinful we may be, but someday we will be as glorious as our exalted Head.

Next we see this blessed hope as the theme which Enoch first preached and afterward exemplified. He was the first prophet of the second coming and when his ministry was finished God bore witness to it by taking him away to realize in his own person the glorious hope to which he had testified.

Noah and the deluge through which he passed set forth in figure some of the greatest truths connected with the Lord's coming. While Enoch represented the translated saints who will be caught up before the storm, Noah represented rather the people of Israel who will pass through the tribulation and come out, as he did, on the other side to inherit the new earth. The times of Noah were typical of the times of the Son of Man, and the whole story of his supernatural deliverance foreshadows the closing days of the Christian age.

Abraham in like manner lived under the power of this coming age. While he received the land of promise in covenant yet he himself was a stranger in it and he died in faith of an inheritance which he should afterwards receive. The very reason why he so sacredly cherished the only spot on the ground he owned in Canaan, the cave of Machpelah, was because it was the burial place of his beloved wife and the pledge of God's covenant of the future inheritance of the land in the glorious resurrection. God's promise to him was for a thousand generations and it is not hard to conclude that those promises must yet be far in the future in their ultimate complete fulfillment.

In like manner Joseph showed his faith in the supernatural hope by giving commandment concerning his bones when dying. He wanted his very dust to have a part in the future inheritance of the land when he, with the saints of Israel, should stand in his lot at the end of days.

Time would fail to trace this hope through the psalms of David and the history of the Old Testament prophets. Suffice it to say that as the old dispensation came to its close amid the wreck of Israel and the utter failure of humanity to accomplish God's purpose, the light of the better hope began to shine amid the gathering darkness. Isaiah, Ezekiel, Jeremiah, Zechariah and, above all, Daniel looked out upon the distant future and saw and told the wondrous panorama of the ages and the glorious coming of Christ which was to be the consummation. Like the New Testament the Old closes with a grand apocalypse of the future.

## The Life of Christ

The ministry of the Lord Jesus Christ was crowned at its highest point with a sublime object lesson of His own future advent. At the very time when He was turning from His marvelous work in Galilee, He took His disciples with Him to the heights of Hermon and for one bright lustrous hour He let the veil fall from the face of His deity and shed forth in all its effulgence His advent glory. In His own transfigured face and form they saw Him as He will come again, while in Moses and Elijah they had the vision, first of the sleeping dead as they will be raised and then of the living as they will be translated. All this, Peter tells us, was a vision of the power and coming of the Lord Jesus intended to cheer his heart and comfort others in view of the dark tribulations which were just before them.

In His last discourse, however, He formulated

the message of His coming with great fullness and, as He sat upon the side of Olivet the last week of His earthly life, He delivered with great definiteness and vividness the successive events of the Christian age and especially of its closing chapter. These wonderful discourses contain the substance of all later prophecies respecting the advent and are worthy of the profoundest study.

But after Pentecost the Holy Spirit unfolded this great truth with greater fullness. All the apostles are witnesses to it. Even on the day of Pentecost they clearly pointed out the connection between the Holy Spirit and the coming of the Lord. The two last promises of Jesus as He went away were the baptism of the Spirit and His own literal return. One of Peter's early sermons referred with great definiteness first to the "times of refreshing" (Acts 3:19) which the Spirit was to bring from the presence of the Lord, and then to the "time . . . to restore" (3:21) which the Lord Himself was to bring when the heavens which had received Him would give Him up for His final advent.

Paul wrote two of his epistles, the letters to the Thessalonians, with special reference to this great truth and again and again refers to it in all his letters as his own blessed inspiration and expectation.

Paul tells much of the "blessed hope" (Titus 2:13) and James, the most practical of them all and furthest removed from mysticism or dreaming of any sort, tells the struggling and oppressed

Christian of his day to leave their wrongs to be adjusted, not by trade unions and labor strikes, but by the coming of the Lord. And John, nearest to the Master's heart, and latest to give out His last messages, closes the sacred canon and seals the book of inspiration with the sublime Apocalypse which is one long bright vision of the Lord's coming and the events which precede and follow it.

The order of the New Testament is similar to the Old in its general scope and structure. There is first the narrative of facts; second, the teaching of the deeper spiritual truth; third, the prophetic revelation of the Father. God cannot trust us with the glorious doctrine of His coming until we are first established in the facts of Christianity and in the depths of the Spirit. Above all doctrines it is the least fitted to play with, to talk about, to lightly hold as a theory. We need to be deeply rooted and grounded in Christ before we can wisely grasp it or give it forth. But after we have received the Spirit in His fullness, one of His special ministries is to show us things to come, to open the gates of vision and unfold the prophetic Word.

## The Visible Appearing of Christ

Now, as the Holy Spirit has revealed this glorious hope, its supernatural character will appear in several particulars.

First, it will bring a supernatural revelation of Christ. If we accept the fact that the Lord Jesus

once resided upon this earth as a supernatural
Man, why should it be thought strange that He
should revisit it and dwell upon it for a longer
time as its sovereign Lord? Christians of every
name believe that the divine Person that once
walked upon this earthly scene is residing somewhere now in the heavens in His actual and
visible personality. It would be but a slight transition for Him to return in person to the world
where He once dwelled. This is the common
sense of the doctrine of the Lord's coming. "This
same Jesus, who has been taken from you into
heaven, will come back in the same way you have
seen him go into heaven" (Acts 1:11). Of course,
His coming will be different in this respect, that
the veil of humiliation which obscured His deity
during His earthly ministry will be forever
dropped and He will shine forth in all the majesty
of His deity and His universal lordship.

That this must mean a literal and visible appearing should scarcely need to be demonstrated.
The strange theory of later centuries, which has
been accepted by so large a portion of the Christian Church, has practically explained away the
force and meaning of this blessed hope. According to this spiritualizing interpretation, the
promise of His coming is substantially fulfilled in
His personal indwelling in the hearts of His
people and the triumph of the truths and principles of the gospel among all nations.

Now, in reply to the first, it is enough to say
that the New Testament apostles enjoyed the in-

dwelling of Christ as fully as any human being may expect to during the Christian age, and yet they constantly looked forward to an actual coming of Christ as the supreme object of their hope.

In respect to the other, it ought to be conclusive to remember that uniformly in speaking of Christ's coming the Holy Spirit represents the world at the time of His appearing as in no sense under the influence of the truth of the Spirit of God but really at the lowest ebb of sin and spiritual declension. If the Lord's coming is really the triumph of the truth, what can we make of such passages as these?

> When the Son of Man comes, will he find faith on the earth? (Luke 18:8)

> As it was in the days of Noah, so it will be at the coming of the Son of Man. (Matthew 24:37)

So far from the horoscope of prophecy revealing a future of Christian progress and worldwide righteousness under the present dispensation, the prophetic vision portrays an age of increasing unbelief, worldliness and sin growing more aggravated toward the close, while the true church of Christ as a little flock stands in the midst of prevailing declension, witnessing for Christ and waiting for His appearing. That appearing is always represented as a clearly marked and unmistakable event, as manifest and as transcendent as the lightning which shines from one end of heaven to the other. It is a great supernatural fact and the central figure of it will be the person of Christ Himself revealed in all His glory not only before the admiring eyes of His saints but before the vision of a startled world.

## *Transformation of Believers*

Second, the believers will be supernaturally transformed. This blessed hope is going to bring not only the glorified Christ but the glorification of His saints. Those who sleep will be raised from the dead by a supernatural and instantaneous manifestation of the almighty power of Christ, and the living will be changed immediately afterwards. The change which will come to both will bring a complete transformation into the perfect likeness of their glorified Head.

The event is described in the most transcendent language. He "who, by the power that enables him to bring everything under his control, will transform our lowly bodies so that they will be like his glorious body" (Philippians 3:21).

In his argument from analogy in the 15th chapter of First Corinthians, the Apostle Paul gives us some hints of the transcending glory of the resurrection body. He tells us it will be a spiritual body and a celestial body. It will be substantially the same as the body that sank to the tomb and yet it will be unspeakably different. The resemblance will be similar to that of the bare grain which we plant in the soil to the beautiful plant which springs from it covered with blossom and abundant fruit. As the orange tree with its fresh and fragrant blossoms and its golden hanging fruit is to a little dry orange seed planted in the soil, so will the body of the glory be to this corruptible form which we lay down at death. "It is sown in dishonor, it is raised in glory; it is sown in weakness, it is raised in power; it is sown a natural body, it is raised a spiritual body" (15:43-44).

The blessed truth of the resurrection and the glorified body is beyond the search of human philosophy and science. It is not a truth that can be learned by the ordinary processes of human knowledge. It is distinctly supernatural, and it must be accepted by faith as a doctrine of divine revelation.

And yet, even nature has some beautiful parables of it. The process of germination from the buried seed is a divine type of the resurrection. The exquisite silver jewel, which the chemist can dissolve in acid until it disappears from view and then by precipitating some new acid into the solution can bring it back again and cast it into the crucible, remaking it in some more beautiful form, is another prototype.

This is man's rude anticipation of God's glorious supernatural redemption. The supreme illustration and confirmation of this stupendous truth must ever be the simple fact that Christ Himself, the Head of humanity, has died and risen from the dead, and His glorified body is the pattern and guarantee of our resurrection.

## Amazing Changes in Nature

Third, the material world will have a supernatural transformation. Not only will man be changed, but his home will be the subject of a transformation quite as wonderful. The traces of sin and the memories of suffering and death will be obliterated. The cemeteries will disappear. The awful fact of death will be but a memory of the distant past and the cemeteries will not only give up their dead but will cease to separate and destroy. The wild and savage instincts of the lower orders of creation will be subjected; the lion will become gentle as the ox; the wolf will lie down with the lamb; the asp and scorpion will cease to sting; the feebler orders of the natural creation will no longer groan under the law that makes them a prey to the stronger.

The very law of gravitation will be changed and in the New Jerusalem the streets will be vertical as well as horizontal and we will pass up and down as freely as we pass to and fro, for earth's attraction will be forever broken and the center of gravitation will be the Lord Himself. The barren desert will "blossom as the rose" (Isaiah 35:1, KJV). Earth's climates will be changed and "The sun will not beat upon them, nor any scorching heat" (Revelation 7:16), nor will the biting frosts and winters distress again in the new earth's summerland of love. Earth will be a heaven below. Paradise will be restored. The curse will be canceled and all that infinite wisdom, love and power can do to make this planet the paragon of nature will crown the glorious work of complete redemption.

## *A Change in Government*

Fourth, this blessed hope will bring a supernatural transformation in the providence of God and the government of the world and the universe. Man's government has been proved and tried and found a pitiful failure.

In the vision of Daniel the kings of earth are represented as a destructive power of so many wild beasts, but the glorious promise is given that the saints of the most High will at length take the kingdom: "Then the sovereignty, power and greatness of the kingdoms under the whole heaven will be handed over to the saints, the people of the Most High. His kingdom will be an everlasting kingdom, and all rulers will worship and obey him" (Daniel 7:27). Christ Himself will be the sovereign Ruler of the world. Zechariah has told us in the most definite language, "The LORD will be king over the whole earth. On that day there will be one LORD, and his name the only name. . . . Then the survivors from all the nations that have attacked Jerusalem will go up year after year to worship the King, the LORD Almighty, and to celebrate the Feast of Tabernacles" (Zechariah 14:9, 16).

This is the very song of the redeemed saints: "You have made them to be a kingdom and priests to serve our God, and they will reign on the earth" (Revelation 5:10).

The very promise of the closing vision of the Apocalypse is, "Blessed and holy are those who have part in the first resurrection. The second death has no power over them, but they will be priests of God and of Christ and will reign with him for a thousand years" (20:6).

Among earth's vast burdens has been the curse of corrupt government; her political and social systems will never be right until He will come whose right it is to reign. Christ's coming is the only remedy for the wrongs of society and the disease of the body politic. Let us be true to the responsibility of Christian citizenship but let us ever remember that our citizenship is in heaven whence we are expecting earth's true King.

The new adjustment of this earth will affect all other worlds. There is a sense in which Christ's redemption is to reconcile all things both in heaven and on earth. Just what all this will mean is impossible even in the light of Scripture to foretell fully, but beyond the millennial years there will certainly be a larger and grander unfolding in the ages of ages resulting at length in the new heavens and new earth, wherein righteousness alone will dwell and the application in some way of the great principle unfolded and established in the story of human redemption to all the distant worlds of space and all parts of God's universal empire. Perhaps these constellations are yet to be distant colonies from this redeemed planet, and the vast dominions and principalities over which the saints will reign as the promised reward of their service and fidelity here.

The forms of human life during these coming ages are sufficiently outlined to make this at least clear: during the millennial age there will be three distinct peoples upon this planet. First will be the nations of earth which will still exist on the human plane as they do today, excepting only that they will be the subjects of Christ's kingdom and enjoy the blessed privileges of His universal reign of righteousness and peace.

The next will be the Jewish nation which is to continue in fulfillment of the promise to Abraham and David for a thousand generations. This will be the supreme nation, and Israel from Jerusalem will exercise a worldwide influence of a sovereign city, governed directly by God Himself and fulfilling the high conception of ancient theocracy without its imperfections and mournful failure. David is to reign over his ancient kingdom as the direct vice-regent of Christ, and Abraham is to enjoy with all his seed the glorious fulfillment of the mighty promises for which he has waited so long, and Israel is to realize literally as a nation the yet-unfulfilled vision of ancient Hebrew prophecy.

But there will be a third race, namely, the risen and translated saints who will reign upon the earth and yet possess a heavenly life and a spiritual body. Their government of the world will be under the immediate direction of the Lord Jesus Christ Himself, their ever-present King.

They will be the executive officers of this kingdom and their power may be similar to that of angelic beings, who now have so prominent a part in the affairs of nature and are employed by God in controlling the affairs of nations and checking and counteracting in human affairs the hate of Satan and the objections and oppositions of wicked men.

The risen saints in the millennial age will have free and constant access to the material world and the whole system of human life, visiting men and often engaging in conflicts with them, but living on a far higher plane. Like the angels who came to Abraham and like the Lord Himself during the 40 days, they will doubtless be able to eat and drink and sit down in simple loving fellowship at human tables and in earth's family circles, but they will not need the nourishment of food, refreshment of sleep or the supply of present physical wants. Their life will be supernatural and directly sustained from the Lord Himself. As Christ has told us, they will be in some sense like the angels who "neither marry nor [are] given in marriage" (Matthew 22:30), neither can they die anymore, being the children of the resurrection. It may be that we will dwell with our glorified Lord not exactly on earth but perhaps above it in the New Jerusalem, which may be the dwelling place of the saints during the millennial age as well as afterwards, a city let down from heaven, yet touching earth and in constant intercourse with its inhabitants.

## Blessings of This Hope

We need, of course, to be careful of ideal or daring speculations respecting things which so far transcend our present range of thought and conception, and yet we know enough of our Lord's resurrection life during the 40 days to inspire our hearts with the most delightful anticipations of the glorified life that awaits us so soon, and of which He has said to us respecting many a fond hope which perhaps we could not prove and yet which we dare to cherish, "If it were not so, I would have told you" (John 14:2).

## Antidote to Humanism

In conclusion, the supernatural hope of the Lord's coming is a present truth because, in the first place, it is a true antidote to the humanism of our age. Self-sufficient man is building his tower of Babel and projecting his future utopias of ambition and imagination. But over all these God is laughing from the heavens and saying, "I have installed my King on Zion, my holy hill" (Psalm 2:6). Let men dream their fond and foolish dreams. Let them make their investments and calculations for centuries to come, but we look for "the city with foundations, whose architect and builder is God" (Hebrews 11:10).

## Explanation of History

Second, this blessed hope is the only explanation and key for facts of human history and providences and the problems and perplexities which they create. All the past becomes plain if we read it in the light of God's plan, and contemporary history is reduced to simplicity as we see in the center of all the movements of our time God's distinct purpose to prove earthly governments a failure, to overrule the affairs of states and nations for the calling out of His people from all lands, to preserve the seed of Abraham distinct from and supremely above all other races, and to put down the systems of iniquity which are hindering His purposes concerning Israel and the Church. Read in the light of prophecy, the rise and fall of Babylon, Persia, Greece and Rome can be understood; we can understand the broken maps of Europe and the dismembered kingdoms of the past; we can understand the rise and decadence of Papal and Muslim powers; we can understand the supremacy of the English people; we can understand the growing strength of Russia in the north; we can understand the Turkish massacres, the Armenian horrors, the outbursts of Muslim fanaticism, the persecution of Israel, and enjoy the remarkable rallying of the nation around the standard of Zion and the hope of a speedy restoration of their national existence. We can understand the increasing commercial activity and strange wickedness of our age. We can see the deeper life of the little flock and the broader enterprise of worldwide missions. He that is Head over all things for His body, the Church, is preparing the last great conflict and marshaling the forces of earth and heaven for the day of the Lord.

## Our Highest Inspiration

Again, this supernatural hope is the highest inspiration of Christian life and work. There is no truth more inspiring, calling us out from this doomed earth to fix our hopes and ambitions in the coming kingdom. There is no truth more sanctifying, impelling us to make sure not only of the white robe of holiness, but the wedding robe of the deeper love that alone can fit us for the meeting with our Bridegroom, and calling us to receive the baptism of the Holy Spirit as the oil in our vessels which will save us from the folly and failure of the foolish virgins.

## Incentive to Service

In like manner, it is the great incentive to diligent and faithful service. We are working intelligently with a well-defined aim and a glorious expectation. We are not beating air and looking in vain for the conversion of the world, but we are cooperating with our coming Lord and giving the gospel as a witness to all nations as the one last condition preceding His advent. Christians are the men most intensely aroused to the necessity and importance of this great work because they understand the times and know what Israel ought to do, and are giving out in the last two movements of our age the message to the streets and lanes of the city, and the message to the highways and hedges and the outcast millions of the world.

## A Convicting Message

And we believe that this blessed supernatural hope constitutes the most convincing and convicting message to lost men, and especially to the unevangelized nations of our time. There seems to be some special emphasis in the phrase, "gospel of the kingdom" (Matthew 24:14), used in connection with witnessing unto all nations before the end comes.

It seems to be suggested at least that the messengers are to go forth with a specific warning of the immediate coming of the King. May it be that we have not used as definitely and emphatically as we might this great message of such world-awakening power.

We remember that when Jonah went to the Ninevites as an ambassador of heaven with a stormy announcement that within 40 days the King of kings would deal in judgment with one of the wicked nations of earth, the whole nation from the king to the lowest slave were moved to fear and repentance, and in sackcloth and ashes sat and obtained the mercy of Jehovah.

We know that when Paul preached to the Thessalonians this must have been his message to them, for he tells them in his first epistle that they turned from idols to serve the living and true God and wait for His Son in heaven.

We remember also that in the last missionary

picture of the Apocalypse, the angel who bears the everlasting gospel to all kindreds and nations and tribes and tongues (Revelation 14:6) proclaims to them that the hour of God's judgment has come and calls upon them with the stupendous call to meet their Judge. This is the present truth not only of the Church of God against the worldliness and skepticism of our Christian lands but especially the present truth which we are to go forth as ambassadors for Christ and deliver with divine authority and emphatic pointedness as His last message to the ungodly nations of the heathen world.

It is an encouraging fact that today the great majority of foreign missionaries at present on the field fully believe this truth. May the Lord give wisdom and power rightly to divide it and mightily to proclaim it to a careless world.

## CHAPTER 7

# *The Supernatural Work*

*We are his workmanship, created in Christ
Jesus unto good works, which God hath before
ordained that we should walk in them.
(Ephesians 2:10, KJV)*

The apostle here declares that our works are
"prepared" (for that is the true translation of
the word "ordained") "that we should walk in
them." They are not our works, but His supplied
to us through the Holy Spirit and the inworking
of Christ, and we just work them out "with all his
energy, which so powerfully works in [us]"
(Colossians 1:29). Our whole life must be supernatural to the close, and our very service must be
received before it can be performed—"receiving a
kingdom that cannot be shaken, let us be thank-
ful, and so worship God acceptably with
reverence and awe" (Hebrews 12:28).

We must have supernatural power for our
work. We must pass the sentence of death upon
our natural enthusiasm, energy and zeal; and,

dying to our own strength, we must receive power through the Holy Spirit and do our work in Him.

Moses had to be rejected when he stepped forth at the age of 40 in his own enthusiasm to deliver Israel. Afterwards, when he came back at 80, a broken man, humbled and conscious of his inefficiency, God could use him, like His own rod, an instrument in the hands of Jehovah.

Christ Himself continually recognized His power for service as divinely supplied. "By myself I can do nothing," He said; "I judge only as I hear" (John 5:30). "It is the Father, living in me, who is doing his work" (14:10). Therefore He did not begin His public ministry until He received the Holy Spirit and there was added to His divine Personality a second divine Personality—the third Person of the Godhead. And as He went through His earthly ministry there were two Persons united in His life work, the Son of God and the Spirit of God. He chose to be dependent upon the Spirit in order that He might be the more perfect type of us in our dependence.

Therefore His disciples were bidden to tarry in Jerusalem until they should be endued with power from on high. They were not permitted to go out in their own strength, but had to lean upon the Spirit for their wisdom, courage, faith and complete efficiency.

## *Wait for the Holy Spirit*

No man is fitted for the humblest service in the

Church of God until he receives the divine baptism of the Holy Spirit. The mother needs it in the nursery, the Sunday school teacher in his class, the preacher in his pulpit, the soul winner in his dealings with the inquirer and the saint in his ministry of prayer in the secret closet.

There is no truth that needs to be more emphasized in this age of smartness and human self-sufficiency than the imperative necessity of the baptism of the Holy Spirit as the condition of all effective Christian work. We must tarry before we go.

It pays to wait. A traveler pursued by his enemies lingered five minutes at the blacksmith's shop to have his horse reshod, and while some might have thought he was foolish thus to delay, yet he was truly wise, for as they drew near at the last moment and shouted their expected triumph he leaped into the saddle and was soon far in the distance. A week spent at the source of faith and power will bring more effective service than years of human effort in the energy of our highest gifts and loftiest genius.

We must have a supernatural plan. In the working out of a military campaign the commander relies upon the intelligent cooperation of his subordinate officers. If one division of the army were to rush into the attack heedless of the plan of the leader, it might hinder instead of help. A very small force judiciously used at the salient point of attack or defense often turns an enemy's flank and changes the issue of a decisive battle.

Christ has a plan in His mediatorial work. He does not send us forth to draw our bow at a venture and run wherever our fancy may dispose us, but He wants us to understand His method and work according to His great purpose. It is foreshadowed in the promise of the Spirit (Acts 1:8), the gospel for the center first, and then for the circumference, and then for the uttermost parts of the earth.

That plan was more fully unfolded at the first great council of the Christian Church in the 15th chapter of Acts and consists of three great sections: first, a visit to the Gentiles to take out of them a people for His name; second, the return of the Lord and the restoration of Israel; third, the millennial reign with the ingathering of all the Gentiles.

A wise worker will work according to this plan. He will not attempt today the ingathering of all the Gentiles, but will be occupied with the outgathering from them of the few who are to be the firstfruits for His coming. He will not be devoting his attention to Israel supremely, for the restoration of Israel is to come with the return of the Lord. His chief business will be to give the gospel to the Gentiles and gather out of them a people for His name.

This will save us many a bitter disappointment. We will not be found trying to convert all the people in the world and stop all the abuses of our time. This belongs to the next dispensation. Rather, we are to be busily occupied in the great missionary work of the age and the bringing back of our King.

## Wait for God's Directing

We must have supernatural direction. It is possible to have a divine plan and yet run at our own impulse in the direction of our work. This was Saul's mistake. God sent him as Israel's king to destroy His enemies, but Saul took the reins into his own hand and, instead of waiting for Samuel to lead, stepped out in front, and by his presumption destroyed himself and his kingdom.

This was Joshua's danger. God had sent him and promised to bless him in bringing Israel into the Land of Promise. Joshua had an idea that he was to lead the armies of Israel, and so God had to meet him with a drawn sword and lay him on his face at the very outset of his career, and remind him that He, not Joshua, was Captain of the Lord's host. Then Joshua became conqueror when he simply followed his conquering Leader.

Very early in the Acts of the Apostles Philip had to learn this lesson. Preaching in Samaria with wonderful success, it seemed on all human principles that this was his immediate duty. But suddenly the Spirit commanded him to go down into the desert, and he was wise and faithful enough to obey, to leave his work in Samaria and to go down 100 miles into the lone wilderness until at last the leading was made plain, and the prince of Ethiopia was converted to God and became the pioneer of the gospel in the great continent of Africa.

Even Paul and Silas had to be severely taught that they must go every moment at the direction of their supernatural Leader. Rushing forward in the accomplishment of their plans into Bithynia, Mysia and Asia, they were suddenly stopped by the Holy Spirit: "the Spirit of Jesus would not allow them to" (Acts 16:7). They had gone beyond their personal Leader, and they were compelled to retrace their steps and get still before God and wait for new orders. They seemed to be doing good, but God was not pleased and would not have it.

He does not even want good work if it is not His very work for us at that very time. It is not true to say, "I am doing some good; I am doing the best I know how." True service is doing the very thing that God has for us, doing it in His strength and wholly pleasing Him. If we are not doing this we may be hindering Him by our very Christian work. It is a serious question whether much of the religious work today is not entirely out of God's will. I believe that many a man that is preaching today in an American pulpit ought to be in some foreign field, and because he is not in God's will he blights his blessings and lets his church run into foolishness, worldliness and sometimes infidelity.

So Paul called a halt and waited for his Leader to point the way, and then he found that way led them out of the field that He was cultivating across the Aegean Sea into the continent of Europe and the kingdom of Greece.

God had a great ultimate purpose in that which Paul could not foresee. He knew that the nations of modern history were to have their theater of action in that great continent. There our forefathers were to be born and thence were we to spring, and well may we thank God that Paul obeyed that divine leading and gave up his own work to the work of the Master.

Beloved, are you doing the very work God has for you? Did He redeem you for the purpose of spending your life in selfish amusement, or even in half-hearted conventional formalism which you call Christian work? Go to your knees and find out whether you are going to discover too late that you have lost your way and have spent your strength in vain.

## God Gives the Increase

Last, we need supernatural efficiency. God must give the increase and bring the fruition as well as lead the way, and He does give efficiency for the humblest ministries which are performed in Him. The seed may have seemed to lie in silence, but it is sure to spring forth and bring the harvest.

A single sentence spoken by Charles Spurgeon in an empty hall that the carpenters were fixing for his next Sabbath's service reached the ear of a mechanic at his workbench in an adjoining shop. Twenty-five years later Spurgeon found, when that man was on his deathbed, that he had been saved through that arrow shot at a venture because it was in the Holy Spirit.

A little English girl lived and died unknown to all but her family and her pastor, but the beautiful story of her life was written by her minister, Leigh Richmond, in a tract called *The Dairyman's Daughter*. That little tract fell into the hands of a young English noble who was wasting his splendid intellect in dissipation, and William Wilberforce arose from his perusal a consecrated Christian and became the emancipator of all the slaves in the British Empire. William Wilberforce wrote a little book called *The Practical View of Religion*, and it fell into the hands of an easygoing Scottish preacher who was actually thinking of giving up his pulpit to teach mathematics, but out of that little book was born the mighty soul of Thomas Chalmers, and out of his life came the Scottish Disruption, the Free Church and the great movement for Christ and mission which that noble church has led and to which many of us owe our Christian hopes.

How marvelous the chain of divine working! How mighty the efficiency of a little word! How immortal the Word of God which lives and abides forever!

We will not always be conscious of the power. Indeed, it is our weakness that God most frequently uses. A little message spoken in great humility will become a seed in some other heart whose fruit will shake like Lebanon, and the blessing cover the earth and fill the heavens.

But God chose the foolish things of the world to shame the wise; God chose the weak things of the world to shame the strong. He chose the lowly things of this world and the despised things—and the things that are not—to nullify the things that are, so that no one may boast before him. It is because of him that you are in Christ Jesus, who has become for us wisdom from God—that is, our righteousness, holiness and redemption. Therefore, as it is written: "Let him who boasts boast in the Lord." (1 Corinthians 1:27-31)

What, after all, is Apollos? And what is Paul? Only servants, through whom you came to believe—as the Lord has assigned to each his task. I planted the seed, Apollos watered it, but God made it grow. So neither he who plants nor he who waters is anything, but only God, who makes things grow. . . . So then, no more boasting about men! All things are yours, whether Paul or Apollos or Cephas or the world or life or death or the present or the future—all are yours, and you are of Christ, and Christ is of God. (3:5-7, 21-23)

# SCRIPTURE INDEX

Also by James M. Russell

*A Brief Guide to Philosophical Classics*

**James M. Russell** has a philosophy degree from the University of Cambridge, a post-graduate qualification in critical theory, and has taught at the Open University in the UK. He is the author of *A Brief Guide to Philosophical Classics*. James lives in north London.

some specific angle or message that reaches beyond their religious origins.

These are intended as examples of titles that may appeal to anyone who has a broad interest in matters of spirituality and religion. Of course, as with the Christian texts, it is impossible to claim any kind of completeness or to deny that many other books could equally have been included.

Each book that we have chosen is described in a few pages. It can be hard to capture the essence of a book in such a short space. Our guiding principle was to try to explain the books in such a way as to convey a brief idea of what each one has to offer the interested reader. But also we wanted to answer the question 'Would I enjoy and understand this book?' which sometimes involves trying to explain the strengths and weaknesses of the book for a modern reader.

The 'Speed Reads' included at the end of each entry aim to deliver a quick sense of what the writer is like to read. They also provide a highly compressed, and occasionally somewhat flippant summary of the main points of the book in question.

Overall we have aimed for a chatty and comprehensible style, even if this occasionally risks criticism for being insufficiently serious. We have tried to explain the books as we would to an interested friend, rather than taking too academic a viewpoint, and we hope that this makes for a readable and interesting journey.

Each entry is self-contained, and there is no reason why the book shouldn't be used for 'dipping into'. However, we have also arranged the book into seven sections, grouping the books together in various ways. Within each section the books are arranged chronologically. While there is no attempt at a joined-up historical approach, the chronological progression at times reveals some interesting juxtapositions and relations between the books included.

There are a couple of general editorial points to be made. First, many of these books are available in a variety of editions and with alternative titles. In these cases we have aimed to use the best-known title. Some of the original publication dates are also uncertain – we have used first publication where this is known, but for some of the earlier books the best we can do is give the correct century or decade. In a few cases the quote given at the start of the section is not from the specific book under discussion – this is because we felt that the best way to give a flavour of an author's writing was to use an alternative quote from their other writings.

In conclusion, we hope that this book will provide entertainment and inspiration and will be a useful, if idiosyncratic guide to a representative selection of the many wonderful spiritual books that have been written over the centuries.

# I
# Early Christian Classics

The story of the early Christian Church is a complex, fascinating one. From the early days of persecution in the Roman Empire, through legalisation in the fourth century, and the gradual spread of the gospel across subsequent centuries, Christianity survived and continued to evolve during some dark times in history. The attitudes of the very early Christians are represented here by two remarkable texts: *The Sayings of the Desert Fathers* and *The City of God*. Both cast a great deal of light onto the early history of the Church.

In the latter part of the first millennium, following the collapse of the Roman Empire, the Church became a major political player in Europe, while the monastic movement developed the theology and philosophy that underpinned the religion.

This was the period in which the Christian Church established its dominion over much of Europe, went into battle with the more recent Islamic faith in the Crusades, established the Inquisition to suppress the unorthodox, and ultimately separated into the Eastern and Roman branches of the Church, a schism that remains today.

In this period, Christianity was primarily a paternalistic religion in which the message of Christ was interpreted for ordinary people by the priesthood. Within the Roman Church, masses and Bibles continued to be propagated in Latin, even as that language died as an everyday tongue and became a historical relic. Texts from this period reveal a great deal of the history and development of the Church, although their reliance on scholastic theology can make them dense and hard to empathise with today.

From a modern perspective, it is more interesting to look at some of the books that started to emerge from about the fourteenth century onwards. From a distance, books of orthodoxy are less interesting than those thinkers who tried to understand their own personal relationship with God. Writers such as Meister Eckhart and Marguerite Porete departed from the orthodox teaching of the Church to one degree or another and suffered the consequences. From this time onwards the invention of the printing press also meant that unorthodox ideas could be rapidly circulated over distances that had been impossible in the Middle Ages.

It is perhaps not surprising that the most enduring writing of this period was produced by thinkers who were starting to question the established Church in one way or another. Teresa of Ávila and St John of the Cross were reacting against the luxury and decadence of their contemporaries in the Church when they founded the Discalced Carmelites. Even John Bunyan, who was writing after the establishment of the Protestant Church of England, was fighting for his own Puritan ideals against the prevailing orthodoxy of his country.

In this section of the book we encounter some mysticism, several puritanical approaches, and the 'back-to-basics' Christianity of St Francis, who dared to take Christ at his word when he implored his followers to spread the word without shoes or money. Several of the authors in this section were condemned as heretical in their time, while others, such as Teresa of Ávila and St Francis, had to battle for their views against stubborn opposition.

To the modern reader the appeal of these books lies in seeing the individual struggling with the demands of trying to live a good life, attempting to reach their own understanding of Christ's message and their own comprehension of the divine, rather than simply relying on received wisdom. Instead of regarding the individualism of these writers as heresy or unorthodoxy, we can understand that they were merely aiming to reach a more complete and authentic understanding of their spirituality.

There is also a great deal of poetry and beauty in titles such as *The Little Flowers of St Francis* and *Dark Night of the Soul*, while *The Pilgrim's Progress* has been a hugely influential work of literature over the subsequent centuries. Beyond their spiritual message, these books are a reminder of the enormous contribution that spiritual writing has made to the cultural and intellectual development of the modern world.

## Sayings of the Desert Fathers

### The Desert Fathers, Fourth Century

'Let us charge into the good fight with joy and love without being afraid of our enemies. Though unseen themselves, they can look at the face of our soul, and if they see it altered by fear, they take up arms against us all the more fiercely. For the cunning creatures have observed that we are scared. So let us take up arms against them courageously. No one will fight with a resolute fighter.'

For an insight into the attitudes of the very early Church, there is no better place to start than with the sayings of the Desert Fathers, which have been published in a variety of collections, sometimes under the Latin name of *Apophthegmata Patrum*. The Desert Fathers were those hermits, monks and ascetics who lived a few centuries after Christ, and chose to follow monastic or eremitic lives in the desert region of Egypt, from the third century onwards. At this stage the life and work of Christ was relatively recent history, so it is fascinating to see how the beliefs and practices of the Desert Fathers reflect their understanding of his message.

The Fathers had mostly fled from the persecution of the Roman Empire, which was going through a turbulent period, during which Christians were often made into scapegoats. The reign of the emperor Diocletian was a particularly brutal one for early followers of Christ and the religion became a fugitive one, operating in small refugee communities away from urban centres.

Christianity in the Roman Empire was legalised in 313 by the Emperor Constantine, but while Christians were now free to live openly, some continued the solitary lives that they had developed during the harsher years. The desert had great appeal as a place where people could live in stoic simplicity – the story of Christ's temptation and fasting on the mountain, having been baptised by John the Baptist, was one that resonated deeply with the early Christians. To some degree they were attempting to recreate the deprivations of his time there. They were also continuing older religious traditions of asceticism and adapting these to a specifically Christian way of life.

By living in isolation in the desert and exercising extreme self-discipline, they aimed to follow in the path of Jesus, rejecting worldly pleasures and seeking a closer relationship with God. The Desert Fathers were revered for their wisdom and holiness, and their sayings and deeds were thus collected by early writers. They also gained a reputation for some highly individual and idiosyncratic practices. For instance, Simeon Stylites chose to live for thirty-seven years on a platform perched on top of a pole, to find a pure form of solitude and sacrifice. This seems rather comical now, but it is an example of the extremes of devout behaviour that were evident in the Desert Fathers.

Over time, their lives as hermits became more formal and less solitary and, under the influence of significant figures such as Anthony the Great and Pachomius, a life of common prayer and meals, together with solitary prayer and meditation, became the basis of the Christian monastic tradition. The fundamental idea of the Fathers – that we can ascend to God through a mixture of self-sacrifice, abstinence and meditation leading to spiritual progress – became a model of Christian practice that is still influential today.

One modern figure who edited a collection of their sayings was Thomas Merton, best known for his twentieth-century exposition of the virtues of the monastic life and solitude. As a young man he had aspired to live a life as holy as those of the Desert Fathers – again this demonstrates how their practices have inspired people across the centuries.

Many different selections of the source material have been published. Some divide the material by subject matter, others by the father (or mother) to whom sayings and deeds are ascribed. It has to be remembered that the sayings of the Desert Fathers can't be seen as reliable history. The collections were originally passed down from the Coptic Church, via Greek translations, and it is impossible to know if the sayings and deeds ascribed to particular Fathers are accurate. But from any of these collections you can get a general impression of the beliefs and acts of these individuals and the state of the Church in their lifetimes.

The sayings cover a wide range of theological and spiritual areas. Obviously there is an emphasis on the ascetic life. There is also a tendency for some of the stories of deprivations and suffering welcomed by the Fathers to seem somewhat grotesque and masochistic by modern standards.

However, one can't help but be impressed by the hardiness of those who were prepared to undergo these deprivations in the name of their beliefs. There are also inevitable moments of misogyny, as the temptation of women is regarded with particular horror by these Fathers. But this has to be seen within the context of the period.

One especially inspiring aspect of the sayings for the modern reader is the extraordinary perseverance that these Fathers show in their attitude to spiritual progress. St John of the Ladder writes: 'Do not be surprised that you fall every day; do not give up, but stand your ground courageously. And assuredly, the angel who guards you will honour your patience.' We can find great inspiration in such attitudes even if we are unlikely to follow the Desert Fathers to their extremes of asceticism. Jesus said, 'Deny yourself, take up your cross and follow me.' Today we rarely take these words as seriously as the early Church did, but the Desert Fathers are examples of believers who took every word of Jesus' exhortation with full seriousness.

Another way we can take inspiration from the Desert Fathers today is with regard to temptation. Anyone who tries to live a good life will know the problem of temptation, whether this be from failing to live up to one's own expectations, or from the temptations of sensuality, over-eating, laziness or whatever may be our personal weaknesses.

Since the Desert Fathers tried to live such ascetic existences, they were constantly faced with the problem of temptation, as even an additional crumb of food might count for them as a failure to live up to their personal standards. Abba Isaiah the Solitary wrote: 'When you pray to God in time of temptation do not say, "Take this . . . away from me", but pray like this: "O Jesus Christ, sovereign Master, help me and do not let me sin against Thee . . ."' Rather than imploring Jesus to deliver him from temptation, Abba Isaiah suggests that we should concentrate on the imperative not to sin, and thus overcome the temptation even when it remains with us. This is a powerful approach to the problem – to pray for the temptation to be taken from us implies that we are not strong enough to reject it. Whereas to pray for Christ's help in avoiding sin suggests that our desire to avoid sin should be powerful enough to overcome the temptation no matter what, which is a far stronger faith.

The power of the sayings of the Desert Fathers lies in many such small moments of contemplation. The sayings make an ideal accompaniment to prayer and meditation, as they can be read in short bursts and each moment inspires us to consider different aspects of faith and belief. Some of the Fathers' words and deeds may seem to be truly archaic, but other thoughts and ideas remain as true today as they were all those centuries ago.

## *Sayings of the Desert Fathers*

### THE SPEED READ

The collected sayings and deeds of the early Christian hermits, monks and ascetics who lived in the Scetes desert in the fourth century AD, either in solitude or in small groups overseen by an elder. Undertaking lives of asceticism and holiness, they represent an extreme but powerful representation of early Christianity, and their sayings retain great power to inspire and teach us today.

# City of God
## Augustine, Fifth Century

'Though there are very many nations all over the earth . . . there are
no more than two kinds of human society, which we may justly call
two cities . . . one consisting of those who live according to man, the
other of those who live according to God . . . To the City of Man
belong the enemies of God . . . so inflamed with hatred against the
City of God.'

One of the most interesting thinkers of the medieval
period was Augustine of Hippo. A North African,
who converted to Christianity, he has to be understood
within the specific intellectual culture of his time. The main
concern of many contemporary writers was to harmonise
Christian ideas with the thinking of the Greek philosophers,
Plato in particular.

The Egyptian writer Plotinus is often seen as the foremost interpreter of Plato in a Christian context in this
period, but the task he set himself was one that many
attempted: to provide a rational foundation for the mystical
and theological aspects of Christian, Jewish or, later, Islamic
belief. In many cases this strand of early Christian writing
makes for fairly dull reading fifteen centuries or so later.

By contrast, Augustine gave a compelling account of his
life in *The Confessions*, which is regarded as one of the first
true autobiographies, in the modern sense. The picture he
paints of himself is not flattering – a follower of Manicheanism
(a belief system that was based on a duality of good versus
evil), he was tempted into evil ways and pleasures of the
flesh. A turning point came when he picked up a Bible and
read a passage from St Paul concerning licentiousness, and
this led to his conversion.

Based on his own early life, Augustine saw mankind as

weak in spirit, and only capable of gaining redemption through God's grace. He moved away from the Manichean belief in evil, instead coming to define evil as the absence of good. This led him to regard rationality as being less important than faith in God. However, he did still believe that philosophy can help us to understand our faith.

He rejected the sceptical belief that we can't know anything with certainty, pointing out that '*Si fallor, sum*' ('If I am mistaken, I exist') – he used this early version of 'I think therefore I am' in the same way that Descartes would in the seventeenth century: as the basis for asserting that we can have trust in our perceptions because we can trust in God.

In *The Confessions*, Augustine also wrote with subtlety and wisdom on questions such as necessary truth and free will. He saw free will as a function of the way that we experience time – God experiences the world without our limitations and knows all our choices. Whereas we have to work out our decisions without knowing the future, and free will is therefore an essential part of how we must live our lives.

In many respects, *City of God* is a more difficult read than *The Confessions*. Augustine wrote it (in Latin) in the early part of the fifth century, following the sacking of Rome by Visigoths in 410. This was a crisis point in the history of Rome – many Romans believed that the sacking was a punishment for having turned away from their earlier gods to Christianity. Augustine's first aim in the book is to counter this idea, suggesting that it is not always necessary for the earthly rule of Christianity to triumph for the City of God to flourish. The book deals with issues such as martyrdom and the suffering of early Christians in this context, and analyses the relationship between the Christian Church and other religions, including Judaism and paganism. The full title of the book is sometimes given as *The City of God Against The Pagans*.

Christianity was now the official religion of the Roman

Empire. But Augustine stresses that the fundamental Christian message is more spiritual than political. So we should look to heaven, rather than focusing on worldly events. In particular, Augustine asks us to contemplate the mystical heavenly city of New Jerusalem. This idea that Jerusalem would be literally or figuratively recreated in heavenly surroundings, a final destination for saints and the redeemed, is a recurring theme in Jewish and Christian texts.

Augustine also considers the long sweep of human history. He contrasts the City of Man with the City of God. Harking back to his *Confessions*, he sees the City of Man as being prone to weakness, licentiousness and failure to recognise Christian values. Whereas the City of God (which is a metaphor rather than a literal place in his writing) is made up of people who are able to resist temptation and devote themselves to the Christian message.

*The City of God* can be heavy going for a modern reader. Augustine makes many digressions in which he seeks to reject pagan beliefs on philosophical grounds, and this makes the book very much of its time.

The book has also been criticised from a different point of view: some believe that it was a powerful influence within Christianity, but in a malign way. This is because it helped to establish the idea that the Christian Church was in a long-term battle against the pagan (or infidel) horde. This idea would influence the Crusaders and the Spanish Inquisition and can still be perceived today in extreme elements of modern Christian evangelism. Of course, Augustine can't really be blamed for the excesses of some of those who followed him, but the confrontational nature of the book does tend to lend itself to such interpretations.

Overall, Augustine's work makes for a difficult but intriguing read. It is interesting to consider the historical context: the struggles of the early Church to establish itself in people's hearts and minds in spite of political turmoil.

Beyond that, there is inspiration to be taken from Augustine's personal determination to overcome temptation, and from his idea that the City of Man is ephemeral, while the eternal City of God is where we should fix our gaze.

### City of God

**THE SPEED READ**

Pagans have wrecked the city of Rome, but do not be disheartened or return to false gods. What you see here is the City of Man, where people are often weak, licentious and lacking Christian virtues. What we are seeking to build is the City of God, where man's innate weakness will be overcome through faith in God.

# The Cloud of Unknowing
## Anonymous, Approx. 1375

'God can be taken and held by love but not by thought.'

*T*he Cloud of Unknowing is an anonymous fourteenth-century spiritual guidebook. It is thought to have been written by an English monk (possibly a Carthusian). It is framed as advice to someone who is setting forth on a life of contemplation, as a young monk might be doing. It advocates the idea that we can only approach God through love, not through knowledge or rational thought.

The author describes our basic human desire to comprehend the world as a stumbling block on the route to reaching God through simple love. He writes that this need to understand will 'replace the darkness which you have pierced to reach God with clear images of something which, however good, however beautiful, however Godlike, is not God'.

It is a short text, made up of brief chapters, and it is surprisingly readable for a modern reader, in spite of the convoluted phraseology. It gives a good insight into medieval mysticism and the spiritual problems that faced a monk of the time. Some writers have even claimed it espouses a Zen-like view of Christianity.

The unknown author of *The Cloud of Unknowing* translated several other religious texts, including a version of the works of the fifth-century Syrian now known as Pseudo-Dionysius (or Dionysius the Areopagite). His work *Concerning Mystical Theology* took its starting point from St Paul's references in Acts 17 to 'the unknown God'. From here he developed the system of belief that later theologians would classify as 'Apophatic Mysticism'. This is an unfortunately daunting bit of theological jargon but it is not as complicated as it sounds.

Pseudo-Dionysius taught that however we try to imagine God, the true nature of God must lie beyond any concept we could hold in our mind. So he directed us towards an 'imageless' approach to the divine being. Apophatic mysticism is sometimes defined as dealing with knowledge of God via a process of negation – this is true in so far as it is a belief system that negates any image of God we might have and insists that God is unknowable.

Instead this 'negative' spirituality emphasises the grand mystery of God, and the transcendence of rational thought that leaves God clouded in darkness to our rational minds. Other writers such as Meister Eckhart and John of the Cross would be influenced by this way of thinking but *The Cloud of Unknowing* is one of the most complete and eloquent medieval statements of apophatic mysticism.

Regarding the impossibility of knowledge of God, the author writes:

> thou hast brought me with thy question into that same darkness, and into that same cloud of unknowing, that I would thou wert in thyself. For of all other creatures and their works, yea, and of the works of God's self, may a man through grace have fullhead of knowing, and well he can think of them: but of God Himself can no man think.

For this author, the fact that God cannot be reached through rational understanding means that we must recognise our own weakness in the face of the divine. The voice of the teacher in the book varies between loving encouragement of the pupil and a harsher tone. In particular, when the author is emphasising the humility we need to cultivate, he takes a strong tone of chastisement:

> Look up now, weak wretch, and see what thou art. What art thou, and what hast thou merited, thus to be called of our Lord? What weary wretched heart, and sleeping in sloth, is that, the which is not wakened with the draught of this love and the voice of this calling.

However, the teacher's aim in insisting that God is unknowable is not to demoralise his pupil. It is merely to prepare him for the idea that we can only approach God through unconditional love. He counsels that prayer should not be a matter of language or rational constructions. Instead we should develop an 'inner silence' – we should push all images and concepts out of our mind into a 'cloud of forgetting'.

Then we should strive with our whole heart simply to love God, even though God will always remain hidden from our conscious understanding by the 'cloud of unknowing'.

At this point the author counsels his pupil to pray by focusing on a single word such as 'God' or 'love', suggesting that by repeating this word one's heart can develop a love for God without the interference of our conscious rationality.

This is a technique that has been adapted by some modern theologians and some Trappist monks, in the idea of 'centring prayer', through which a single word becomes the entire prayer. However, here we also see why some modern writers see a connection between *The Cloud of Unknowing* and Eastern religion, in both Zen Buddhism and the meditational practices of Hindu gurus.

Rather than encourage pupils to conceptualise God, the teacher is advising them to reject extraneous thoughts, and to focus only on the love for God. But we can't know God, so we do not know what it is that we are loving. All we can do is to try to send a 'sharp dart' of love to attempt to pierce the cloud of unknowing:

> And therefore, although it be good sometimes to think of the kindness and the worthiness of God in special, and although it be a light and a part of contemplation: nevertheless yet in this work it shall be cast down and covered with a cloud of forgetting. And thou shalt step above it stalwartly, but Mistily, with a devout and a pleasing stirring of love, and try for to pierce that darkness above thee. And smite upon that thick cloud of unknowing with a sharp dart of longing love.

This is a medieval, monastic author and as a result his voice can often be stern. However, there is a generosity and encouragement in the writing for anyone considering a contemplative existence. The author writes that it is 'not what you are nor what you have been that God sees with his all-merciful eyes, but what you desire to be'. So even though God can't be known, the presumption is that as well as loving God we will be loved and forgiven by the divine being.

This emphasis on the unknowability of God makes apophatic mysticism a precursor of some elements of later philosophy. Rationalist philosophers of the renaissance, such as Descartes, would attempt to ground philosophy in certain knowledge derived from God. However, Spinoza and others insisted on the impossibility of knowledge of God, arguing that we could only work within the limits of our rationality.

Eventually Kant, in dividing the world into noumena and phenomena, would argue that in trying to understand the noumenal world (the world of things as they are rather than as we perceive them) we inevitably come up against the 'bounds of reason'. He argues that, as rational beings, we behave as though we can have knowledge beyond the world we perceive, in order to escape the intolerable possibility that life is meaningless.

Kierkegaard would then seize on this idea and suggest that to approach God we must make a 'leap of faith'. In each of these thinkers one can hear a belated echo of the apophatic mystics' conviction that God was unknowable, and that rational thought could not allow us access to the divine being.

*The Cloud of Unknowing* has inspired many mystical and contemplative thinkers over the centuries and is still a readable and inspiring book. We may not know who the author was, but their personality shines through in the text and the message is one that resonates in many surprising ways with modern spiritual thought.

## *The Cloud of Unknowing*

### THE SPEED READ

So you want me to teach you how to live the contemplative life? First you need to realise that you are a weak wretch, and that no image you hold in your mind can approach the mystery and majesty of God. So in a condition of utter humility you must try to remove rational thought from your prayers and, in order to approach an unknowable God, you must use the simplest prayer of your heart. Then you will be able to send sharp darts of love into the cloud of unknowing that surrounds God.

# *The Mirror of Simple Souls*
## Marguerite Porete, Fourteenth Century

'God has nowhere to put his goodness, if not in me, no place to put himself entire, if not in me. And by this means I am the exemplar of salvation, and what is more, I am the salvation itself of every creature, and the glory of God.'

The story of *The Mirror of Simple Souls* provides an insight into the medieval Church and the paths it might have taken. The book was written by Marguerite Porete, also known as Marguerite of Hainaut. She lived in an area of modern-day Belgium, and wrote in Old French (Latin was the approved language for religious texts of the period). She was burned at the stake in 1310 after a trial in Paris, having been accused of heresy because of her book. Copies of the book were burned, and the text only survived because of foreign translations, while it took until 1965 for careful scholarship to establish that Marguerite was indeed the author.

Why was this book so offensive to the church authorities of the period? Its full title was *The Mirror of the Simple Souls Who Are Annihilated and Remain Only in Will and Desire of Love*. The title is a reference to the ecstatic annihilation a believer can find in God. It takes the form of a conversation in prose and poetry between personifications of Love, Reason and the Soul.

The book details the seven stages of spiritual growth one must go through on a journey to union with God. In this respect it is similar to the later works *Dark Night of the Soul* by St John of the Cross, and *The Interior Castle* by St Teresa (see pp. 32–5 and pp. 29–32), which also guide the reader through the metaphorical journey towards divinity.

For Marguerite, the noble soul is one that will resonate to the love of God. Souls resonate like bells do, and some respond more clearly than others to the love of God. The path towards God is one in which the soul is eventually annihilated, in the sense that the soul no longer wills in a selfish way but wants only what God wants. In this union with the divine, the self disappears, leaving only God.

This all seems simple enough but the Church saw traces of the heresy of the free spirit in her writing and asked her to recant. She died refusing to withdraw her own words. She was also accused at her trial of being a Beguine. We should take a moment to explain each of these accusations in more detail.

In the thirteenth and fourteenth centuries, a tradition grew up in the Low Countries of Europe whereby individual women, not aligned to religious orders, chose to live a life of solitary prayer and contemplation. There were various influences on this choice, including the spread of Franciscan ideals, and the fact that many men departed on Crusades in this period. The Beguines were lay communities that grew out of this tradition. They were not nuns – they did not renounce property, and they took no vows. But they grouped together on the edges of towns and cared for the poor, living lives that in many respects were deeply simple and holy. A parallel movement of men, the Beghards, also grew in this period.

The Beguines and the Beghards may have been influenced by the Albigensians and Cathars, divergent branches of the Church that had been suppressed by the Roman Church. The main concerns for the official Church were that they were not official organisations that could easily be absorbed and controlled, and the suspicion that they held antinomian beliefs – meaning that they felt that it was not necessary to hold to an established code of ethics that was legislated by a central authority. This worried the Church, as it felt the need to dictate its understanding of Jesus' teaching to its followers.

The Church also suspected the Beguines of holding to the heresy of the free spirit. This means that it felt they believed it was possible to have a personal relationship with God rather than one which was directed through the intercession of the Church. Obviously a great deal of the Church's power in this period rested on its claim to be the sole channel to God, and the hierarchy was appalled by any suggestion that individuals could choose to bypass the Church.

The free spirit doctrine taught that through austerity and contemplation it was possible to achieve perfection and union with God in this world. This was characterised by the Church as meaning that believers in the free spirit felt themselves beyond sin, although this seems to have been a wilful misinterpretation of the real ideas being disseminated. Either way the heresy of the free spirit was something that the central authority of the Church was keen to suppress.

It is not certain whether Marguerite Porete actually was a

Beguine. At one point in her writing she lists them among her critics, and it may be that she was falsely accused at her trial. But for the church authorities it would have been enough that her writing shared elements of the same doctrine, in particular the fact that it stressed a personal relationship with God.

So when *The Mirror of Simple Souls* started to be read and revered throughout France, the Church reacted and, as was common at the time, it acted brutally to suppress the book. Marguerite Porete was burned in the Place de Grève in France in 1310 and the book would have been lost to posterity if the Church had succeeded in its aim of destroying every copy.

Today, it is not an easy book to comprehend. It is poetical and uses some arcane language. Even when the language is simpler it is hard to unravel the references to popular and biblical ideas. You need an edition with a good introduction to make sense of the book if you are not a scholar of medieval spirituality.

However, it can be an interesting read in spite of its difficulty, because it offers a glimpse into the medieval period and into the kind of thinking that the Church worked so hard to suppress. If the Church had not been so diligent in crushing elements such as the Albigensians and the 'heresy' of the free spirit, modern Christianity might look very different indeed. Certainly it would have a wider canon of classic works to draw on, and we are lucky that this one survived.

The heresy of the free spirit went on to be smeared by association with witchcraft. Two fifteenth-century works, *Formicarius* by Johannes Nider and *Malleus Maleficarum* by Heinrich Kramer, cemented the idea that it was a part of the belief system of witches. This provided part of the justification for the widespread witch-burning which, together with the reign of the Inquisition, did so much to damage the reputation of the Church in the later Middle Ages.

At one stage Meister Eckhart was reputed to be an exponent of the heresy of the free spirit, but today his reputation is being rehabilitated in the Roman Catholic Church. However, Marguerite Porete has never been officially rehabilitated or pardoned for the 'crime' of writing her poetic, spiritual work on oneness with God.

### The Mirror of the Simple Souls

#### THE SPEED READ

A debate between Love, Reason and the Soul. This book describes the seven stages of spiritual growth on the path to God, and the ways in which a soul can resonate to the love of God. The eventual union with God is described as an annihilation of the soul. The book was suppressed by the Church, on the basis that it expressed the 'heresy of the free spirit', and the author, Marguerite Porete, was executed. It remains a glimpse into what the medieval Church might have become if it had not been so determined to suppress all alternative interpretations of the message of Christ.

# The Little Flowers of St Francis
## Anonymous, Fourteenth Century

'As our Lord Jesus Christ says in his Gospel, I know my sheep and mine know me, so the holy St Francis, like a good shepherd, knew, through divine revelation, all the merits and virtues of his companions, and also their defects and faults.'

*The Little Flowers of St Francis* is one of the most enchanting, inspiring and downright funny spiritual texts you could ever hope to encounter. It was written in the fourteenth century, and was based on earlier texts about the life of St Francis. It has been credited to a Brother Ugolino, although its true authorship remains uncertain.

The beauty of this little book is the way that it encapsulates the anarchic, humble nature of the early Franciscan movement. St Francis drew to him a motley crew of followers and this book gives a touching but unflinching account of some of their vagaries.

Everyone knows of St Francis as a gentle lover of animals, and a saintly advocate of a life of simplicity and poverty. What is sometimes forgotten is the degree to which the ideals of the Franciscan movement challenged and undermined the Church of its day. He was born in approximately 1181, the son of a wealthy cloth merchant. He had an artistic temperament as a young man, and one anecdote relates how he gave all his money to a beggar who asked him for alms in the marketplace.

Following a serious illness in 1203 and, apparently, a mystical vision of Jesus Christ, Francis became increasingly absorbed in religious contemplation. The turning point came in 1209 when he heard a sermon based on the passage from the Gospel of Matthew in which Christ asks his followers to go forth proclaiming the Kingdom of Heaven, taking no money or even shoes for their travels.

This inspired Francis to take up a new kind of monastic life in which he would travel in poverty and humility. He travelled barefoot around his native Umbrian region preaching, and within a year had gathered a group of followers, including the wealthy Brother Bernardo, who gave up a life of luxury, and donated all his money to the work of the emerging Franciscan movement.

They worked with lepers and the poor, the hungry and

oppressed. But they not only helped them; they joined with them and lived among them. St Francis also chose not to subject his followers to any kind of rules (beyond the requirements of their austere lifestyle) or hierarchy. Each Franciscan was free to make his own decisions about his actions, meaning that they practised a form of anarchy within the movement.

After Francis travelled with his followers to Rome, Pope Innocent gave them the protection of the Church. But on Francis's return to Assisi, the movement became increasingly popular to the point where the papacy started to see it as a revolutionary threat. One of his new followers was St Clare, who would later be remembered as the inspiration behind the Poor Clares.

Francis travelled to Egypt in 1219, where he put his non-violent principles into practice by preaching to the sultan about his view of Christianity. On his return he found that the Church had attempted to impose standard monastic rules on his movement. This was the start of a long period during which the more revolutionary members of the Franciscan movement were gradually suppressed or sidelined by the Church. After Francis's death in 1226, the Franciscan order would become a far less radical entity than it had been in its early days.

St Francis left behind a Testament, and was also an early advocate of the radical idea that ordinary people should pray in their own language rather than the arcane Latin of the Catholic Church. He always wrote in his native Umbrian himself. He was quickly beatified by the Church, and subsequent accounts of his life spread his fame, as well as distributing legends such as the accounts of him preaching to the birds, and taming the Wolf of Gubbio. But the most popular and enduring account of his life would be provided by the various versions of *The Little Flowers of St Francis*.

The book is a collection of short chapters giving pithy accounts of events from the life of St Francis and his followers. Some of the stories seem simply absurd, others quite beautiful. His sermon to the birds is given an eloquent description:

> St Francis lifted up his eyes, and saw on some trees by the wayside a great multitude of birds; and being much surprised, he said to his companions, 'Wait for me here by the way, whilst I go and preach to my little sisters the birds'; and entering into the field, he began to preach to the birds which were on the ground, and suddenly all those also on the trees came round him, and all listened while St Francis preached to them, and did not fly away until he had given them his blessing.

However, some of the most memorable moments in the book come from accounts of the exploits of St Francis's companions, in particular the frequently hilarious accounts of the activities of Brother Juniper.

Juniper is a strange figure, a devout, simple man who personifies the early Franciscan ideals, yet frequently behaves in a bizarre manner. One chapter of the book describes how, when a crowd approached him, impressed by his holiness, he proceeded to play see-saw with a child in order to abase himself and repel their admiration. On another occasion he takes lodging with some fellow Franciscans and ruins their entire week's supply of food by tipping it all into a single inedible stew.

The Juniper stories are more complex than they look. For instance his shortcomings as a cook showed up the fact that this particular group of Franciscans were not fully embracing St Francis's love of simplicity and poverty – and their response to his act reveals their discomfort in this knowledge. However, regardless of the message, the stories about

Brother Juniper have a simple charm and humour that persists to this day.

Modern editions of *The Little Flowers of St Francis* date from a couple of centuries after St Francis's death when the current selection of stories first started to circulate. It was only translated into English quite late, in spite of having long been a popular favourite in Italy. Possibly the title implied a fluffier, less entertaining book, or perhaps it just took a while for anyone capable of translating it to come across it.

Either way, it is a valuable, light-hearted book. As well as being a very enjoyable read, it raises genuine questions about the meaning of Christ's exhortations to poverty and simplicity. The Catholic Church has always tended towards pomp and wealth, and the early Franciscan movement and its successors are rare examples of this tendency being seriously challenged from within.

### The Little Flowers of St Francis

In this book are the Little Flowers of St Francis, meaning testimony concerning his miracles, pious examples of behaviour and his teaching. St Francis drew followers such as Brother Bernard, St Clare and Brother Leo to him at Assisi. He explained to them that perfect joy would be to accept all kinds of sufferings, impoverishments and abasements in the name of one's love of Christ. Brother Juniper took his love of abasement and poverty to such a degree that he often appeared absurd, yet even in stories of his foolishness, one can catch glimpses of genuine holiness.

# Sermons and Treatises

## Meister Eckhart, Fourteenth Century

'The eye with which I see God is the same eye with which God sees me.'

Eckhart von Hochheim was a German theologian and philosopher who was born in 1260 in Thuringia. Best known to posterity as Meister Eckhart, he was a religious thinker who put forward some unusual ideas at a time when unorthodoxy was dangerous. This was the period of the decadent Avignon Papacy, during which members of the Franciscan and Dominican Orders had a frequently antagonistic relationship. Eckhart joined the Dominicans as a young man, travelled around Europe, and became a teacher in the Dominican schools.

The Dominicans were representatives of the Thomist way of thinking – which means that they followed in the footsteps of Thomas Aquinas in trying to find ways to marry a rational system of thought to Christian basics. Eckhart was also known as a Neo-Platonist – this was the section of the Church which attempted to interpret Christ's teaching in the light of Greek philosophy, in particular that of Plato (at least as he had been interpreted by medieval scholars such as Plotinus).

Part of Eckhart's writing is thus within the traditional scholastic tradition of dry theological debate. However, he is a more interesting figure in church history than this suggests. His thinking has real psychological insight, and he uses a fascinating range of metaphorical devices to communicate his beliefs. Writing of the mysteries of God's love he describes it as a fertile overflowing, and talks about the spark of the soul, and the birth of the Word in the heart. Many of these metaphors convey ideas that are notably out of line with the Church of his time.

He is also known for a series of sermons that he delivered in vernacular German, in an attempt to explain the mysteries of the Bible to ordinary people. A few centuries ahead of the Protestant schism, he was already concerned by the exclusivity of the Church and tried to make it more democratic by explaining the gospel in everyday language.

So it's not surprising to discover that the Church of his time was uncomfortable with his activities. He came under the scrutiny of the Inquisition, which was by now largely under Franciscan control (something which would certainly have appalled their gentle founder, St Francis). Eckhart was eventually silenced by being tried for heresy in 1327.

He defended his beliefs, insisting that he had said nothing wrong. He argued that in his sermons he had only meant to inspire in listeners the desire above all to do some good. It is unclear whether Eckhart died or disappeared as a result of his persecution; we only know that the trial marked the end of his public life.

Hilariously, a church decree was subsequently issued denouncing preachers such as Eckhart who 'endeavour to preach subtle things which not only do [not] advance morals, but easily lead the people into error'. Subtlety was not appreciated in the medieval Church, let alone giving the common people ideas 'above their station'. Eckhart's influence lived on in the Friends of God movement, but he is still a controversial figure in official Vatican circles.

So what did he actually say that was so problematic?

By the standards of his time, some of Eckhart's ideas were indeed revolutionary. He talked of how the individual soul had the capacity to become one with God, counselling the faithful to look inside themselves to find God. He talked of the human soul as being superior to the angels. He talked of passively emptying oneself of consciousness and allowing God to flow through us – and he talked about going 'beyond God' to a still desert, a place where all things were created. These concepts sound closer to Lao Tzu's Taoism or to Buddhism than to the traditional Christian faith of the time.

For modern readers, Eckhart's sermons can be fascinating reading. One of his primary concerns was to educate his listeners on how to search for God. He admonishes people to look for God inside themselves, suggesting they try to do this by finding a state of disinterestedness, or detachment. He talks of the birth of the Word, a kind of union with God which happens deep in our souls. He emphasises that this alchemy can only happen if we are living a good Christian life. But he also stresses the importance of passivity in reaching this state.

By talking of passivity or disinterestedness he is not suggesting we should be weak or negative. Instead, he asks us to place all the attributes of our self and self-interest to one side and to allow God into our being. And if we can achieve this, he suggests that we can live with God inside us: 'A man should accustom himself to having God present always in his disposition and his intention. Believe me, if you were constant in this way, no-one could come between you and the God who is present to you.'

So, through this special kind of passivity, we experience the birth of the Word inside us. And how do we recognise this moment? 'You must know that God is born in us when the mind is stilled and sense troubles us no longer.'

For Eckhart, the spiritual life leads us to a condition where God is within us and we notice only God in all things. This sentiment has appealed to proponents of Eckhart's links with Eastern religion and to pantheists, but it is also a very specific interpretation of the Christian message, which was not welcomed by the Church of his time.

Another way Eckhart's teaching was contrary to orthodoxy came in his attitude to monastic retreat. Following St Augustine, a large part of scholastic Christianity revolved around the theory that the ideal path to God was to retreat from the activities and distractions of everyday life and seek God in solitude. So the monks and priests of the Church were granted a privileged relation with God because of their withdrawn role. But Eckhart acknowledges that we can't all live in retreat from the world, and emphasises that even in ordinary life we can have God in our souls:

> Whoever truly possesses God in the right way, possesses him in all places: on the street, in any company, as well as in a church or a remote place or in their cell. Grasping all things in a divine way and making of them something more than they are in themselves cannot be learned by taking flight, but rather we must learn to maintain an inner solitude regardless of where we are or who we are with.

To the modern mind this is not such a surprising idea, but in an era when the priesthood was exalted, it was a powerful thought, especially when allied with Eckhart's decision to preach in language that ordinary people could understand.

Meister Eckhart was offering the Church a big idea when he suggested that the contemplative life was not innately better than the active life. He was putting religion at the centre of our everyday lives, and suggesting that through a good life and through overcoming the self, we could have God in our hearts, whatever kind of life we lived. The Church wasn't ready for his ideas, but they are inspiring to read, even eight centuries later.

## Sermons and Treatises

### THE SPEED READ

If we live a good Christian life, we can discover the birth of the Word inside ourselves. We must become passive, devoid of self-interest and then we will be able to find God in our

souls. We can do this whether we live an active or contemplative life, as not everyone can live in a monastery or be a
priest, but God can be in every individual. When the word is
born inside us, we will see God in everything.

# The Interior Castle
## Teresa of Ávila, 1577

'I began to think of the soul as if it were a castle made of a single
diamond or of very clear crystal, in which there are many rooms, just
as in Heaven there are many mansions. Now if we think carefully
over this, sisters, the soul of the righteous man is nothing but a
paradise, in which, as God tells us, He takes His delight.'

The life of Teresa of Ávila (also known as St Teresa of
Jesus) can be seen in at least two ways. On the one hand
she was a determined reformer who overcame considerable
obstacles to set up the Discalced Carmelites, an austere
branch of her order which went back to the basics of poverty
and simplicity. On the other hand she was a mystic who
experienced visions of Jesus and had a deeply passionate
belief in her religion. It is impossible to understand her life
without reconciling these two separate aspects.

Teresa was born in 1515 in Ávila, and first entered the
Monastery of the Incarnation of the Carmelite nuns when
she was nineteen. She was a deeply religious child and was
fascinated by the lives of the saints and martyrs. When she
became a nun she suffered from a series of illnesses, but also
experienced spiritual visions and moments of epiphany as

she studied paths to God through the religious literature of her time.

After a two-year period in which she experienced many visions of Christ, she became determined to set up a new monastery in which she could put her personal vision of the religious life into practice. She felt that her contemporaries had allowed their practices to become lax, and wanted to obey Christ's strictures on poverty and simplicity in a more literal manner.

With the aid of wealthy backers she succeeded in this aim, setting up St Joseph's in 1562. She was a deeply controversial figure in the Carmelite movement and Catholic Church of her time, and faced serious opposition from those who didn't want her to succeed. But she was able to negotiate the difficult path to achieve her goals, along the way calling on the help of St John of the Cross and Anthony of Jesus, both of whom were strong supporters of her vision.

If this were all that we knew about Teresa, she would still be an interesting figure for her vision and determination in overcoming many obstacles. However, we also have her writing to remember her by. She was a reluctant writer, only writing when told to by her spiritual supervisors. These included Fray Diego, her confessor, who apparently persuaded her to put pen to paper, but only after she received a vision from God giving her permission to do so. Teresa herself wrote of her reticence thus: 'For the love of God, let me work at my spinning wheel and go to choir and perform the duties of the religious life, like the other sisters. I am not meant to write: I have neither the health nor the wits for it.' She was so detached from her writing task that she never reread a word she had written. However, we should be enduringly grateful to those who persuaded her to commit her inner life to paper. *The Life of St Teresa* is a fascinating account of her life story and gives us a clear insight into her mind. But *The Interior Castle* is an inspiring book in a rather different way.

In her visions from God she found the starting point for her work:

> A most beautiful crystal globe, made in the shape of a castle, and containing seven mansions, in the seventh and innermost of which was the King of Glory, in the greatest splendor, illuminating and beautifying them all. The nearer one got to the centre, the stronger was the light; outside the palace limits everything was foul, dark and infested with toads, vipers and other venomous creatures.

Teresa used this as a metaphor for the soul's journey of faith. She described the soul as a castle with a series of chambers, which could be compared to the seven heavens mentioned in contemporary religious texts. Each chamber represented a step closer to God.

In this way, she describes the way that a soul progresses through prayer, leading an exemplary life, and on through an increasingly close relationship with God to a spiritual marriage with the divinity. As the soul progresses through these stages it increasingly withdraws from outside life into the interior castle and absorption with God.

She exhorts her readers to set foot on this journey, and to seek God. There is something deeply passionate in the language she uses, comparing the soul's search for God to that of a lover seeking their soulmate.

Throughout Teresa's writings there was a thread of mysticism centring on the ascent of the soul. She often spoke of the journey that starts in contemplation and prayer, then leads to the subjugation of the will to God. She experienced many moments of spiritual ecstasy herself, and describes the ideal religious life in terms that include such passionate engagements with God. But one need not have her temperament to appreciate her descriptions of the soul's journey through life.

There is an everyday simplicity in her descriptions of the act of praying. She writes that 'mental prayer is nothing else than a close sharing between friends; it means taking time frequently to be alone with him who we know loves us'.

This familiar relationship with her God is one of the aspects of her writing that makes her so appealing to readers today. When talking about daily devotions, she manages to combine a mystical, medieval view of religion with something very modern and simple.

And somehow, in spite of the great humility her writing shows, her lively and engaging personality always shines through. We may not be able to take every step of the spiritual journey with her, but she is certainly a good companion to have on our own paths.

## The Interior Castle

### THE SPEED READ

There are seven mansions in the interior castle. In the first mansion, our souls are surrounded by sin, with prayer the only salvation. In the second and third mansions we find the practice of prayer and exemplary life. As we pass through the fourth and fifth mansions we gradually give up our wills and do only as God wills. In the sixth mansion we pass from betrothal to a closer relationship with God. Finally, in the seventh mansion we achieve perfect clarity and spiritual marriage to God.

# Dark Night of the Soul

## St John of the Cross, Sixteenth Century

'What more do you want, O soul! And what else do you search for outside, when within yourself you possess your riches, delights, satisfaction and kingdom – your beloved whom you desire and seek?'

O ne of Spain's best-loved poems is *Dark Night of the Soul* by St John of the Cross. It is a short, mystical account of the soul leaving the body and reaching up towards its 'beloved', God. Together with the commentaries written by its author, this is one of the most exquisite pieces of writing on the journey of the soul that can be imagined.

John was born in 1542, grew up in a village near to Ávila in Spain, and was christened Juan de Yepes y Álvarez. His father had come from a wealthy background, but had been disowned when he married a weaver's daughter, John's mother. The family struggled with poverty after the father's death and they were forced to move around Castile, eventually settling in Medina del Campo.

There he worked in the hospital with people who suffered from mental problems and incurable disease. The Society of Jesus (Jesuits) had recently been founded by St Ignatius Loyola, and the young John studied at one of their schools from the age of sixteen to twenty. At twenty-one he became a member of the Carmelite order, and studied philosophy and theology in Salamanca. Here he was taught by Fray Luis de Leon, who had translated the Song of Songs into Spanish.

This was an important encounter for John. The translation of biblical text into Spanish vernacular was still against church rules – because the Church wanted to control how this information was transmitted to the common people. So this was a controversial translation, but also a deeply inspiring one as it brought John into direct contact with the beauty of biblical poetry.

John intended to join the Carthusians, where he would have engaged in a life of solitary contemplation. However, he came under the influence of Teresa of Ávila (Saint Teresa) and she asked him to help in her plans to reform the Carmelite order.

The two are remembered as founders of the Discalced Carmelites. Discalced means barefoot – in practice the Discalced Carmelites followed a devout, disciplined path, and reformed the relatively lax religious orders of the day. This was inevitably met with some opposition by their contemporaries, who did not want to live a more austere religious life.

As a result of his reforming activities, John was imprisoned and tortured by his fellow Carmelites. In 1577 he was placed in confinement, and suffered the humiliation of regular public lashings. He was also kept in a tiny cell, where for nine months he suffered great deprivations. This was where he started to compose the poetry for which he would later become famous.

Finally he managed to escape from his confinement and spent the rest of his life pursuing his ambition of establishing the Discalced Carmelite order. His writings were not published until after his death in 1591.

*Dark Night of the Soul* is, along with *Spiritual Canticle*, his best-known work. He also wrote a commentary to the poem, which helps to explain its metaphorical meaning and intentions. The first part of the poem speaks of how the senses are purified as the soul leaves the body in search of God. In the second part he describes the ten steps that the soul needs to take up a ladder of love, an idea which derives from St Thomas Aquinas.

It reads almost like a love poem at times, as the delicate language describes the soul's search for God. The poem also introduced the concept of the dark night of the soul into common usage. In essence this refers to the condition of despair that is felt by a believer who feels that their prayer is empty and unrewarding. While prayer can sometimes involve us in an experience of satisfaction and epiphany, there are times in the life of a religious person when they feel only emptiness when they pray to God.

This can feel as though God has abandoned us or is refusing to listen. It can also lead us to confront our deepest doubts and uncertainties about our religion and beliefs. However, the dark night of the soul may also lead to a more positive experience in the end. Instead of performing acts of virtue for the happy feelings they engender in us, we are left performing these for no immediate reward, only for the love of God.

While this love may feel unrequited, persisting in a life of virtue and prayer can lead us to a deeper understanding of that love, and we can recognise that we are acting purely from love of God, not from a surreptitious interest in self-satisfaction. Mother Teresa is one well-known figure who went through a long dark night of the soul, but emerged from it with a deeper faith and happiness.

Just as the dark night of the soul can be a spiritual experience in the end, St John's long months in captivity led him on to greater belief and achievements in the remaining part of his life. John's poems have outlived him by centuries, and have been a source of great consolation and inspiration to many people, especially those who have suffered their own dark nights of the soul.

## Dark Night of the Soul

### THE SPEED READ

The fastest way to acquaint oneself with *Dark Night of the Soul* would be simply to track down a copy of the poem and to read it. But to fully understand it, you can also read commentaries that explain it at greater length. In essence, the poem simply describes a soul leaving the body, searching through the dark night for its beloved, climbing the 'secret ladder' and eventually finding peace and abandonment with the beloved, God. But there is so much more to this poem that it somehow feels insulting to attempt to reduce it to a summary, in spite of the brevity of the original text.

# The Way of Christ
## Jacob Böhme, 1623

'When Man will enter upon *Repentance*, and with his Prayers *turn to* God, he should, before he beginneth to pray, seriously consider the State of his own *Soul*.'

Jacob Böhme is an intriguing figure, a Christian mystic of the seventeenth century who influenced writers as varied as Angelus Silesius, William Blake, John Wesley, John Milton and William Law. He was born to poor but devout Lutheran parents in 1575 in eastern Germany. He was always religious and thought deeply about issues such as the salvation of the soul. One of his mystical visions was an epiphany in 1600 when he was observing the beauty of a beam of sunlight and its reflection in a dish. He felt that he had had a glimpse into the spiritual structure of the world.

He was not able to devote himself to writing at first. His work kept him busy, both as a shepherd and as a shoemaker. But he set himself to studying scripture and to spiritual contemplation. He became somewhat melancholic in his studies, saying that

I knew the Bible from beginning to end, but could find no consolation in Holy Writ; and my spirit, as if moving in a great storm, arose in God, carrying with it my whole heart, mind and will and wrestled with the love and mercy of God, that his blessing might descend upon me, that my mind might be illumined with his Holy Spirit, that I might understand his will and get rid of my sorrow . . .

Böhme started to write in 1612 and would eventually pen thirty books. His first book, *Aurora*, led to him being persecuted and censored. A local pastor acquired a copy of the work and denounced it for heresy. For some time Böhme wrote no more, but eventually he was persuaded to start writing again.

*The Way of Christ*, published in 1623, was his first printed book (previously his works had been circulated as handmade copies): he was exiled to Dresden because of its publication.

In the years after his death, Böhme's work gradually became more widely read. *The Way of Christ* is one of the most complete statements of his theology, focusing on the problems of sin and redemption. Following Lutheran ideas, he wrote that mankind had fallen from a state of grace to the world of sin and misery.

He wrote of fallen angels who were on the side of evil. A more controversial aspect of his writing was the way he treated the Fall: as a crucial part of the evolution of the universe. In his theology, man has to go through hell in order to reach God and a state of grace.

Thus for Böhme, mankind must depart from God and undergo conflict and suffering in order to make spiritual progress. He compares a person's spiritual journey with the fall of Satan from heaven, and the inevitable separation of Adam and Eve from the Garden of Eden. He sees free will as central to man's existence. God seeks to interact with mankind, which is both part of his creation and a separate entity. Indeed, for Böhme, God is in some sense incomplete without the act of creation. By making the gift of free will to mankind he gives us the opportunity to find a new state of harmony.

This was one of the respects in which he departed radically from Lutheran teachings – the idea that God might be imperfect or in some way incomplete without mankind was seen as heretical by his contemporaries. Böhme also departed from his Church by emphasising the need for self-awareness and faith rather than the blind pursuit of dogma. As so often, the suggestion that the believer might have to follow their own conscience caused offence to the Church, which was striving to impose orthodoxy on its followers.

It is important to remember that Böhme's writing is constantly informed by his mystical visions. The Church of his time took issue with theological details of this vision, but it is perhaps better to take Böhme's writing as a personal, poetical view of God's relationship with man.

As well as inspiring a group of followers, who became known as Behmenists, his writing became influential among those who appreciated its theological and poetical depth. John Wesley suggested him as reading for his preachers, while the theologian William Law wrote that 'Jacob Böhme was not a messenger of anything new in religion, but the mystery of all that was old and true in religion and nature, was opened up to him . . . the depth of the riches, both of the wisdom and knowledge of God.'

Meanwhile the suggestions of mysticism and anti-authoritarianism in his work attracted followers as varied as William Blake and the later Theosophists.

*The Way to Christ* is not an easy read today. The text is dense and hard to decipher. It consists of nine separate chapters or treatises, and Böhme intended it as a meditation guide. He regarded his work as being dictated by the Holy Spirit, which he also described as the principle of life.

His unique vision of the Trinity as being constructed of fire and light and his obscure references to the role of Mary and her virginity can be hard to follow on a casual read. But there is nonetheless something fascinating and absorbing in his writing, and *The Way to Christ* remains a thought-provoking glimpse into the mind of a seventeenth-century mystic.

## The Way to Christ

### THE SPEED READ

A meditation guide, based on the mystical visions of a seventeenth-century mystic in the Lutheran tradition. Focusing on the problem of sin and redemption, Böhme suggests that mankind must suffer the hell of the ordinary world of suffering in order to travel back towards a state of grace with God.

# *The Pilgrim's Progress*
## John Bunyan, 1678

'If you have sinned, do not lie down without repentance, for the want of repentance after one has sinned makes the heart yet harder and harder.'

The full title of John Bunyan's classic work is *The Pilgrim's Progress from This World to That Which Is to Come*. This is one of those books that is such an ingrained part of literary and spiritual culture that even those who haven't read it will be familiar with much of its content. The allegorical hazards and places encountered by the hero on his journey include the 'Slough of Despond', the 'Valley of the Shadow of Death', 'Doubting Castle', 'Enchanted Ground' and 'Vanity Fair'. All of these and many other phrases and names from the book have passed into popular usage in the same way that phrases from biblical texts or Shakespeare have done.

Bunyan started to write the book while he was in prison in Bedfordshire in England. He had been sent there for contravening rules that prevented people from holding religious services other than within the official Church of England. Bunyan was a Protestant, but he was a Puritan, an independent opponent of the state-sanctioned version of the Christian religion.

He had fought for the Parliamentary Army during the English Civil War and started writing the book in the later years of the Republican Government. The Puritans wanted the Church to be purified, casting aside the remnants of Catholicism that had been retained by the Church of England. His writing was rooted in the revolutionary times he lived through: he contrasted ideas of authoritarian government and law with the joy one can find through saving one's soul.

The plot initially revolves around an everyman character called Christian, and his attempt to travel from the City of Destruction to the Celestial City. It uses a dreamlike narrative, involving strange encounters with other travellers and symbolic meetings with allegorical figures, to represent a soul's journey towards redemption. The book starts with Christian becoming weighed down by a terrible 'burden' as he reads a religious text, and his realisation that he must set out on his journey.

He is guided on his way by Evangelist, but is frequently sidetracked. First he makes the mistake of trying to relieve his burden through the law, on the advice of Mr Worldly Wiseman. But then a character called Good Will (who is later revealed as Jesus Christ) guides him on his way once again to the 'place of deliverance'. Here Christian is finally relieved of his burden as the straps holding it break loose at the open sepulchre of Christ.

Following a battle with the mighty Apollyon in the Valley of Humiliation, Christian continues his journey through terrors such as the Valley of the Shadow of Death, and Doubting Castle, where he is imprisoned by the Giant Despair. At times he is accompanied by companions such as Hopeful and Faithful, although they gradually fall by the wayside.

One crucial turning point comes when Christian's courage returns to him after he hears the words of the 23rd Psalm: 'Yea, though I walk through the valley of the shadow of death, I will fear no evil: for thou art with me; thy rod and thy staff they comfort me.'

Finally Christian and Hopeful get beyond the Enchanted Ground to the Land of Beulah, then finally they cross the River of Death to reach Mount Zion and the Celestial City, where they are welcomed.

Bunyan also wrote a second part to the book, which is often published in a single volume with the first. In this one Christian's wife Christiana sets off on the same route as her husband with members of her family. This journey is a longer, more realistic one. The narrative focuses more on the everyday life of the pilgrims and emphasises the joy of the pilgrimage itself as well as the struggles they go through on their path towards the Celestial City.

Bunyan's tone throughout *The Pilgrim's Progress* is quite tough – his idea of how to live the holy life is a very specific one and some of the wayfarers who make mistakes are harshly punished. But at the same time the book has a kind of fairy-tale appeal that makes it popular even with children. And certainly it is one of the most powerful and influential allegories of a soul's journey that has ever been written.

The book was hugely successful, being translated into more than two hundred languages. It quickly reached America, where it was widely read in the new Puritan communities. And to this day the book has remained in print somewhere in the world.

It influenced many successors, who either imitated its allegorical, dreamy style or who found other ways to relate the journey of a soul through life. It has also been influential in a purely literary sense, as many writers have either imitated or parodied its style, in particular in the names of the characters and places involved in Christian's journey. One can even see remnants of its influence in such disparate modern children's writers as Enid Blyton (who wrote her own version of the book, *The Land of Far Beyond*) and J. K. Rowling.

It is not always an easy or comforting read, as its Christian message is a very specific, purist one, in keeping with Bunyan's Puritan beliefs. However, it can be an inspiring read for both young and old, and has to be regarded as one of the most influential religious books in history.

### The Pilgrim's Progress

#### THE SPEED READ

One day Christian realised he was carrying a heavy burden. He set off to relieve himself of this burden, making a difficult and danger-fraught journey. Along the way he encountered a series of people and places with allegorical names that identify their role. His journey was a metaphor for the Christian journey through life, towards redemption. Guided by, among others, Jesus Christ and Evangelist, he managed to rid himself of his burden, and to travel on to finally reach the Celestial City. Then his wife made the same journey, meeting even more fantastical characters along the way. Life is difficult and the way is narrow, but faith in Christ can save us in the end.

# 2
# Later Christian Writings

The last few centuries have been an age of great advances in science and rationalism. As a result, religion has at times seemed to be under threat from relativism and nihilism. So it is not surprising that some of the most interesting twentieth-century writings on Christianity are those that consider the underpinning of religion in the modern world.

The first book in this section, *The Way of a Pilgrim*, is something of a throwback to a simpler age. The pilgrim's faith in God is inspiring and a reminder of simpler times. However, it is a book that examines some of the most basic aspects of faith, and tries to establish an understanding of what it means to live a life devoted to God.

The other books included here are all from the twentieth and twenty-first century, and all address the basic problems of faith in the modern world. *Orthodoxy* by G. K. Chesterton is an interesting book because it makes an argument that you don't see too often, which is that we should defer to the authority of the Church. Writers, even spiritual writers, tend to be individualists, so they are perhaps less likely than other people to wish to make the argument that we should conform to orthodoxy, but Chesterton makes an engaging argument for this point of view.

*The Screwtape Letters* is similarly focused on the essential problems of faith and temptation, but is a more humorous book. The works of Francis Schaeffer and Henry Nouwen each take a look at the essential roots of Christian faith, Meanwhile Timothy Keller's 2008 book *The Reason for God* returns to the old-fashioned tradition of Christian apologetics. Keller looks at the arguments for scepticism and for rejecting Christianity and calmly debunks the certainty of the non-Christian position.

These titles are all ones that have their own value in an age when doubt and scepticism are rife. It could perhaps be said that the two great dangers of the modern world are excessively dogmatic religious movements and the forces of nihilism and faithlessness. The task facing the modern believer is how to steer a reasonable path between these extremes.

## *The Way of a Pilgrim*

### Anonymous, Nineteenth Century

'My worldly goods are a knapsack and some dried bread in it, and a Bible in my breast pocket. And that is all.'

In 1 Thessalonians 5.17, St Paul gave believers a notoriously impossible command, when he exhorted them to 'pray always'. The classic Russian work *The Way of a Pilgrim* is a direct response to this question. It is a charming book, about the author of which little is known. It is not even clear if it is an autobiographical account of the wandering of a hermit, or a well-constructed piece of spiritual fiction. Either way the book has been instrumental in popularising both the Jesus Prayer and the idea of silent prayer.

The book is squarely within the Orthodox Christian tradition, taking its authority from the Orthodox text the *Philokalia*, in which the Greek Church Fathers advocated the idea of *hesychasm*. This is based on Christ's instruction in Matthew's Gospel to 'go into your closet and pray'. In practice this involves turning inwards to find a still centre from which you can achieve a knowledge of God.

The specific method recommended in *The Way of a Pilgrim* involves repeating the Jesus Prayer endlessly to oneself. Rather than getting bogged down in theological detail, the anonymous narrator chooses simply to start praying and to continue doing so. The *starets* (religious father) who teaches him how to use the prayer advises him to study the *Philokalia* and instructs him thus on the use of the Jesus Prayer:

> Sit down in silence. Lower your head, shut your eyes, breathe out gently, and imagine yourself looking into your own heart. Carry your mind, that is, your thoughts, from your head to your heart. As you breathe out, say, 'Lord Jesus Christ, have mercy on me.' Say it moving your lips gently, or simply say it in your mind. Try to put all other thoughts aside. Be calm, be patient, and repeat the process very frequently.

The book is an account of the pilgrim's wanderings and his attempt to come to terms with praying ceaselessly, as advised by the *starets*. One of the reasons for its popularity today is the engaging style of the narrator. He starts the book by telling us this about himself: 'By the grace of God I am a Christian man, by my actions a great sinner, and by calling a homeless wanderer of the humblest birth who roams from place to place.' Then he tells us of his travels and of the various sinners, drunks and homeless people he meets along the way. The pilgrim himself remains a cipher, or everyman:

we discover relatively little about him, not even his name. The small amount of information he reveals about his family only gives us a few hints.

His parents died while he was young and he grew up with his grandfather and elder brother. The latter accidentally injured him in a rough game in their childhood, leaving him with a crippled left arm, meaning that he was unable to do much manual labour. The elder brother became an alcoholic. After the death of their grandfather, he burned down the house, which the younger brother now shared with his young wife, in a fit of jealousy. The wife ended up dying of a fever, leaving the pilgrim to wander the world alone.

The book's depiction of nineteenth-century Russia is one that will ring true to anyone familiar with the novels of Dostoevsky or Tolstoy. Having heard of St Paul's admonition to constant prayer, the pilgrim rejects the material world and sets out to discover how he can achieve this goal. This is the journey that leads him to the *starets* and the Jesus Prayer.

The book is divided into four sections, through which the pilgrim's travels and experiences develop. There is also a sequel, *The Pilgrim Continues His Way*, which is often included with the first book in a single volume.

The books first came to light on Mount Athos, and many believe that the first book was written by a Russian traveller, while the second may have been a continuation of the work written by a Greek monk from the holy mountain. Certainly the ideas advocated in the book – of living as a hermit in simplicity and constant prayer – would have been given an enthusiastic reception in the rarefied atmosphere of Mount Athos. The second book definitely feels more dry and theoretical than the first, although whoever wrote the first was clearly well informed, and demonstrates a knowledge of religious figures such as St Simeon the New Theologian, Ignatius, Peter the Damascene and John Climaticus.

At first, the pilgrim repeats the Jesus Prayer 6,000 times a day, although he soon doubles this to 12,000. Eventually the prayer synchronises with his breathing and walking to become a natural part of his life. After working on a farm, he decides to travel to Siberia in search of greater silence. He walks sixty miles a day, begging for no more than dry bread, salt and water from the villages and farms along the way. His life as a wanderer plays almost as strong a role in his spiritual development as his use of ceaseless prayer.

Some of the pilgrim's encounters are especially charming. At one stage the children of a family accost him, calling him 'Dear little beggar' and inviting him to their house, because their mother is so fond of beggars. The pilgrim stays with this family for a while, passing on what he has learned in a series of conversations.

However, the pilgrim also encounters adversity. He is forced to fight off a wolf, and is jailed and flogged after an incident with a young woman – she was facing a forced marriage and the pilgrim advised her to flee. After she catches up with the pilgrim on the road, he teaches her about prayer, but the groom discovers them and the pilgrim is accused of seducing her away. The pilgrim describes such unfortunate incidents in a stoical tone that suggests he sees them merely as lessons from God.

After his travels, the narrator ends the book by revealing that he has travelled to Kiev and is planning to move on to Jerusalem. It is not a long book, but he feels obliged to end with the self-effacing comment: 'I have already chatted far too much. And the holy fathers call even spiritual talk mere babble if it lasts too long.' The popularity of this sweet and profound little book was boosted when it was used by J. D. Salinger as a central part of the plot of *Franny and Zooey*. Part of its modern appeal comes from the fact that the wanderer's spirituality revolves around his travels, and the easy way he relates the incidents that happen to him on his journey.

Some modern readers have also related the idea of the Jesus Prayer to meditation, and the use of koans and mantras within Eastern religion, although the book sits easily within the mainstream of Orthodox Christianity. It can be read as a simple theological introduction to ideas that can be pursued further by reading the *Philokalia*. But it can also be read as a profound meditation on silence, receptiveness and inward prayer.

## *The Way of a Pilgrim*

### THE SPEED READ

After my miserable Russian childhood, I chose to wander the world, trying to discover what the Bible meant when it advised us to pray ceaselessly. A wise man told me how to use the Jesus Prayer, 'Lord Jesus Christ, have mercy on me', as a constant prayer. Through this prayer and my ongoing solitary wanderings, I came to a deeper understanding of spirituality and how prayer can lead us to God. Now, I have kept you for long enough. Time for me to continue my journey.

# *Orthodoxy*
## G. K. Chesterton 1908

'This, therefore, is, in conclusion, my reason for accepting the religion and not merely the scattered and secular truths out of the religion. I do it because the thing has not merely told this truth or that truth, but has revealed itself as a truth-telling thing. All other philosophers say the things that plainly seem to be true; only this philosophy has again and again said the thing that does not seem to be true, but is true.'

*O*rthodoxy is an unusual book because it is a defence of the idea that not only should we accept the teaching of the Church, but we should be prepared to respect the specific authority of the Church and accept that as being superior to our own individual judgement. Many books address problems of faith from a more individual viewpoint, but there are not many modern books by writers of note that recommend subjugating ourselves to the Church.

Chesterton, the English writer and journalist, wrote the book as a companion to his earlier book *Heretics*. In the preface he explains that he had decided to 'attempt an explanation, not of whether the Christian Faith can be believed, but of how he personally has come to believe it'. His views at this point were specifically Roman Catholic, and the book needs to be read with this in mind, as part of his project is a defence of the Church's historical actions.

He describes Christianity as being a natural answer to human needs, the solution to the problems we face, and a solution that is naturally superior to other solutions. As a metaphor for his spiritual search Chesterton describes a man setting off from his hometown, travelling for many days, only to arrive back where he started. His point is that the man would now see his hometown through new, clearer eyes, and this is the viewpoint he hopes he is able to bring to the idea of Christianity.

To describe the book, it's necessary to briefly describe the logic of its argument. He starts by describing mankind's spiritual needs and proposing that Christianity might be a reasonable solution to those needs. To support this he takes some time to consider and dismiss some of the contemporary alternatives.

This section sees Chesterton at his most infuriating – his rejections of the ideas of pragmatism, evolution, enlightenment rationalism and the continental ideas of thinkers such as Nietzsche and Schopenhauer are mostly based on paper tigers, inadequate accounts of the actual ideas involved. At one stage he argues thus, in defence of the oppressive systems of past religious authorities:

> The creeds and the crusades, the hierarchies and the horrible persecutions were not organized, as is ignorantly said, for the suppression of reason. They were organized for the difficult defence of reason. Man, by a blind instinct, knew that if once things were wildly questioned, reason could be questioned first. The authority of priests to absolve, the authority of popes to define the authority, even of inquisitors to terrify: these were all only dark defences erected round one central authority, more undemonstrable, more supernatural than all – the authority of a man to think.

As a defence of Christianity over rationalism, this is a very weak argument. Historically, it is clear that many parts of the Church, including the Inquisition, were indeed intent on the suppression of reason. And the failure to acknowledge this fatally undermines an argument that might otherwise be effective. This is unfortunate because Chesterton does touch on some fascinating points – in particular the idea that the complete rejection of orthodox religion in favour of science and rationalism can lead to a nihilistic, relativistic void, into which new mythologies and authorities will step.

The rise of communism and fascism over the ensuing decades would bear out this analysis to some degree. A far more rigorous version of this argument would eventually be made in *The Dialectic of Enlightenment*, in which Max Horkheimer and Theodor Adorno argue that the apparent victory of subjective reason over objective reason as a result of the Enlightenment had in fact created a new and more dangerous age of myth, as people were cut loose from the old certainties and faiths.

So the slackness of Chesterton's argument in these sections is disappointing. He fails to explain why a reasonable person should reject rationalism and science for Christianity. When it comes to evolution he argues that 'if evolution simply means that a positive thing called an ape turned very slowly into a positive thing called a man, then it is stingless for the most orthodox; for a personal God might just as well do things slowly as quickly, especially if . . . he were outside time'.

But rather than follow through on the promise of this argument Chesterton rejects the idea of evolution on the basis that he prefers to accept the orthodoxies of the Church than to allow them to adapt to modern science. This may be one of the reasons why Chesterton's book is now popular with evangelical Christians and others who prefer to hold to a fundamentalist interpretation of Christianity rather than allow the Church to grow and adapt to modern science.

Chesterton moves on to talk about man's basic attitude to the world. He talks about how it is reasonable for us to view the world in wonder, to believe that it holds meaning, that it has been designed for a purpose, and to react to this idea with humility and respect. He goes on to consider the views of those who reject Christianity.

Again this section is flawed by overly simplistic rejections of opposing arguments. Basically he argues that because people have attacked Christianity from a variety of opposing positions they can't all be right and there must be something peculiarly right about Christianity. This of course isn't a remotely logical argument, even though Chesterton makes his case in an engaging and appealing way.

Finally Chesterton moves on to a rather personal view of the structure of Christian thought and the reasons why he believes it to be the best and most reasonable answer to human spiritual needs. The book really comes alive in these passages, as Chesterton devotes more time to explaining his own faith.

He also talks engagingly about the reasons why we should accept the authority of the Church. He talks about a child who learns to trust their father when they are told that, for instance, a flower will smell a certain way. He points out that the child need not come up with a complex scientific reason to trust their father, or to justify the parental authority with resort to psychology or other rationalisations. They simply trust their father because he has always been the person they trust the most. They have found him to be someone who tells them the truth about the world, so why wouldn't they trust him?

In sections such as these, Chesterton writes powerfully. And in the book as a whole there is an argument that almost but not quite succeeds. One can accept his overall thesis that the result of rationalism is for people to lose their faith in orthodoxy and that, as a result, we lose something valuable. But his argument is idiosyncratic and unlikely to persuade anyone who doesn't share his specific beliefs.

*Orthodoxy* is an enjoyable read, in spite of its flaws. Sometimes it provokes one to argue with the writer, other times to nod in agreement. It is probably not as good an apology for simple Christianity as *Mere Christianity* by C. S. Lewis, to which it is often compared. But it is an honest and interesting account of one writer's reasons for trusting in his Church. As such it makes an interesting read for anyone who believes that it is important to respect some form of religious authority, whether that be a trusted preacher, the official Church, or simply the teaching that is passed down to us from our families.

*Orthodoxy*

### THE SPEED READ

Mankind has certain spiritual needs and has to balance different aspects of human nature. Christianity is the best solution to this problem and something that any reasonable person could or should believe in. Enlightenment rationalism and science answer questions but don't satisfy the soul. Pragmatism, nihilism and all the currently fashionable 'isms' are piffle. People attack Christianity from different viewpoints, so they must all be wrong. In the end one trusts the Church as one might trust a parent – because they have proven themselves to be the best path to truth and a good life.

# *The Screwtape Letters*
## C. S. Lewis, 1942

'Your man ... doesn't think of doctrines as primarily "true" or "false," but as "academic" or "practical," "outworn" or "contemporary," "conventional" or "ruthless." Jargon, not argument, is your best ally in keeping him from the Church.'

C. S. Lewis is one of the great popular writers on Christianity. In titles such as *Mere Christianity* and *The Problem of Pain* and *Miracles*, he dealt in a succinct but inspiring way with many of the basic problems and objections to the Christian faith. But one of his most entertaining books on the subject is a more humorous title, *The Screwtape Letters*, in which he takes the point of view of a devil in order to satirise and analyse the obstacles a believer must overcome.

Lewis had been baptised in the Church of Ireland, but drifted away from the Church in his youth, feeling it to be a chore and irrelevant to his life. However, he reconverted, joining the Anglican Church after a long struggle with his beliefs. Part of his inspiration came from his fascination with myth and history, in which his studies led him to conclude that there were certain ever-present themes in the human condition, themes that could only be dealt with in a moral way from the religious standpoint.

Today, C. S. Lewis is most famous for his children's books, the Chronicles of Narnia, which were published in the 1950s. The Narnia books often contain clear Christian messages, albeit in allegorical form. The figure of Aslan contains elements of God and Christ, and there are numerous storylines that revolve around faith, redemption and forgiveness. Lewis preferred not to see the Christian content as 'allegory', instead describing it as an imaginative recreation of what Christ might be like if there were a real world like Narnia where he underwent experiences such as those that Aslan faces.

The Narnia books retain great popularity and power to this day. But Lewis was already a well-known writer and broadcaster long before he started work on them, renowned for his wartime broadcasts on the subject of Christianity.

In his faith he was always careful to take a broad, non-sectarian approach. He didn't want to exclude any branch of the Christian Church, believing that the message of Jesus was of far more importance than whether one chose to follow that message through the Quaker, Baptist, Roman Catholic, Anglican or any other route.

In *The Screwtape Letters*, Lewis chose a satirical form to convey his message. The book takes the form of a series of letters from the experienced demon Screwtape to the junior tempter Wormwood. Wormwood is in the process of attempting to win a human soul for the forces of evil, and to keep his man from discovering the road to God. Screwtape gives him humorous advice on how to achieve his goal, advice that centres on genuinely interesting problems of faith and belief.

Some of the humour in the book is rather broad – hell's bureaucracy is called the Lowerarchy, and Screwtape's references to 'Our Father' and 'the Adversary' are reversed from the usual Christian understanding of those terms. Lewis dealt with the problems and challenges that face doubters and believers at greater length in *Mere Christianity* and his partial autobiography *Surprised by Joy*. But the pithy and entertaining way that Screwtape deals with these problems from his demonic point of view makes Lewis's point as well if not better than those more sober books.

Screwtape often advises Wormwood on the usefulness of the 'modern' point of view in befuddling the human mind. The many distractions that can be used to distract the man from God, the relativism, and belief in scientific solutions that can be used as justifications for rejecting faith – all of these are presented as the natural allies of the tempting demon. Lewis's own views are clear throughout, sometimes enlightened, sometimes a little fuddy-duddy and anti-modern, but always presented with the best intentions.

The book deals with sinful situations as varied as sex, love, pride, gluttony, and war. It also focuses on the small everyday acts of pride, weakness and selfishness that can turn us away from God just as effectively as the more obvious sins. Lewis presents self-interest and greed as human attributes that can be exploited by Wormwood to distract the man from the path of virtue and godliness.

Throughout the book Wormwood seems a slightly hapless figure and many of his attempts at temptation backfire, to the impatience and irritation of his older mentor Screwtape. In the end the man's soul escapes Wormwood's clutches and he is left facing the inevitable wrath of 'our Father'.

While it is a funny book in many ways, it is not one that Lewis enjoyed writing. He found it difficult and morally ambiguous to place himself in the role of Screwtape and to have to think about the world from the opposite viewpoint to his own. Lewis also went out of his way to point out that his use of demons as the main characters in this book did not imply that he believed in hell and demons in the old-fashioned sense.

He eventually resolved to stop writing the letters because of his unease about these issues, although he wrote one sequel, *Screwtape Proposes a Toast*, many years later, in which he dealt with what he saw as the evil of progressive education. One of Lewis's weaknesses as a religious writer is his tendency to let his political views distract from the wider message, and thus to detract from his more powerful messages. But this is a minor cavil about a writer who wrote some marvellously interesting and inspiring books about spirituality.

The fundamental message of *The Screwtape Letters* is as relevant today as when it was written. For a vision of the small obstacles and temptations that can confuse and distract us from a spiritual path, it has rarely been bettered.

## The Screwtape Letters

### The Speed Read

My dear Wormwood,

As ever you are not making a terribly good job of distracting and befuddling your human patient, and keeping him from God. Follow my advice, focus on everyday weaknesses, pride and self-interest, and steer him towards "modern" relativistic thinking, teach him to value "real life" over the life of the spirit, and you'll be halfway to saving his soul from heaven.

Your affectionate uncle, Screwtape.

## True Spirituality
### Francis A. Schaeffer, 1971

'Christianity is not just a series of truths but Truth – Truth about all of reality.'

Francis Schaeffer is an intriguing figure in twentieth-century Christianity who makes arguments that are more complex than some of his critics might accept. In the 1940s the Schaeffer family moved from the USA to Switzerland, where he and his wife set up the L'Abri community, which still exists as a centre of Christian thinking. This was a time when people were struggling to find meaning in the world after the horrors of the Second World War. Schaeffer personally went through a crisis of faith and his book *True Spirituality* should be read with the knowledge that it describes a personal progress more than it prescribes a path for others to follow.

It is an inspiring book in many respects that describes how Schaeffer examined the roots of his own faith, came to the simple conclusion that Christianity is true, and made this realisation the foundation stone for his life.

It is important to note that Schaeffer has been credited with inspiring the modern activism of right-wing evangelism in the USA, in particular its militant opposition to abortion. This is partly because of his belief that America (and any Christian nation) should adhere to biblical rather than humanistic principles.

Schaeffer is also often associated with *presuppositional apologetics*. To briefly explain this term, there is a theological opposition between two theories of how to approach the idea that God and scripture should hold primacy in one's thinking. Evidential apologetics follows Thomas Aquinas in attempting to find ways to demonstrate the existence of God, and the truth of his word; ways that rely only on facts that can be acknowledged by any rational human, whether they be Christian or not.

Presuppositional apologetics rejects this starting point. Instead it suggests that it is impossible to find such a neutral starting point, that the Christian worldview is the only coherent one and that any attempt to start from a neutral viewpoint is confused or contradictory.

Schaeffer certainly started from the idea that Christianity is true. But he did accept that a rational conversation could be had with a non-Christian – he felt that any non-Christian viewpoint was inherently contradictory but that this was because even those who rejected Christianity could not bring themselves to reject all that was clearly true, and that there was thus part of the Christian idea already in their thinking. Thus he saw it as the Christian apologist's job to expose the contradictions in other lines of thought, in order to demonstrate that Christianity was the one truth.

Schaeffer was adamant in his viewpoint that society had become bogged down in relativism, modernism and what he referred to as humanism, the idea that man is the measure of all things. He thus called for a robust Christian response to those ideas which, in his view, led to the negative and hopeless outlook of such modern theories as Marxism and existentialism.

For Schaeffer, any attempt to comprehend the world without starting from Christ's message was doomed to founder in confusion and contradiction. He felt that the

angst of contemporary political and philosophical ideolo-
gies was inspired by a failure to recognise this truth. He had
started out by studying philosophy himself, but felt that it
failed to answer the important questions about life, death
and the spirit, and that he had only made any real progress
once he started studying the Bible instead.

It is also worth reading *True Spirituality* to get a more
complex view of someone who has been taken up as a guru by
some parts of modern Christianity. There are evangelists who
admire his call to personal action on issues he felt strongly
about, while others have criticised him for encouraging the
move towards a kind of modern theocracy as the ideal of
Christianity.

In his writing there are more nuances than have been represented by some who followed in his footsteps. For a start
he warned several times about the dangers of 'wrapping
Christianity in the American flag'. This is a writer for whom
the idea of personal conscience is of paramount importance.

He wants to persuade others to his point of view, which
he believes is the only valid one, but he nonetheless recog-
nises the difficulties inherent in linking politics and religious
conviction. Schaeffer believed in the First Amendment,
guaranteeing freedom of religion for all, and specifically
rejected any serious step towards theocracy (the rule of religious law).

In a modern world where we perceive dangers both in the
lack of faith and conviction of modern relativisms, and in
the excess of certainty that fundamentalists of both Christian
and non-Christian faiths evince, Schaeffer is a problematic
read. But he must be acknowledged as a powerful voice that
makes a case for religious certainty as a personal, moral
choice. And *True Spirituality* is also a persuasive account of
one man's spiritual journey.

*True Spirituality*

### THE SPEED READ

The Bible and its message of salvation carry the 'true truth'. When we understand this we have a responsibility to demonstrate the falsehoods and inconsistencies of non-Christian belief systems. Christianity is not something we practise only in church or in prayer, but something that is present in the truth and spirituality of our actions in everyday life, in education, social policy and business.

# *The Return of the Prodigal Son*
## Henri Nouwen, 1992

'Home is the centre of my being where I can hear the voice that says:
"You are my Beloved, on you my favor rests" – the same voice that
gave life to the first Adam and spoke to Jesus . . .'

Henri Nouwen (1932–96) was a Catholic priest who wrote many books on spirituality that are popular with readers of different denominations. He was born in the Netherlands, but spent most of his life in the US and Canada. In 1986 he left his life as a teacher at institutions such as Yale and Harvard to live at the L'Arche community near Toronto called 'Daybreak', where he helped to care for mentally handicapped people. He wrote a deeply moving book called *Adam: God's Beloved* about his friendship with a member of the community who suffered from severe disabilities.

One of his most fascinating books is *The Return of the Prodigal Son*. After an exhausting lecture tour of the US, Nouwen was staying in a different L'Arche community in France in 1983. There he found himself contemplating a reproduction of Rembrandt's painting, which provided the name for his book. It was partly as a result of his meditations on this painting that he eventually chose to give up his lifestyle and take his place in the Canadian L'Arche community.

His meditation on the painting, and on the biblical story that inspired it, considers different perspectives within the narrative. In turn he identifies with the younger son, the elder son and the father. In each of his writings he emphasised the idea that we are all beloved sons and daughters of God. He takes this line of thought further by looking at each character in the story, and by pointing out that we are all capable of playing the different parts.

In the younger son, he identifies the part of us that wants to be loved and forgiven, even though we may not truly deserve to receive those blessings. In the elder son he sees someone who is 'doing everything right' but feels depressed that the love and forgiveness that he has 'earned' are given freely to the younger son who has not deserved the same treatment as him.

Both of these characters' motivations are comprehensible. But Nouwen emphasises that God's love and forgiveness are unconditional. The only character in the story who shows this is the father, and we all have it in us to emulate the father rather than either of the two sons. We are capable of expressing love and forgiveness in spite of the faults, pride and weaknesses of others. The father is also the only truly happy figure in the story, because he is the one who is at spiritual peace.

In this sense, Nouwen is bringing out a less obvious aspect of the story. Jesus is not only trying to teach us to accept God's love, as the prodigal son does once he realises he is forgiven. If anything the moral of the story derives from the unconditional love the father offers to the son. This is the example that Jesus would prefer us to follow.

The book also has a powerful message for those who can identify with the elder son – feeling that they follow all the rules but are not appreciated. This part of the writing may have been informed by Nouwen's own personal circumstances. He struggled with depression at times and also felt restricted by his role as a priest. It may or may not be relevant that he struggled with homosexual feelings in his life – meaning that as well as having to deal with the difficulties of abstinence, he found it hard to be honest about the exact way that those difficulties affected him.

There seems to be an echo of this in his sympathetic portrait of the depression felt by the elder son. And anyone who has been 'good' and 'dutiful' in their life may recognise the feeling that virtue is not always its own reward. However, when he discusses the father's point of view, Nouwen also shows a way to reach beyond this depression or perception, by seeking to emulate God in his unconditional love and forgiveness, rather than by seeking spiritual rewards for one's correct behaviour.

In a later book, *Bread for the Journey*, Nouwen wrote this:

> Although we tend to think about saints as holy and pious, and picture them with halos above their heads and ecstatic gazes, true saints are much more accessible. They are men and women like us, who live ordinary lives and struggle with ordinary problems. What makes them saints is their clear and unwavering focus on God and God's people.

The point he is making so eloquently is that the holiest and most admirable people were not born as perfect paragons. They struggle with their own problems as we all do. And this understanding can inspire us to reach out and try to improve our own behaviour and virtue, rather than making us feel inadequate. Nouwen's writing is inspiring for anyone who has ever struggled to live up to their own spiritual standards, as it reminds us that we are all only human, but can nonetheless aspire to become closer to God.

## The Return of the Prodigal Son

### THE SPEED READ

Contemplating the story of the Prodigal Son, you can identify with the different characters in different ways. We can all be like the younger son – undeserving and living a bad life until we perceive the unconditional love of God. The elder son suffers from depression when his worthy behaviour is rewarded no better than the wayward behaviour of his younger sibling. Meanwhile the father shows us how Jesus would want us to behave, because he shows unconditional love and forgiveness to both of his sons.

# The Reason for God
## Timothy Keller, 2008

'During my nearly two decades in New York City, I've had numerous opportunities to ask people, "What is your problem with Christianity. What troubles you the most about its beliefs or how it is practiced?"'

Timothy Keller, the pastor at the Redeemer Presbyterian Church in New York City, is the author of *The Reason for God: Belief in an Age of Skepticism*. This is a defence and explanation of Christianity for the modern world, in the tradition of Christian apologetics that also includes books such as *Mere Christianity* by C. S. Lewis and *Orthodoxy* by G. K. Chesterton.

While Keller is a Presbyterian, he takes a broad approach to Christianity, addressing the basic problems of faith rather than more detailed theological debates. In fact, one could argue that his work in New York City, where he preaches to an audience that will regard itself as relatively cultured, sceptical and even cynical, provides the perfect background to writing a book of this sort. Keller patiently but powerfully looks at the most common arguments against Christianity and explains his own reasons for rejecting those arguments.

The book has been described as being for 'sceptics and the believers who love them' and provides a blueprint for anyone who feels the need to defend their faith. He draws on secular material, including philosophical and literary classics and scientific accounts of anthropology, to make his case.

Keller starts by observing that this is an age in which attitudes towards religion are becoming more polarised. He writes that 'skepticism, fear, and anger toward traditional religion are growing in power and influence . . . But, at the same time, robust, orthodox belief in the traditional faiths is growing as well.' As a result he decided to write a book addressing some of the fundamental issues in this argument.

Keller's approach is to address sceptics, and to ask them what the foundation is for their doubts. He argues that even sceptical doubts about religion are themselves based on assumptions and beliefs, and that by questioning those assumptions you can show that the sceptical position is less certain than sceptics assume.

Seven chapters in the first half of the book address some of the most common objections to Christianity. He responds to the ideas that a good God would not allow suffering, that the Church has been responsible for great injustices, that science has superseded Christianity and that the Bible is mere myth, not to be taken literally.

In each case he calmly points out the assumptions that underpin the sceptical position and deconstructs them to show that they have their own difficulties and problems.

In the second half of the book he moves on to positive reasons to believe in God. He deals cogently and persuasively with issues such as the problem of sin. He also continues to insist that even those who deny 'supernatural' explanations of the world have their own views of spiritual truth.

Critics have questioned details of Keller's explanations – for instance, the way he argues for 'theistic evolution', an approach which allows a Christian to accept that evolution is real, but still believe in God as the creator of that evolution. But one of the most powerful aspects of the book is the way that he addresses the whole issue of scepticism and shows that the sceptics make their own non-rational leaps of faith, just as they accuse believers of doing.

While we live in a world where both scepticism and faith seem to have increased in strength, much recent publishing has focused on the sceptical side of the argument. From Richard Dawkins to Christopher Hitchens there has been a stream of books that claim that all the problems of the world stem from religion and that the only answer is atheism.

Keller's book is a useful antidote to this tendency. He may not persuade every sceptical reader, and not all Christians will agree with some of his specific interpretations. In addition, he occasionally relies too much on arguments derived from Lewis's *Mere Christianity*. But the main line of his argument is a strong, robust defence of the Christian faith that will genuinely be of interest to nonbelievers as well as those who are already Christians, and which is ideally geared to the modern world.

## The Reason for God

### THE SPEED READ

In my church in New York, I've spent a lot of time discussing belief with sceptics. Here are some of the most common arguments I have come across against God, and here are my arguments as to why they are not convincing. Even sceptics are falling back on assumptions about spiritual truth, even when they claim to 'believe in nothing'. And there are many positive reasons for believing in God as well.

# 3
# Approaches to Prayer

One of the most basic religious practices is prayer. We talk to God to plead for intervention, for daily comfort, for spiritual inspiration and for many other reasons.

But what is the best way to pray? Where do you start, and what is the best way of using prayer to develop a fuller spiritual existence? Should you set aside time for prayer on a daily basis, pray in church, or attempt to stay in constant contact with God? These are such obvious questions that we may sometimes forget to ask them.

This is one reason why the books in this section are of great appeal. Several of them, including John Baillie's *A Diary of Private Prayer* and Anthony Bloom's *Beginning to Pray*, can be used as introductions to the art of praying. Bloom's book in particular is a marvellous examination of what is happening when we pray, and addresses questions such as 'Why should we get upset if God doesn't seem to be listening to us, when we so often fail to heed his call?'

Madame Guyon's *A Short and Easy Method of Prayer* is a rather different work. Condemned as heretical in its own time, it is a passionate examination of our relationship with God. Like the anonymous author of *The Way of a Pilgrim*,

Madame Guyon concludes that we must practise 'constant prayer'. Frank Laubach reaches a similar conclusion in *Letters by a Modern Mystic*, in which he takes a detailed look at how we might have God in our lives every moment of the day.

The remaining two books in this section, *A Testament of Devotion* by Thomas R. Kelly and *The Pursuit of God* by A. W. Tozer, cover a wider range of topics, but, like the other books described here, they focus on the very basics of our daily spiritual existence. Tozer subjects our religious foundations to an intense examination, while Kelly's approach is more meditative. However, both books deal with one of the most difficult spiritual problems: how do we face up to complexities of modern existence and still keep room for God in our lives? And beyond that, how can we make God the centre of our daily existence?

These titles all offer different approaches to the problems of prayer and religious practice. Different readers will be drawn to different approaches, as the writers represented here have such varying personalities. But each in their own way is trying to understand the most fundamental issues of how we should engage with God.

## *A Short and Easy Method of Prayer*
### Madame Guyon, 1685

'May I hasten to say that the kind of prayer I am speaking of is not a prayer that comes from YOUR MIND. It is a prayer that begins in THE HEART . . . PRAYER THAT COMES FROM THE HEART IS NOT INTERRUPTED BY THINKING!'

Madame Guyon (1648–1717) is an intriguing mystic, a French widow whose book *A Short and Easy Method of Prayer* led to her imprisonment for seven years for heresy. The history of the Christian Church is sadly full of cases where people's heartfelt beliefs or theories led to their persecution in the name of the prevailing orthodoxy of the time. It is valuable to return to the actual ideas that caused such offence and examine what value they might have for us in the modern world.

In the case of Madame Guyon, the specific heresy was 'Quietism'. This form of Christian philosophy was popular in Southern Europe in the seventeenth and eighteenth centuries. The Quietists believed that perfection could be achieved through a path of intellectual stillness and passivity. It was this emphasis on internal meditation rather than public duty that was largely to blame for the opposition of the Catholic Church of the time. For a start, it was dangerously close to the Cathar or Albigensian idea that man could seek perfection and become sinless.

However, Quietism has interesting precedents (for instance in Meister Eckhart and, arguably, in Eastern philosophy) and has had an influence on thinkers as varied as Teresa of Ávila, Watchman Nee, the Moravians and Quakers, and even John Wesley.

Madame Guyon was widowed at the age of twenty-eight after an unhappy marriage. She had been introduced to mystical ideas by Père Lacombe, a Barnabite priest. She moved from France to Annecy (in Switzerland) and renewed her acquaintance with him in the early 1680s. There she started to circulate her ideas. *A Short and Easy Method of Prayer* advocated constant prayer, and an approach to God which relied more on a passive heart than on the mind.

However, back in France, Madam Guyon ran into opposition. Quietist ideas had been declared heretical and she would be forced to recant and withdraw her statements on various occasions. Over three hundred copies of her books were burned by the authorities. Eventually, after a seven-year imprisonment from 1695 to 1703, she withdrew from public life, choosing poetry as her only public means of expression.

Her followers, however, continued to circulate her ideas and works. She had advised a life of constant prayer, in order that we might always be with God. Like the author of *The Way of a Pilgrim*, she was fascinated by St Paul's advice to pray ceaselessly. She wrote that 'prayer is the key of perfection and of sovereign happiness; it is the efficacious means of getting rid of all vices and of acquiring all virtues; for the way to become perfect is to live in the presence of God'. In this pursuit she also advocated an inner stillness, a passivity that would allow one to become one with God.

One of the long-running disputes within Christianity regards the relationship between grace and works. Guyon (like St Augustine, St Thomas Aquinas, Calvin and others) believed that salvation could only come from God. She thus concluded that a state of grace was of more significance than holy works.

The danger she identifies is that those who perform good works will do so in the belief that these will take them a step closer to heaven – in this case their actions are rooted in pride and a sense of entitlement rather than true holiness. Thus Guyon concludes that even a wicked sinner, who submits passively to God, may achieve a state of grace that makes them spiritually stronger than someone who seeks the approval of God through their actions.

This is a difficult conundrum, one that goes to the heart of the problem of free will – because, if someone has free will, then surely their actions define the choices they have made, whereas if we are mere vessels of God's will, then all that can make us more or less spiritually pure is the grace and passivity with which we carry out the will of God.

Madame Guyon's formulation of the problem may not satisfy modern readers, but it is an interesting take on a problem that still has relevance to believers today.

Another aspect of Madame Guyon's writing that can be jarring is the strain of anti-intellectualism that she shows. She writes: 'Of course, there is a kind of reading the scripture for scholarship and for study – but not here. *That studious kind of reading will not help you when it comes to matters that are divine.*' In a number of passages she seems to be suggesting that we should instinctively sense the message of the Bible rather than comprehending it with our rational minds. Of course there is a danger here of falling back into the kind of interpretive thinking shown by medieval scholasticism in which the Bible becomes a web of 'secret messages' which can be sensed but not rationally understood. In many cases it seems safe to assume that the meaning of the Bible is intended to be one that can be understood rationally rather than mystically deciphered.

One aspect of Madame Guyon's writing that disturbed the church authorities came in a chapter entitled *The Ultimate Christian Attainment*, where she writes that the final stage of prayer is union with God. Like many Christian mystics she talks of a ladder of prayer, and sees petitionary prayers as the most basic form of praying. She believes we must move beyond asking God for favours towards a state where we annihilate the self and actually become one with God.

When St Teresa of Ávila and St John of the Cross describe a ladder of prayer, they both stop short of allowing this possibility – for them God remains a separate, superior entity. The annihilation envisaged by Madame Guyon seems to have more in common with the declared goal of transcendental meditation than it does with standard Christian belief.

Nonetheless, there is much to enjoy in the work of Madame Guyon, and, as with other writers who were condemned, studying her can give us a broader understanding of the ways in which orthodoxies developed over the centuries, and of the branches of mysticism that were rejected by mainstream Christianity.

### A Short and Easy Method of Prayer

#### THE SPEED READ

Constant prayer is the path to perfection, because it is the best way to always be in the presence of God. When studying the scripture, you should sense the meaning with your heart rather than rationalise it, and cultivate a quiet and passive mind. The ultimate goal of prayer is annihilation of the self and union with God.

# A Diary of Private Prayer
## John Baillie, 1936

'Where deed of mine can help to make this world a better place for men to live in, where word of mine can cheer a despondent heart or brace a weak will, where prayer of mine can serve the extension of Christ's kingdom, there let me do and speak and pray.'

John Baillie (1886–1960) was a minister in the Church of Scotland, a professor at Edinburgh University and a well-known theologian, who wrote about the way our experience of God affects our spiritual lives. However, he is best remembered for his book *A Diary of Private Prayer*.

In essence this is a devotional, a collection of prayers. But there have been many less interesting devotionals, with no great depth or significance. Baillie's book is a different matter. It includes thirty-one morning and evening prayers, as well as extra prayers for Sundays. The subjects of the prayers are extremely varied. Some deal with personal confession, or with the spiritual life, while others centre on ideas about family and neighbours or about the state of the world.

The prayers draw on a variety of source material, from ancient prayers, and Christian liturgies, to biblical texts, although they are expressed through Baillie's own interpretation and style. At times this style is somewhat archaic: 'Give me a stout heart to bear my own burdens. Give me a willing heart to bear the burdens of others. Give me a believing heart to cast all burdens upon Thee, O Lord.' On a first read, this can seem a stiff, old-fashioned type of prayer. But the content of the prayers is the real inspiration in this book. Baillie writes with honesty about the problems that assail a believer in daily life, and his prayers crystallise immense wisdom while being constantly thought-provoking.

Not everyone would want to use these prayers as a blueprint for their own prayer. They are mostly too specific and too wordy to be used in that way. But they provide a wonderful model of prayer for those who might need inspiration or ideas for spiritual meditation.

One of the reasons this prayer book is so enduringly popular is the way that it deals with the mundane issues of everyday life. Baillie focuses on issues like getting on with the neighbours, staying polite and civil, fulfilling one's daily duties, and keeping self-control.

He also focuses on temptation, and constructs the prayers in such a way that the reader can fill in their own weaknesses and sins. This means that the book provokes a degree of soul-searching, in a way that the average cheerful devotional title does not.

This is a small book, but a powerful one. Baillie's love of God and desire to live a holy, spiritual life shines out from every page and provides an inspiration to the reader.

*A Diary of Private Prayer*

### THE SPEED READ

Morning and evening prayers, with extra Sunday prayers for a month's worth of prayer. Much more than a standard devotional book, this book provides inspiration by giving an example of how one might choose to pray on a daily basis.

## *Letters by a Modern Mystic*
### Frank Laubach, 1937

'But why do I constantly harp upon this inner experience? Because I feel convinced that for me and for you who read there lie ahead undiscovered continents of spiritual living compared with which we are infants in arms.'

*L*etters by a Modern Mystic is a collection of letters by Dr Frank Charles Laubach (1884–1970), written about the time he spent working as a Christian missionary in the Philippines in the 1930s. Laubach later became known as the 'Apostle to the Illiterates'. This was because he was the founder of the 'Each One Teach One' literacy programme, a scheme that subsequently spread worldwide, teaching millions of people to read. Laubach had a deep concern with alleviating poverty and illiteracy as a tool towards spreading peace in the world, and in his later years he achieved extraordinary results in his work with Laubach Literacy.

However, when the letters in this book were written this was all in the future. He was having a difficult time in his missionary work in the Philippines. He hadn't yet mastered the language and felt an outsider, spurned by the locals, many of whom were Muslims and not particularly receptive to his help.

He spent a lot of time contemplating his religion and resolved to embark upon an experiment in prayer. He was thinking about the passage in St Paul's letters to the Colossians which recommends the virtues of constant prayer. He resolved to try to live his life in constant contact with God.

This is an idea that had been approached in earlier works such as Brother Lawrence's *The Practice of the Presence of God*, a charming account of a seventeenth-century monk's attempt to walk in the constant presence of God, and *The Way of a Pilgrim* (see pp. 44–8), in which a Russian wanderer used the Jesus Prayer as a form of constant prayer.

Laubach brings a more experimental, twentieth-century approach to the subject. He writes frankly of his early difficulties in finding ways to live with God in the forefront of his thoughts at all times. But gradually he finds more success in his attempts. He writes thus:

> Yesterday and today I have made a new adventure, which is not easy to express. I am feeling God in each movement, by an act of will – willing that He shall direct these fingers that now strike this typewriter – willing that He shall pour through my steps as I walk – willing that He shall direct my words as I speak, and my very jaws as I eat!

Gradually as Laubach became more successful at keeping God in his mind at all times, he found that, while the effort of achieving this did not lessen, the other difficulties in his life started to feel far less problematic. He made significant progress in his missionary work, not only learning to speak the local language but also inventing a transcription method by which the local Moros could write down their words. This would be the starting point for his later literacy work.

In an age when it is often assumed that Christianity and Islam are opposing forces (largely because of the growth of extreme fundamentalist approaches to both), it is noteworthy to see how Laubach approached the Muslim religion of the locals. While he always proclaimed himself a follower of Jesus, he was happy to study the Qur'an as well as the Bible, and to pray alongside the local Islamic elders. As a result of his tolerance, the local priests recommended his teachings on God to their followers, he became known as a Friend of Islam, and this helped him to spread his message.

In fact one could argue that his relationship with Islam went deeper than this. Traditional Islamic lore emphasises the importance of submission to God, and this became a major part of Laubach's thinking, whether out of respect for or healthy competition with his Islamic contacts. At one point he suggests approaching each moment in the day with these questions in one's mind: 'What, Father, would you desire said? What, Father, would you desire done this minute?'

Later in life Laubach would write the influential pamphlet 'The Game With Minutes', in which he suggested that in order to keep God constantly in mind one should think of God for one second in every minute of the day. Of course this is just one of many approaches to the problem. In *Letters by a Modern Mystic*, he suggests that each person might want to experiment with different ways of keeping God in mind, since we all have specific circumstances and mindsets, and what works for one person might not work for another.

However you approach the problem, the goal seems a

worthy one in his writing. Laubach describes the state of mind achieved when you manage to concentrate on God as a peaceful state in which God permeates the soul and the world is transformed into one where, instead of individual striving, we seek only the will of God.

Perhaps the experiments described by Laubach go beyond the levels of devotion and concentration that most people can apply to their spiritual lives. But this is a deeply inspiring book. For some it will create the desire to follow in the path of Laubach, to experiment with techniques for keeping God constantly in mind. But even for those who do not feel able to go so far, it is a reminder to make room for God in our daily lives, and a vivid example of the benefits that can accrue from doing this.

## Letters by a Modern Mystic

### THE SPEED READ

While engaged in missionary work in the Philippines, I decided to try to stay in constant touch with God. I experimented with different ways of achieving this, and gradually managed to make God a part of my life in every moment. As a result I find that 'this concentration upon God is strenuous, but everything else has ceased to be so!'

# A Testament of Devotion, 1941,
## Thomas R. Kelly

'Let me talk very intimately and very earnestly with you about Him who is dearer than life. Do you really want to live your lives, every moment of your lives, in His Presence?'

Thomas Kelly was a respected college professor at Haverford College, a well-known Quaker school. On 17 January 1941, he reportedly told his wife that this was going to be the greatest day of his life. His elation was partly because he had just written to an editor at Harper and Brothers, a New York publishers, about a meeting to discuss the book he wanted to write on the subject of devotional practice. But this actually was to be the last day of Kelly's life. He collapsed with a massive heart attack that evening while drying the dishes, and died soon afterwards.

Kelly was forty-seven and had been developing a reputation as a thinker of note. Fortunately he was championed after his death by his good friend, the philosopher Douglas Steere, who carried on working on the planned publication. When it was issued, *A Testament of Devotion* consisted of five essays on devotional subjects, which were introduced with biographical notes that put the ideas into the context of Kelly's life.

Kelly was brought up in the Quaker faith in Ohio. Something of a perfectionist, he was also a warm-hearted young man, interested in science, motorbikes and carpentry as well as more spiritual pursuits. After studying at a variety of colleges, including Haverford, he trained as a missionary. As a teacher, he frequently had to move around the country in pursuit of work in difficult times – he was a young man during the First World War and his adult life was lived partly under the shadow of the Great Depression. He finally became established at Haverford College in 1936, succeeding D. Elton Trueblood in a chair of philosophy there.

At this time he was still studying for a PhD. It was in 1937 that his life went through a transformation. His dissertation had been well received but he had a disaster when he went to explain his work at an oral examination and suffered from a severe memory lapse. This seems to have been the trigger for a spiritual crisis in Kelly's life. Douglas Steere, who was also there for him as a friend in this difficult time, wrote this:

> He moved toward adequacy. A fissure in him seemed to close, cliffs caved in and filled up a chasm, and what was divided grew together within him. Science, scholarship, method remained good, but in a new setting . . . out of it seemed to come a whole new life orientation.

In this period Kelly threw himself into a deeper examination of his relationship with God. The Quaker faith is known for stressing the 'inner light', and the individual's relationship with God. Rather than preaching dogma, Quakers believe that each individual must discover his own way to God.

The change in Kelly showed immediately in his teaching and way of life. He went to Germany in the summer of 1938, to support the Friends in a dark time in the history of that nation. He was clearly deeply moved by the suffering he saw there, but he was also going through a very direct experience of his faith: he wrote later that he had been 'melted down by the love of God' in this period.

It was the teachings and writings that he created in the years between then and his tragically early death that built on his reputation, leading up to the offer of publication that sadly he would not live to see to completion.

*A Testament of Devotion* is a fascinating book. While it is not too heavily burdened by theological jargon, a passing knowledge of Quaker terminology is helpful in understanding it. Kelly discusses the ways in which ordinary people, living everyday lives, can search for that inner light that he saw so clearly. He writes in a gentle unhurried style about the complexity of modern life and the distractions that can keep us from discovering God.

For Kelly, our relationship with God is not a complex one that requires any great intellectual effort, but it must be one of absolute submission. He cautions us against looking for God in the external world, advising us instead to look inwards. He suggests that once we find God, the only thing we need to understand is how we can will the same thing as God wills. In another of his published writings, he says this:

> Did you start the search for Him? He started you on the search for Him, and lovingly, anxiously, tenderly guides you to Himself . . . It is as St. Augustine says: He was within, and we mistakenly sought Him without. It isn't a matter of *believing* in the Inner Light, it is a matter of *yielding your lives* to Him.

Kelly also writes penetratingly of the relationship between the individual and the Church and his or her fellow seekers. He was gently critical of some of the secular tendencies he observed among his contemporaries in the Quakers, but he saw the religious community as having a supportive role in the life of the individual: 'The disclosure of God normally brings the disclosure of the Fellowship . . . It is the holy matrix of "the communion of the saints"; the body of Christ which is His church . . . Yet can one be surprised at being at *home*?'

From the day *A Testament of Devotion* was published it was widely acknowledged as a classic of spiritual writing. Throughout the five essays in the book, Kelly makes a compelling case for his view of God. He tells us to treat God as the central point of our lives, to search for peace among the whirl and noise of modernity, and to find satisfaction in submission to God's will and in the spiritual journey that this entails.

### A Testament of Devotion

#### THE SPEED READ

Modern life is complex, but rather than get drawn into look-ing for God in our external environment we need to find the peace to search within ourselves for the inner light. We must recognise the voice of God in ourselves, and aim to will whatever God wills. Life is a spiritual journey, a search for divinity, in the course of which we will eventually find the spiritual satisfaction we crave.

# The Pursuit of God
## A. W. Tozer, 1957

'. . . it would seem that there is within each of us an enemy which we tolerate at our peril. Jesus called it "life" and "self," or as we would say, the self-life. Its chief characteristic is its possessiveness: the words "gain" and "profit" suggest this. To allow this enemy to live is in the end to lose everything. To repudiate it and give up all for Christ's sake is to lose nothing at last, but to preserve everything unto life eternal.'

There are some books which bring us back to the absolute basics of religious life. *The Pursuit of God* by A. W. Tozer is one such book. The author's engagement with the simple problems of prayer and a simple life are a reminder to examine the foundations of our own belief, whether or not we agree with every part of his argument.

Tozer was a Protestant pastor from Pennsylvania who

converted to Christianity in his late teens and became a minister in his twenties. He spent many years as a pastor and spent much of his life campaigning for a return to simplicity in the Church, and opposing what he saw as the dangerous drift towards worldliness in modern religion.

In his own life, he chose a path of great austerity and simplicity, even after he had become a well-known and successful author. He donated most of his royalties to worthy causes, never owned a car, preferring to use public transport, and his family lived a simple life, reflecting his views on the message of the Bible.

He wrote many books, but *The Pursuit of God* is the most widely read. He composed most of it in the course of a train trip from Chicago to Texas, in a single burst of inspiration. According to some accounts, much of it was written while he was on his knees, praying for guidance from God. In spite of the speed of its creation, this went on to become his most popular book, selling over a million copies and being translated into many languages.

One key aspect of Tozer's thought was a focus on the absolute basics, such as how to pray. He had a strong belief that one could find God through the simple practice of prayer methods. He was fascinated by the Christian mystics and saw their devotion to daily worship as an inspiration to all. He would personally often pray sprawled face down on his study floor, in order to find the total detachment necessary to work towards a true spiritual experience.

He doesn't instruct his reader to copy his example. Instead he subjects them to an interrogation concerning their commitment to the teachings of the Bible. He accepts that we all have our own paths to God, and recognises that a pure way of seeking goodness is valid, no matter how varied our paths may be.

The book takes various elements of the spiritual life one by one and gives a robust, fundamental account of their meaning. In each chapter Tozer looks at a different aspect of the search for and desire for God in our lives. With a few simple quotes, and a concluding prayer, he outlines his views and urges us to remain steadfast in our beliefs and faith.

Some readers find the language used in the book difficult. Tozer comes across as something of an autodidact and employs some fairly arcane theological language. Words and phrases such as *adamic*, *hymnody* and *summum bonum* may drive the reader to the dictionary on a regular basis.

In general though, Tozer's focus is on a very simple point. He argues that at the heart of all religious experience is our personal relationship with God and with the word of God. Thus we must devote ourselves to the best of our ability to prayer and contemplation, and, through our study of the word of God, we must seek to live better lives. For such simple and refreshing insights into the spiritual life, this is a book that can provide much inspiration.

### The Pursuit of God

#### THE SPEED READ

My aim is to help people in their search for God. I don't claim to be saying anything new, only to be interpreting ancient truths in the hope of helping others who are seeking for God.

'Others before me have gone much farther into these holy mysteries than I have done, but if my fire is not large it is yet real, and there may be those who can light their candle at its flame.'

# *Beginning to Pray*

## Anthony Bloom, 1970

'First of all it is very important to remember that prayer is an encounter and a relationship, a relationship which is deep, and this relationship cannot be forced either on us or on God.'

Anthony Bloom was a well-respected archbishop in the Russian Orthodox Church in the United Kingdom. This short book was first published in 1970 and is also known as *School for Prayer*. In many ways this was the perfect title for the book. While acknowledging that we are all beginners together when it comes to our search for God, Bloom comes across as a wise man who offers some very basic advice on how to approach prayer. There are surprisingly few books on how to pray, possibly because it seems like such a basic topic, but this book is invaluable for its simple approach to the problem.

In recent editions, the book starts with an interview with Bloom, who was also a popular broadcaster. This provides valuable additional information about his personality and life, although it might have been better added as an appendix at the end of the book: the first chapter, *The Absence of God*, is such a strong starting point, and provides a huge amount of food for thought. Bloom focuses on the relation-ship we have with God when we pray. He acknowledges that all prayer is in some sense a moment of crisis. We pray because we are already in crisis, or we risk putting ourselves in crisis by asking God to pass judgement upon us. And this means that we may receive either condemnation or salvation as a result.

Bloom talks persuasively, but kindly, of the Old Testament idea that to be in the presence of God is a terrible thing. By this he means that when we place ourselves before God we have no defences left and are revealed as we truly are, and this can be an uncomfortable experience.

By the absence of God, he means the feeling we some-times have that God is not listening when we pray. He gently reminds us that our relationship with God is an uneven one, and that there are also times when God may feel that we are shunning him, and not listening to his voice – so what right do we have to complain if we sometimes feel that he is in turn failing to listen to us?

> If you look at the relationship [us and God] in terms of mutual relationship, you would see that God could complain about us a great deal more than we about Him. We complain that He does make Himself present to us for a few minutes we reserve for Him, but what about the twenty-three and half hours during which God may be knocking at our door and we answer 'I am busy . . .'

So when we pray, we are sending messages into the unknown with no certainty that God is listening. And this is only natural from Bloom's point of view. To imagine anything else would be presumptuous of us.

He recommends the virtues of silence and peace as a prelude and accompaniment to times of prayer, and dis-cusses what avenues of prayer might suit different people. One person might choose a personal appeal to God, another might focus on a repetitive prayer such as the Jesus Prayer, while another might choose to work their way through the Psalms as a mode of prayer.

The book discusses ways in which we might experiment with different types of prayer to find out what works for us, and this is one of the most valuable contributions it makes in terms of teaching us how to pray. It can be hard to admit that we don't always know how to pray, but Bloom is a patient teacher who does not make one feel bad for one's weaknesses in this respect.

For Bloom, the most important thing is to keep trying and not to allow distractions to keep us from regular prayer. Crises in our life can become excuses to avoid praying, whereas those are the times when we most need to keep the conversation with God going.

One whole chapter focuses on how we might best manage our time to make sure that we are always able to continue with our practice of prayer. And Bloom emphasises the importance of praying wholeheartedly, and with an appropriate degree of seriousness at all times.

In the later stages of the book, he focuses more closely on our personal relationship with God. He criticises any attempt to have a functional relationship with God, where we see God as serving a purpose for us. Instead he urges us to get to know God on a personal basis and to have a direct, intense relationship with Him.

In the end Bloom argues that if we are hoping that God will listen to us, the only way to move towards achieving that ambition is to pray sincerely and with all our hearts. And if we are not sure how to go about doing that, there is no better place to start than this book.

## Beginning to Pray

### THE SPEED READ

Sometimes we feel that God is not listening to us. But on the other hand, how often can we say that we are truly listening to God? If we want to have a real relationship with God we must learn how to pray. This may mean experimenting with different approaches to prayer. The crucial thing is to learn how to set aside silent time in which we can pray wholeheartedly to God.

# 4
# Meditations and
# Praise of Solitude

In this section of the book we start to move away from formal religious doctrines and ideas into a broader spiritual realm. Some of these books are from specifically Christian backgrounds, while some (such as *Walden by* Henry David Thoreau or *One Day in the Life of Ivan Denisovich* by Aleksandr Solzhenitsyn) are not formally religious works at all. What all of these books share is that they deal with basic spiritual needs.

Kierkegaard is one of the writers here who does write from a Christian viewpoint. *Purity of Heart Is to Will One Thing* is a book that addresses our relationship with God directly. However, Kierkegaard's writing also represents an intense attempt to come to grips with the whole question of spiritual faith, coming to the conclusion that the religious life always involves a 'leap of faith' but that it is necessary for us to be brave enough to make that leap.

*Walden* and Catherine de Hueck Doherty's *Poustinia* are books that examine the idea of solitude and retreat from the world from a spiritual angle. In each case the simplicity of life in retreat is put forward as a way to find peace and to advance one's spiritual condition. *One Day in the Life of*

*Ivan Denisovich* is a rather different book as it is a study of someone in forced captivity where the simplicity of their existence is a punishing one. However, it also draws out the way we can find meaning in tiny blessings, and incidentally reminds us how lucky many of us are in our lives to be blessed with relative prosperity and security.

*Gravity and Grace* by Simone Weil also focuses on spiritual suffering: it examines our relationship with God, reminds us that Jesus always empathised with those who suffered the most in life, and represents a passionate reminder to look beyond our own lives in our spiritual pursuits.

In a different way, this is the message of *Leaves from the Notebook of a Tamed Cynic* by Karl Paul Reinhold Niebuhr. Niebuhr was a well-known theologian who covered a range of subjects in his writing. But this early book deals with his experiences as a young preacher in Detroit. With humility and wisdom it discusses the ways in which spirituality can be a communal experience. Niebuhr learns as much from his congregation as he teaches them, and is led by this to contemplate the degree to which we are all interconnected.

Collectively these books make up a series of meditations on the spiritual life that is grounded in religion, but that reaches beyond orthodoxy to aspects of the common human experience.

# Purity of Heart Is to Will One Thing
## Søren Kierkegaard, 1846

'What kind of life do you live, do you will only one thing, and what is this one thing?'

Kierkegaard was a Danish philosopher who wrote in an intense and perceptive way about problems of faith and the individual. He can be difficult to read, but is rewarding to study as he is such a clear, unflinching thinker. He faces up honestly to the difficulties of a religious life, and by doing so puts them into context.

He was an outwardly gregarious man who suffered from depression. He had a difficult childhood and a father who had turned against God as a result of his misfortunes. This may have contributed to Kirkegaard's intense reading of biblical stories such as the Book of Job and the story of Abraham and Isaac.

He used the latter as an example of a key concept, 'the leap of faith' in his book *Fear and Trembling*. As with most of his books, he wrote this under a pseudonym. In his philosophical writing he often spoke of the *angst* (existential anxiety) we feel when we are confronted by the borders of reason (a term that had been used by the philosopher Kant to describe the limits of our knowledge, the point at which we confront the unknowable). This is the point at which an individual is confronted with, and terrified by, the prospect of their own freedom.

Kierkegaard identified three ways that people cope with human existence. The aesthetic life is one in which we live for the moment, and hold beauty and aesthetic truth as our guiding principles. The ethical life is one in which we seek to live in accordance with rationally deduced moral truths. Kierkegaard sees both of these ways of life as incomplete

– they cannot be rationally justified, and they ultimately fail to satisfy our wills.

He proposes a third way, the religious life, as the only alternative. He is impressively ready to acknowledge that the religious life cannot be justified on grounds of 'objective truth'. Instead he argues we have to live our lives in a condition of 'subjective truth', and suggests we must make that 'leap of faith' to live a good life.

Abraham's acceptance of God's instruction to take his son Isaac's life is interpreted by Kierkegaard as a moment when Abraham's subjective truth and faith forced him to make an apparently irrational choice. Kierkegaard transforms this unsettling story (why would God want Abraham to kill his son?) into a metaphor of faith. He also forensically describes the 'fear and trembling' that an individual feels when he or she is forced to make that leap of faith and to embrace his or her own freedom.

So this is Kierkegaard's starting point when it comes to the idea of faith. But during a period of intense creativity between 1842 and 1848, he also wrote a series of 'Edifying Addresses' under his own name. These are extended sermons in which he expanded upon his ideas of Christian faith in far more detail. One of the most fascinating of these is *Purity of Heart Is to Will One Thing*.

In this text, Kierkegaard confronts two questions. The first is: 'What kind of life do you live, do you will only one thing, and what is this one thing?' – while the second is: 'Do you live in such a way that you are conscious of being an individual?'

To explain this further: Kierkegaard violently rejected any form of thinking that detracted from personal responsibility, and sees the mass or the crowd as something in which an individual can hide from that responsibility. His entire drive in this sermon is to force the individual to confront their own weaknesses and evasions and to bring them in front of God, alone and undefended, to face up to their own freedom. He talks of how badly individuals can behave *en masse*:

> Take the highest of all, think of Christ – and think of the whole human race, all that have been born and will be born. Now the situation is one where Christ is alone, so that someone as an individual alone with Christ stepped up to Him and spat upon Him: the man was never born and will never be born, who possesses the courage or the audacity to do this: that is the truth. As they became a crowd, however, they had the courage to do it – oh, terrible falsity.

So Kierkegaard labours to remind us that in the perspective of eternity, and in the eyes of God, we are individuals, not members of a crowd. In this respect he is rejecting the philosophy of Hegel, who had treated individuals as being less significant than the 'world-spirit', but he is also making a deeper religious point. He was disappointed by Protestantism's failure to break more fully with Catholicism – he despised the organised Danish Church for its cosy, political comforts, and felt that man's relationship with God must be an intensely personal one.

He also addresses Christ's comments that we should love our neighbour. He points out that Christ never advised us to love men *en masse* – only to love them as individuals. We are not equal, we have very different attributes and weaknesses. The only level on which we are equal, in Kierkegaard's view, is in our relationship to God, in which we are all as children to a parent. And we owe each other love on an individual basis: 'That one shall honour each individual man, without exception, each man: that is truth and is reverence and is neighbour-love.'

Kierkegaard lived a life of physical suffering, and was driven by a vocation to write, often spending his entire waking hours on his work. He neither embraces nor ignores his sufferings in his writing. Instead he interprets them for us in a revealing way. He acknowledges that his individual relationship to God is not for all. Instead he continually challenges the reader to study their own life.

He dialectically examines the idea of 'willing the good'. He argues that the only way we can 'will one thing' without being 'double-minded' is to will good without evasions, and without keeping back one little bit of selfishness for our own comfort.

For Kierkegaard, only someone who is 'conscious of themselves as an individual' can truly will one thing in this way. We have to come before God as individuals, stripped of all our defences and evasions, and we must decide what our vocation really is. How can we single-mindedly will the Good, how can we use our faith to live a good life in the eyes of God? And this life must be one that we can defend as individuals who live a life of faith.

Kierkegaard is simultaneously terrifying and exhilarating to read. He allows his reader no excuses, no evasions, and his forensic examination of his own faults leads us to contemplate how often we live lives of bad faith. He forces us to consider our individual relationship to God. One can argue with his writing – his views on faith sometimes suggest that a passionate faith in something false or immoral would be better than a lukewarm faith in truth and goodness. And one can question whether every individual needs a life of such absolute vocation as Kierkegaard depicts.

He is also a notoriously hard writer to understand at first. Some of his books are indeed dense and complicated. But *Purity of Heart Is to Will One Thing* makes a surprisingly good introduction to his work. Here he is simply making the case for his very passionate and individual type of Christianity. One can agree or disagree with his conclusions, but either way he is a deeply inspiring thinker who challenges us to question the very foundations of our faith and relationship with God.

*Purity of Heart Is to Will One Thing*

### THE SPEED READ

If we can will one thing, then we must will the Good, for the Good alone is one thing. To will the Good, a man must be conscious of himself as an individual, and not just as a face in a crowd. If we will the Good, but only up to a certain point, then we are being double-minded. We must be prepared to accept any kind of suffering or deprivation in our pursuit of the Good. 'What kind of life do you live, do you will only one thing, and what is this one thing?' The religious life is based on a leap of faith and we can express our love of God by finding our true vocation in life.

## *Walden*

### Henry David Thoreau, 1854

'A man is rich in proportion to the number of things which he can afford to let alone.'

*Walden; or Life in the Woods* by Henry David Thoreau is an American classic. It is a much-loved book that is often filed under natural history. But it is also a spiritual classic in its own humble way, as it reflects on the simple life, and the basic virtues that make us human.

Thoreau wrote it about a period of two years, two months and two days that he spent living in a cabin near Walden Pond, which is in the woods near to Concord, Massachusetts, on land which was at the time owned by Thoreau's friend Ralph Waldo Emerson.

Emerson was known as one of the main figures in the transcendentalist movement, a movement characterised by philosophical, literary and religious ideas that stood in opposition to intellectualism, and that stressed man's spiritual and intuitive sides. The transcendentalists were mostly opposed to established religious doctrine, preferring to trust their transcendental intuition.

This was part of the thinking behind Thoreau's experiment with nature. He aimed to live as simply as possible and in relative solitude in his cabin. His account of the time he spent there simplifies the actual events in some respects – for instance, he compresses the timescale into a year's sojourn.

Thoreau has sometimes been mocked for claiming to live as a hermit while staying close to family and friends in Massachusetts, and enjoying meals and social occasions away from his cabin. However, he does not pretend otherwise in the actual book, making reference to such occasions and being honest that his seclusion is not the total isolation of a hermit, but a retreat from the complexities of modern life.

In many respects the book is a straightforward account of the simple, self-reliant life Thoreau lived. He starts with a chapter on economy where he outlines the four necessities of food, shelter, clothing and fuel, and considers how simply he could achieve these necessities. He makes it clear that he is not praising poverty as an inherently better condition, merely examining the spiritual benefits that can be achieved by simplifying one's lifestyle.

Thoreau first considers the idea of owning a farm, although he sees the labour involved as more of a millstone than anything. Instead he chooses to live in the cabin, explaining that he wants to 'live deliberately, to front only the essential facts of life, and see if I could not learn what it had to teach, and not, when I came to die, discover that I had not lived'.

This is where the spiritual nature of Thoreau's adventure becomes apparent. He removes as much of his ordinary everyday life as he possibly can and then, in the absence of clutter and complexity, attempts to achieve a clearer understanding of who he is and who he could be.

His life at Walden was far removed from a monastic lifestyle. He extols the virtues of reading classical literature, and entertains a number of interesting visitors, from Emerson himself to a runaway slave. At times his writing on his rural surroundings is quite beautiful, if a touch naïve. He spends one chapter ruminating on all the sounds he can hear in the woods – the noise of the wind in the trees and the wildlife around him, the whip-poor-wills in the trees and the nearby church bell – and contrasting this with the industrial sound of a passing train whistle.

However, he certainly doesn't argue that we should all live in such rural simplicity at all times. In fact he goes out of his way to assert that we need to consider the balance between simplicity and sophistication in our lives, not just to reject all sophistication on principle.

In spite of Thoreau's love of solitude, he is pleased to receive occasional visitors to his cabin, commenting that if one sits still long enough all kinds of interesting things will come to one's front door.

At one point he takes refuge from a storm in the hut of John Field, a poor labourer who nonetheless holds to the American dream of working hard to achieve a life of luxury. Thoreau fails to persuade him of the benefits of giving up on this dream in favour of a simple life, although Thoreau's comfortable family background makes this story a bit uncomfortable for the modern reader.

His life in the book becomes rather more complicated when he is arrested for non-payment of taxes. Thoreau wasn't an anarchist as such, but he was opposed to excessive government and refused to pay taxes to a government that supported slavery. Given his meagre earnings from the year (he made about eight or nine dollars from the beanfield that he lovingly tended), the amount concerned can't have been too huge, and in fact his aunt paid off the debt after he had spent a single night in jail.

The net effect of these misadventures is a slightly comical one, but Thoreau's writing on non-cooperation has had an enduring influence. Gandhi was one famous figure who was inspired by his writing on civil disobedience – indeed he borrowed that phrase directly from *Walden* for his own political purposes. Meanwhile Martin Luther King read *Walden* as a young man. He wrote that after reading it, he 'became convinced that non-cooperation with evil is as much a moral obligation as is cooperation with good. No other person has been more eloquent and passionate in getting this idea across than Henry David Thoreau.'

Towards the end of the book, Thoreau, having survived a winter in his cabin, observes the first growth of spring, as the ice on Walden Pond melts. This is a moment of epiphany: it is as though the author is reborn, drawing on all the experiences great and small that he has had in his retreat from the ordinary world.

One of the great virtues of *Walden* is the way it makes you reflect upon your own life. You don't need to agree with everything that Thoreau writes to find the idea of his retreat inspiring. And in a world where the materialism and consumerism that Thoreau was reacting against is even more entrenched in everyday culture, the vision he presents of a simple life is a deeply inspiring one to many who sometimes feel overwhelmed by the modern world.

*Walden* is not a simplistic rejection of material comforts – instead it is a plea for us to think about each part of our world and to compare it with simpler alternatives. In some respects, such as in his love of classical literature, Thoreau believed in a more advanced society than the one in which he lived. Elsewhere, for instance in the degree to which the industrial age has made us into consumers, he raised valid doubts about the direction in which society was headed.

By focusing on self-reliance, close contact with nature and solitude, Thoreau questions the 'desperate' existence that he saw in the life choice of many people, and forces us to consider the ways in which we might be able to improve our own lives by turning away from material things to a more spiritual existence.

## *Walden*

### THE SPEED READ

I withdrew to the solitude of nature in my cabin near Walden Pond for a period of time. There I lived a simple life, tending my beans, listening to the sounds of nature in the woods, and only receiving occasional visitors. I spent a night in jail for refusing to pay my taxes to a government that supported slavery, visited friends in town, then returned to the silence of the woods. In the end, by making me see what I could live without, my life of self-reliance and simplicity taught me a great deal about who I am.

# Leaves from the Notebook of a Tamed Cynic
## Karl Paul Reinhold Niebuhr, 1930

'Without an adequate sermon no clue is given to the moral purpose at the heart of the mystery, and reverence remains without ethical content.'

Reinhold Niebuhr (1892–1971) was a Protestant theologian who was well known for his work relating theology to the realities of modern life. *Leaves from the Notebook of a Tamed Cynic* is not especially representative of Niebuhr's lifetime of writing – he wrote more complex theological works in later life. But it is still his best-known work, and an unusually honest and compelling account of the difficulties that face a preacher – it is about his time as a young man in Detroit, where he struggled with the responsibilities of a congregation. He would later refer to this book as an immature work, so it is probably fairest to start with an overview of his life.

Niebuhr was born in Missouri, and studied in Illinois, Missouri and Yale, before being ordained a pastor in the German Evangelical Church in 1915. He was sent to serve in Detroit, where his congregation numbered less than a hundred people. This was a time of great industrial growth in the town and by 1928, when he moved on, his church had grown to 700 members.

At this stage Niebuhr was a pacifist. He also became involved in social causes, campaigning against the industrial practices of the manufacturers and against the Ku Klux Klan in particular. In 1928, he published *Leaves from the Notebook of a Tamed Cynic*, a journal of his time in Detroit. From there he moved on to New York City, where he became a professor of Practical Theology at Union Theological Seminary. His lectures there were highly influential on a generation of students, including Dietrich Bonhoeffer, who travelled from Germany to New York in the 1930s.

The Second World War proved a significant challenge to Niebuhr's pacifism and communist sympathies. He gradually came to believe in the idea of a just war and to support the military fight against fascism and communism. This was a dark, challenging time for the world, and Niebuhr was forced to face up to the idea that one might have to choose the lesser of two evils when faced with tyranny.

His 1952 book *The Irony of American History* captures the transformation of his views to the 'Christian Realism' he now espoused. His thinking of this period is also presented in *The Nature and Destiny of Man*, a collection of the Gifford Lectures, which he gave in Edinburgh in the 1940s. He retained some of his former beliefs and always campaigned for social justice, but this was now grounded in a different framework of beliefs about the world and the necessity for democracy to defend its freedom. He saw America as a nation in which hard-won freedoms could be used as a basis to move towards a society of greater social equality and justice.

His thinking was influential on Martin Luther King, among others, in particular the vision of America as a mythological agent of justice, and of a future in which America's freedoms would create a better land for all. Fifty years later, we also find Barack Obama quoting Niebuhr's influence:

> I take away . . . the compelling idea that there's serious evil in the world, and hardship and pain. And we should be humble and modest in our belief we can eliminate those things. But we shouldn't use that as an excuse for cynicism and inaction. I take away . . . the sense we have to make these efforts knowing they are hard, and not swinging from naïve idealism to bitter realism.

Niebuhr's influence has in other respects waned as his Christian realism was superseded by other movements within Protestant theology. But he is still a writer that theologians take seriously, and in whose writing there is much of value.

Going back to *Leaves from the Notebook of a Tamed Cynic*, it is easy to see why Niebuhr saw the book as a piece of writing from an earlier, more innocent period of his life. However, while the book lacks the theological complexity of his later work, it is a wonderful read in a different way.

By writing so engagingly about the problems he faced in Detroit, Niebuhr gives a clear picture of life as a preacher. He talks of the difficulties he has in thinking of new subjects for sermons, the inspiration he takes from his parishioners, and the fact that he sometimes feels intimidated by them. He discusses the fact that there can be more spirituality in a factory or a front room than in a church where the sermon is uninspired. At one point he writes that: 'A prophet speaks only when he is inspired. The parish preacher must speak whether he is inspired or not. I wonder whether it is possible to live on a high enough plane to do that without sinning against the Holy Spirit.' And in writing of these problems he also brings out the fact that ministry is a two-way process. The pastor may leave the seminary full of confidence and belief in the grace of God, but he comes up against the realities of people's lives and learns as much from them as they do from him. We see him progress through the war years and on to a more mature understanding of his place, and at every step of the process there are illuminations from his intelligence and humility in the face of the challenges he faces.

Spirituality can be a private experience, in which we withdraw from the world or go into retreat to examine our own relationship with God. But far more often, our spiritual lives are rooted in our community.

Niebuhr's book is well known as an introductory text for young preachers who can learn from his experiences. But it has something to say to anyone who sees their spirituality in the context of their community. In our daily struggles, worries and joys, we find our own path, and we learn from the paths of those around us, just as they might learn from us.

### Leaves from the Notebook of a Tamed Cynic

#### THE SPEED READ

'There is something ludicrous about a callow young fool like myself standing up to preach a sermon to these good folks. I talk wisely about life and know little about life's problems.' In my time as a pastor in Detroit, I learn as much from those good folks as they do from me. And one thing I come to understand is that I must always stay humble in the face of these problems, but that a good sermon can be the difference between a spiritual moment and a church that feels empty.

# Gravity and Grace
## Simone Weil, 1947

'It is only the impossible that is possible for God. He has given over the possible to the mechanics of matter and the autonomy of his creatures.'

Simone Weil was a French philosopher and social activist who was born in Paris in 1909. In her early life she was drawn to the radical politics of contemporary Marxism and

anarchism. She campaigned on behalf of the proletariat, the poor, and tried to fight in the Spanish Civil War, although chronic ill health defeated her in this ambition.

She was a contemporary of Simone de Beauvoir's at the École normale supérieure and became a teacher of philosophy. Most of the writing for which she is remembered was published posthumously. This includes some interesting philosophical and political thought, but the aspect of her thinking which concerns us here is best represented by the book *Gravity and Grace*.

This is an aphoristic collection which was compiled by Gustav Thibon, and was made up of selections from her notebooks. Weil had experienced a religious epiphany in 1937 while in a church in Assisi, in the same place where St Francis had once prayed. From this moment onwards her writing started to take a more spiritual angle, even when she was dealing with social issues. Thibon was a devout Catholic – Weil herself was from a Jewish family and decided not to be baptised into the Christian Church, although she did study under a Dominican friar.

Weil was against any attempt to synthesise religions and reduce them to a universal religion, but she did believe that there were many different paths to God. She was fascinated by non-Christian religious sources such as the Upanishads and Mahayana Buddhism. And even within Christian tradition, she took her own path: for instance, her influences varied from the Philokalia to the works of St John of the Cross.

She also focused strongly on the New Testament, largely rejecting the role of the Old Testament in her view of the world. We need to remember while reading *Gravity and Grace* that this is a selection that has been made by a friend with a particular interpretation of her work. However, Thibon does not allow his own interpretations of her work to intrude. Instead we are left to comprehend her subtle thinking for ourselves.

Some of Weil's writing focused on the problem of evil, and how we can reconcile this with God's love. She views the world as being caused by God's love, but also stresses the importance of the idea of God's absence. God's perfection means that our creation and existence happens to some degree in the absence of God. The afflictions and evil that we feel are not punishments or injustices but something that propels us in the direction of God. In other words the only way we could come into existence at all as imperfect beings was to be less than holy.

When Weil talks about affliction she speaks of something more than mere suffering. She suffered from very poor health herself and was also prone to bringing suffering on herself in sympathy with those for whom she campaigned. Even at the age of six she was refusing to eat sugar in sympathy with the soldiers at the Western Front.

Later in life she was driven to try to live life like the poor and unemployed for whom she felt a strong empathy. Her early death in 1943 was partly caused by this inclination – following a period of illness in exile in England, she refused to eat as well as she could have done to recover, preferring to restrict her eating to the rations that she felt her compatriots in occupied France were being kept to. Sadly, this contributed to her death.

These anecdotes reveal someone who showed a level of sensitivity to the suffering of others that could even be characterised as neurotic, and that certainly led to self-destructive behaviours. But they can also be seen as saintly, or at least spiritual impulses. Affliction for Weil was something that affected those souls who were closest to spiritual growth – the realisation of suffering was therefore part of the path towards God's love.

Of course, Weil did live through a period of great suffering. Her childhood was in the shadow of the First World War, she then lived through the deprivations of the Depression,

before going into a Second World War in which her country was once again invaded. In her short life there was little peace and much suffering and she was driven to try to understand the reasons for this in her writing.

So in her analysis of suffering, Weil was both urging us to try to see the world from the point of view of the oppressed, poor and miserable (a message that echoes the sayings of Jesus) and also arguing that affliction is in itself a spiritual opening. She described affliction as being like God holding one's hand tightly, pressing hard, and said that if we could get beyond the sound of our own lamentations, we would discover the silence of God beneath.

The separation we feel from God is for Weil partly illusory. She uses an old term from Greek philosophy, *metaxu*, which means something that both connects and separates at the same time. She uses the metaphor of a blind man's stick to describe the way that the physical world both separates us from God, and at the same time allows us to feel and grope our way towards him. Even his absence in the physical world is something which we can use to start thinking about his reality.

Beyond *Gravity and Grace*, Weil's spirituality also shines through in her political writing. She interprets the golden rule of Jesus in terms of obligations, and the obligation we have to respect and love others. She also speaks of spirituality as an absolutely everyday part of our lives.

In the religious practices of icons such as St Francis or St John of the Cross she saw lessons for how we can start to approach the affliction of our lives, and also for how we must empathise with those more wretched than ourselves. Thus politics and spirituality become intertwined in her thinking.

*Gravity and Grace* is a curious book to read. It doesn't present a consistent, ordered argument, as it is a series of reflections from the notebooks. The first thing that strikes you is that much of the writing is beautiful and inspiring, but it takes a while to discern a wider picture of Weil's spiritual beliefs. However, it is a book that repays patience and that has become a beloved favourite of many readers over time.

*Gravity and Grace*

**THE SPEED READ**

'We can know only one thing about God – that he is what we are not. Our wretchedness alone is an image of this. The more we contemplate it, the more we contemplate him.' God is absent in the physical world, and we suffer from afflictions. We must try to live like the poor and the slaves in order to understand their suffering. But the afflictions and sufferings we feel are the start of a path to God as we can find God's presence in the shadow of his absence.

# *One Day in the Life of Ivan Denisovich*
## Aleksandr Solzhenitsyn, 1962

'You should rejoice that you're in prison. Here you have time to think about your soul.'

*O*ne *Day in the Life of Ivan Denisovich* is a product of a very particular period of Russian history. The author Aleksandr Solzhenitsyn had been a victim of Stalin's repression. Having been a loyal Soviet citizen and soldier, he wrote a letter towards the end of the Second World War questioning the tactics of the leaders and referring to Stalin derogatorily as 'the whiskered one'.

For this 'crime' he ended up spending eight years in the labour camps in the Gulag. He was not released until 1953, having suffered deeply in the harsh environment of the camps. Between 1957 and 1962 he worked on a book that was a lightly fictionalised account of his time in prison. At the time this was more or less unpublishable due to the censorship in the Soviet regime.

However, the intellectual atmosphere thawed somewhat when Khrushchev came to power. Solzhenitsyn approached the editor of *Novy Mir*, a literary magazine, who was deeply impressed by the book. He submitted the book to the Soviet Central Committee for permission to publish it and it was eventually sanctioned by Khrushchev himself, albeit with a few minor revisions.

The publication of *One Day in the Life of Ivan Denisovich*, initially in *Novy Mir*, caused a sensation in the Soviet Union. Many had not known much of the Gulag, and those who knew that it existed did not know the level of detail that was exposed in the book. The vagaries of Soviet life meant that since the regime now embraced Solzhenitsyn, with their approval he became a celebrity for a few years.

However, as the mood of liberalisation faded, and Khrushchev was ousted from power, Solzhenitsyn was censored and repressed once again. He ended up as a non-person, and was eventually deported, not returning to his beloved Russia until many years later in the post-communist period of glasnost.

Meanwhile, Solzhenitsyn's international reputation had been made by his powerful writing in *One Day in the Life of Ivan Denisovich*. The book centres on Ivan Denisovich Shukhov, who has been imprisoned in the camps after being falsely accused of being a spy. The book is fictionalised, but clearly based closely on Solzhenitsyn's own time in the camps.

The spiritual aspects of the book arise from the way that it deals with the human response to hardship. There are different types of people in the camps. Some of the warders represent genuine sadism and evil, while others are simply doing their job yet failing to acknowledge the immorality of the situation.

Meanwhile the lives of the prisoners revolve around tiny triumphs and setbacks. The acquisition of food or a few moments of snatched warmth in the miserable, freezing Siberian cold become of overwhelming importance. Shukhov spends time queuing to get supplies that he can swap for favours. The prisoners sometimes help each other, but always with a knowledge that there is a limit to how far they can go. But the strength of their spirits shine through in the tiny details of the terrible life that they are enduring.

In Ivan Denisovich, we see how a man can lower his expectations to deal with a terrible life. The small achievements of his day come to him as moments of great joy. He delights in seeing the sun at its height, meaning that it is nearly lunchtime and the morning of hard graft has passed faster than it might have done. Rather than focusing on the setbacks he encounters throughout the day, or the dreadful nature of his plight, he ends up seeing the day as a good one – at the end of the day he 'went to sleep fully content. He'd had many strokes of luck that day.'

Denisovich also focuses on the way that a prisoner maximises the pleasure he gets from his few free moments – first thing in the morning, last thing at night, and in the brief meal breaks. At these times, he can be still within himself, for a few moments free of the constant supervision, roll calls, searches and fear of punishment.

Ivan is an engaging character, and at times his story can even be curiously uplifting, but it leaves the reader in absolutely no doubt as to how dehumanising the camps are – the things that Denisovich escapes from in these moments are a terrible source of anxiety and worry that rob the prisoners of their dignity, leaving them forced to scrabble after small favours.

This is a brilliant book, one that illuminates a fearful time in history and the spiritual costs of imprisonment in a deep but simple way. As a study in humanity in times of hardship and injustice, it is hard to better. We see both the injustice of the overall situation, and the small ways in which the human spirit can still triumph.

As we gradually realise that this is a good day for Ivan Denisovich because of the small things that go right, we simultaneously know that the bad days must be truly awful ones. And we know that tens of thousands of people suffered this fate under Stalin, many never winning their release, just as many people today continue to suffer imprisonment on unjust grounds.

The book can also provide spiritual consolation of an unusual sort. No matter how bad our lives may seem, few of us suffer deprivations or hardships as demanding as those faced in the Stalinist labour camps. Ivan Denisovich's ability to find joy in small moments through his day is an inspiration to remember that if we live in the here and now, there are many things we should give thanks for. So it can work as a reminder that difficulties can be transcended if only we find the right way to transform our life into a spiritual celebration.

## One Day in the Life of Ivan Denisovich

### THE SPEED READ

Ivan Denisovich is woken at five a.m. in the freezing cold by a hammer banging on the rail of his prison hut. He is serving ten years in the Gulag for false accusations of crimes against the state. For waking late, since he is sick, he is forced to clean the guardhouse. He spends the day in hard labour with the 104 squad, conserving any food he can, and treasuring the small moments he gets of peace and solitude. In the evening he trades services with fellow inmate Tsezar in return for scraps of extra food. He goes to bed content. It has been one of the good days.

## *Poustinia*

### Catherine de Hueck Doherty, 1975

'Acquire inner peace and a multitude will find their salvation near you.'

Catherine Doherty was born and baptised as a Russian Orthodox Christian. After her later emigration to America and Canada, she popularised the Orthodox idea of *poustinia* in the West. A poustinia is a small cabin, furnished as minimally as possible, to which you retreat to pray and fast. The literal translation of poustinia is 'desert' and this gives a sense of the isolation that you would expect from such a retreat. The hope is that in this condition of solitude, one can feel that one is in the presence of God.

In Russia there was a strong tradition of hermits and *starets* (religious leaders) living in poustinia, and in some cases staying there permanently (in which case they were known as *poustiniks*).

Catherine Doherty's own life made a fascinating story. She helped to set up retreats and poustinias in North America, and had many disagreements with the established Church. In particular, at a time when the mainstream Church frequently ignored pressing social issues, she fought for economic justice and against racial segregation. She also worked extensively with the poor, sometimes living in poverty herself.

In Ontario, she set up Madonna House, a Catholic lay

community offering a retreat from the 'marketplace' of the ordinary world. The houses there were communal quarters, in which those who went on retreat renounced individual ownership. At Madonna House one could choose a life of spiritual modesty, and embrace old-fashioned vows of chastity, obedience and poverty. The established Church gradually embraced her slightly maverick approach, and the retreat movement is now a significant part of the Catholic Church in particular.

It was against this background that Doherty wrote her popular book *Poustinia*. The book champions the ideal of the poustinia as a spiritual remedy. The essential purpose of a poustinia is to use the solitude to search for meaning. You eat only bread and water, for anything from four to thirty days. The only reading material provided is the Bible. You can take short walks, or exercise. You can choose to sleep long hours. You can pray if inspiration leads that way, but it is not the only way to search for spiritual consolation in the retreat. Catherine Doherty had overseen many people who went through this process at Madonna House, and as a result had a deep understanding of the process and of its merits.

She believed that in the confusion of the modern world, the search for silence was even more important than ever before: 'It seems strange to say, but what can help modern man find the answers to his own mystery and the mystery of him in whose image he is created, is silence, solitude – in a word, the desert. Modern man needs these things more than the hermits of old.' Doherty also relates her Western retreat to memories of her Russian childhood and the hermits and *starets* that she encountered. She describes Peter, a friend of her father, who gave up his wealth to wander alone, a barefoot pilgrim (reminiscent of the narrator of *The Way of the Pilgrim*, or the original Franciscans who heeded Christ's exhortation to travel barefoot and in poverty).

Years later her father spotted this friend, apparently an idiot, among a group of beggars. Something of Peter's former self returned to his face when he saw his old friend, and the two of them embraced. When her father asked Peter why he was abasing himself in this way, he replied that he was atoning for all those men who had called Christ a fool during his life and in the many centuries since.

Such memories, and those of the hermits who would live on the edge of town in a self-imposed solitude, tolerating visitors but not inviting them, obviously made a deep impression on Doherty. She goes on to describe the set-up at Madonna House, and the conditions under which those undergoing a poustinia would live. The book also includes talks and addresses given to staff and visitors to the community.

This is an inspiring book in two distinct ways. First, the whole idea of setting up such a community and of bringing the Russian tradition of hermits and solitude into Western religion is an intriguing one and a valuable experiment. Second, the concept of a retreat is something that seems increasingly hard to achieve in the modern world.

Whether we find our own way of fulfilling Doherty's idea of a poustinia, or whether we try to make a formal retreat from life, there can be great value in taking an ascetic break and re-evaluating our life and direction. Sadly it is one that only seems to be achieved for some people in rehabilitation, rather than in the purer surroundings of a poustinia.

It is east to understand why this simple book has been such an enduring spiritual classic and why so many people have been inspired by it to take a long look at their own lives and to wonder whether a period of genuine silence and solitude may be the remedy their soul is waiting for.

## *Poustinia*

### THE SPEED READ

In my childhood I was familiar with the Russian Orthodox tradition of *poustinia*. This is a retreat where one lives in solitude and silence and through prayer and reflection comes into the presence of God. We need this more than ever in the modern world. The modern person who undergoes a poustinia can take the solitude of the desert back into their everyday life with them, and live a better life having been through this experience.

# 5
# Lives of Inspiration

In this section we have gathered some of the books which focus on remarkable individuals who, for one reason or another, can be seen as an example or inspiration to us in our own lives.

The first two selections are the journals of well-known figures from the Quaker movement, George Fox and John Woolman. Each in his own way showed great bravery and persistence in the face of adversity. Fox was largely responsible for founding the Society of Friends, but his message of listening to one's inner light was unwelcome to those of more orthodox views: he had to be a man of extraordinary talents to overcome the opposition he faced. Meanwhile John Woolman's opposition to slavery was one of the turning points in American attitudes to that iniquitous institution, and a brave stance for him to take against the contemporary status quo.

Leo Tolstoy is someone who had drifted away from religion, but was brave enough to rethink all his assumptions in life. He re-examined the foundations of Christian belief and realised that his earlier rejection of spirituality had been for weak reasons. He also had to persist in the face of opposition: his new thinking was unpopular within his own family, something that caused him a good deal of unhappiness.

Thomas Merton (*The Seven Storey Mountain*) may not have suffered in the same way, but he made a similarly brave decision to reassess his life and to make a commitment to the religious life.

In Dietrich Bonhoeffer (*The Cost of Discipleship*) and Watchman Nee (*The Normal Christian Life*) we see two writers who went through extremes of suffering for their beliefs. In the early Church many Christians showed great bravery in being martyred for their beliefs. Bonhoeffer's courage in standing up to the Nazis is equally extraordinary, and we are lucky to have his own account of the problem of conscience and discipleship to Jesus. Meanwhile, Watchman Nee also made the decision to stay in his own country in spite of a repressive regime: as a result he endured twenty years of imprisonment for his beliefs.

Finally, Mother Teresa and Jean Vanier both showed considerable self-sacrifice and love in their charity and generosity towards those less fortunate than themselves. Of course there are many other writers and books that could have been included in this section. The final selections are all books that have a particular beauty and wisdom, but there have been many other people throughout history who have lived good lives that should continue to inspire us today.

## *The Journal of George Fox*
### George Fox, 1694

'Then the Lord let me see why there was none upon the earth that could speak to my condition, namely, that I might give Him all the glory; for all are concluded under sin, and shut up in unbelief as I had been, that Jesus Christ might have the pre-eminence who enlightens, and gives grace, and faith, and power.'

George Fox (1624–91) was the principal founder of the Religious Society of Friends, usually known as the Quakers. He lived through a tumultuous period of history, which included both the English Civil War and the restoration of the monarchy. It was a time of fervent political and theological debate, with groups such as the Ranters, Levellers and Diggers becoming the radical exponents of new thinking.

Fox was a rather eccentric figure, who liked to rebel against authority. His parents had hoped he might become a priest but he was not impressed by the conventions of the established Church. Instead, he became a travelling preacher in 1647 after experiencing a series of visions.

(There has been some debate about Fox's mental state of mind – he suffered from severe depressions and mood swings – and whether or not we should take this into account when judging his teachings.)

In his preaching Fox rejected any part of the Church that he could not regard as being based on the Bible. In this respect he was a part of the mainstream Protestant religion that had developed since ordinary people had gained access to scripture and had been able to make their own judgements as to whether the Church was based on the teachings of Jesus or not.

Fox was also opposed to the idea that worship needed a church, derisively calling them 'steeple-houses' and arguing that one could worship God anywhere, and that anyone could lead prayer, even women and children (a view that was deeply controversial at the time). He encouraged his followers to trust their 'inner light' and to have a direct relationship with God. The Quakers refused to take oaths, they were against slavery and war, and emphasised personal spiritual experience over formal religious practice.

Predictably, the Quakers (including Fox) were widely attacked for their beliefs both in Fox's native England and in other European countries. Fox was imprisoned on eight separate occasions. He argued passionately for tolerance of his beliefs and managed in turn to persuade both Oliver Cromwell and Charles II to lessen their persecution.

Fox would often go to church services and start debates with the priests on theological grounds. As an example of his argumentative nature, even his court appearances were marked by arguments with the judges as to whether the Bible insisted that defendants should wear hats or not. As he travelled around preaching, he was also frequently attacked or beaten by those who took exception to his beliefs.

He travelled widely in Europe and America and inspired a wide variety of responses, from those who considered him dangerous or mad to those who came under his influence. The Quaker movement grew after his death into the world-wide institution that it is today, and while later Quakers moved away from Fox's position on some issues, his basic beliefs lie at the heart of Quakerism.

*The Journal of George Fox* was first published in 1694. It was edited by Thomas Ellwood, a friend of John Milton's, and had a preface by William Penn, who had travelled with Fox, and had founded the American Quaker colony of Pennsylvania. *The Journal* was partly dictated by Fox, although parts were constructed by the editors and written as though they were his work.

It is the story of Fox's life, his visions, imprisonments and travels. A dense read, it is probably best first read in an abridged version. But it contains some fascinating writing, and gives us a clear picture of the times Fox lived in, and of the awkward, questioning, loving figure that he was. Walt Whitman, whose parents were inspired by Quaker thought, wrote that 'George Fox stands for something too – a thought – the thought that wakes in silent hours – perhaps the deepest, most eternal thought latent in the human soul. This is the thought of God, merged in the thoughts of moral right and the immortality of identity. Great, great is this thought – aye, greater than all else.'

Quakers were often accused of antinomianism – which means that they were thought to be saying that they were beyond the existing religious law and subject only to their own consciences. The history of the Christian Churches is an ongoing struggle between those who asserted various orthodoxies and those who sought to challenge or rebel against them.

Fox's journal presents us with a case study in the virtues of rejecting orthodoxy. From a modern viewpoint, many of his beliefs seem self-evident. He was in favour of a simpler Church in which all were brothers or sisters. He rebelled against the dominance of ceremony, established tradition and rote learning in favour of a more passionate, personal spirituality. It is the way that, in making these points, he had to struggle against persecution and wilful incomprehension that makes him an inspiring figure to us today.

## The Journal of George Fox

### THE SPEED READ

We have an inner light that connects us to Jesus. True religion doesn't come from obedience to ritual but from personal spiritual conversion. It is the Holy Spirit that qualifies one to be a minister, not theological study. God is within us all and we can feel his presence. We can worship him anywhere as he is present in all places, not just in the 'steeple-house' of established religion. I have travelled England and the world teaching these lessons, in spite of many imprisonments and beatings along the way.

# The Journal of John Woolman

## John Woolman, 1772

'As I looked to the Lord, he inclined my heart to His testimony.
I told the man that I believed the practice of continuing slavery to this
people was not right.'

John Woolman was a Quaker preacher who travelled around the American colonies in the eighteenth century. He was an opponent of slavery, and always an advocate of peace and understanding rather than military and domestic force and violence. The *Journal* is Woolman's own beautifully simple account of his life and beliefs.

He was born in 1720, into a family of Friends (Quakers) who had been among the earliest settlers of New Jersey. One of his first recollections, as recorded in the *Journal*, is of an incident that happened when he was a young boy. He found a robin's nest with young robins inside. Being a foolish young boy, he started throwing rocks at the mother robin, and ended up killing her. He realised that the baby robins would not survive without her, so for the sake of mercy he took the nest down and killed them too.

While many young people might have shrugged or laughed this off, the young Woolman pondered what he had done and became full of remorse. He would always remember this feeling in later life – he wrote:

> In this case I believed that Scripture proverb was fulfilled, 'The tender mercies of the wicked are cruel.' I then went on my errand, and for some hours could think of little else but the cruelties I had committed, and was much troubled. Thus He whose tender mercies are over all His works hath placed a principle in the human mind, which incites to exercise goodness towards every living

creature; and this being singly attended to, people become tender-hearted and sympathizing; but when frequently and totally rejected, the mind becomes shut up in a contrary disposition.

After this incident Woolman developed a sense of love and protectiveness for all living creatures. This would also influence his thinking in a different way when he was older, following another key moment. When he was twenty-three he was asked to write a bill of sale for a slave. He did so out of duty to his employer, but writes that 'at the executing of it I was so afflicted in my mind, that I said before my master and the Friend that I believed slave-keeping to be a practice inconsistent with the Christian religion'.

This was a time when the Friends had not settled on a consistent theory with regard to the practice of slavery. Many individuals were uneasy with the widespread keeping of slaves in the new colonies and regarded it as a sin, but, like Woolman, they suppressed their doubts or withheld from a universal condemnation of the practice. However, Woolman, rather than try to shake off his unease, carried his concerns through into action. He started to personally campaign against slavery.

From this time onwards he travelled widely through the colonies, He was non-confrontational, but managed to persuade many individual Quakers that slavery was wrong. Some of those Friends had acquired slaves in order to treat them better than their original owners, but now Woolman argued that the relationship of master and slave between two human beings was innately wrong. He refused to use goods such as dyed clothes or silver cups and plates that he believed to have been produced using slave labour. He also insisted on paying other people's slaves for any labour they did from which he benefited.

Woolman was even sensitive to the use of animals for forced labour, preferring to avoid the use of stagecoache where he felt the horses were being treated unkindly. A large part of Woolman's argument was about the inequality between people. He was against slavery in all cases, but was more forgiving of those slave-owners who worked in tandem with their slaves and treated them well than he was of those who lived a life of ease on the back of their slaves' labours.

No one man could defeat such a widespread practice as slavery single-handedly. But Woolman did succeed in provoking significant changes in attitudes. His book *Some Considerations on the Keeping of Negroes* was published in 1754 and widely read, while his *Journal*, published in 1772, remained in print for centuries to come. During his lifetime, a large part of the Quaker movement travelled from uncertainty about slavery to a more robust condemnation of the practice, and this was influential in the growing campaign to have slavery abolished over the following decades.

Woolman also campaigned on other issues – in the spirit of his belief that humans of all races should be treated with equality, he spoke directly to Native Americans at a time when many disdained them as savages. He also refused to pay taxes when he believed they were going to support contemporary wars. But it is his achievements in helping to turn the tide against slavery for which he is best remembered.

*The Journal* tells the story of his preaching and opposition to slavery in a simple, direct manner. The inspiring example of his spirituality has made the book enduringly popular. It is also a fascinating historical document. Woolman was travelling in the American colonies before the US became independent. This was a time of considerable political and moral uncertainty. A nation was being shaped and it was as yet uncertain what shape that nation would take. It is to the great credit of John Woolman that he was able to help guide it towards a future in which slavery was regarded as unacceptable.

### *The Journal of John Woolman*

#### THE SPEED READ

As a young man I killed a family of robins. I felt such remorse I vowed to be kind to my fellow creatures in future. At the age of twenty-three I wrote a bill of sale for a slave, but again my conscience spoke and I knew that it was wrong for any man to keep another as a slave. I travelled the early American colonies spreading the message of peace and campaigning against slavery, and this journal records those travels for posterity.

# *A Confession*
## Leo Tolstoy, 1884

'The whole of the people possessed a knowledge of the truth, for otherwise they could not have lived. Moreover, that knowledge was accessible to me, for I had felt it and had lived by it. But I no longer doubted that there was also falsehood in it . . . But where did the truth and where did the falsehood come from? Both the falsehood and the truth were contained in the so-called holy tradition and in the Scriptures. Both the falsehood and the truth had been handed down by what is called the Church.'

Leo Tolstoy, or Count Lev Nikolayevich (1828–1910), was one of the world's greatest novelists. His two best-known works, *War and Peace* and *Anna Karenina*, are each in their separate ways classics. But Tolstoy was also a remarkable spiritual thinker.

The turning point in his thought came with the short book *A Confession*, which was first distributed in Russia in 1882 before being published two years later. In his two great novels he had taken a rationalist position – he describes the philosophical message of those books in *A Confession* as being 'that one should live so as to have the best for oneself and one's family'.

He had also taken the position that history was an inexorable process in which you can have little control over your life. This led him to suggest a rather passive submission to your place in life. But by the later stages of *Anna Karenina*, Tolstoy had come to find his own philosophical position unsatisfactory and he turned back to religion for solutions.

*A Confession* is an autobiographical discourse on how Tolstoy's religious beliefs were formulated and modified. In searching for the meaning of life, Tolstoy no longer found a passive acceptance of fate to be an acceptable solution. He had lost his faith in Christianity at a young age. However, looking back, he came to feel that what he had lost faith in was partly the Church itself and the uncomfortable mixture of truth and falsehood he felt it enshrined.

After eliminating such possible solutions as science and Eastern wisdom, as well as existing political theory, Tolstoy moves on to acknowledge the simple Christian faith of everyday people as having the utmost importance. While he feels that there are always falsehoods among those beliefs, he no longer thinks that this is a reason to reject faith per se.

Instead he returns to the New Testament to make his own decisions as to what he can still have faith in. This means that he rejects some of the positions and customs of the contemporary Christian Church (meaning the Russian Orthodox Church, and other established Christian Churches in Europe).

Tolstoy focuses on the moral lessons of the Gospels, in particular the Sermon on the Mount. He takes Christ's injunction to 'turn the other cheek' with the utmost seriousness and explores its meaning for us today. He concludes from this that the only political means to achieve change must be pacifism, and non-violence.

Tolstoy's political beliefs at this time were somewhat anarchistic – he rejected the compulsion of the state and the organisation of a central Church. However, his non-violence led him to reject communist and anarchist calls for violent revolution. In this way he would come to be a significant influence on twentieth-century figures such as Gandhi and Martin Luther King, who also chose passive resistance as their preferred means of struggle against oppression.

Some of the specifics of these ideas were spelled out more clearly in his later books, *My Religion*, *The Kingdom of God is Within You* (which became one of Gandhi's inspirations) and *The Gospels in Brief*. But *A Confession* remains the most powerful statement of Tolstoy's spiritual crisis and journey to the kind of Christian anarchism that marked his later years.

As a result of his religious writings Tolstoy gathered a following who regarded themselves as Tolstoyans rather than as Orthodox Christians. He became a cult figure, and intellectuals and spiritual leaders from across Europe would travel to his home to speak to the great man.

Ironically it is this very celebrity that gives one most pause for thought in reassessing Tolstoy's spiritual significance today. Even in *A Confession* there is a tendency to self-aggrandisement, of a subtle kind, that makes one feel that Tolstoy is not merely putting forward spiritual ideas but also asserting his own importance. In his fame he came almost to be seen as the founder of a new religion and, while his later years were not his happiest (because his family was estranged by his new beliefs), this perhaps adversely affected his writing on spiritual matters. While reading, you tend to wonder if the importance of his writing was over-rated by contemporaries, who were judging his importance partly on the basis of his astonishing literary work.

However, in its most simple and humble moments, *A Confession* is still a powerful book. It is the testament of a serious and deep thinker who wants to understand why his faith has been allowed to lapse and who chooses to contemplate Christ's actual words to try to rediscover that faith. We may not share all of Tolstoy's conclusions, especially those which are too closely related to the political theories of their time, but we can nonetheless admire the sincerity of his exploration of the meaning of life.

## A Confession

### THE SPEED READ

When I was very young I accepted religion, but as I grew older I lost my faith as I rejected the weary ritual and formalities of the Church. I went on to seek the meaning of life, but I came to find all other explanations unsatisfying, so I returned to Christ's words to examine the real meaning, especially his Sermon on the Mount. As a result I came to realise that the simple faith of everyday folks should not be rejected merely because it contains some falsehoods. Instead we should focus on the part of that simple faith that we can recognise to be the truth.

# The Cost of Discipleship
## Dietrich Bonhoeffer, 1937

'Cheap grace is the mortal enemy of our church. Our struggle today
is for costly grace.'

One of the most uncomfortable questions you can ask
about history is to ponder how you might have reacted
to the rise of Hitler. Which of us can be absolutely sure that
we would have the moral strength to oppose the rise of
fascism, to resist a dictatorship, even at our own cost?

Dietrich Bonhoeffer provides an inspiring example of
someone who did exactly that. He refused to be cowed by
the Nazis and refused to accept that his Church should not
stand up to them. *The Cost of Discipleship* is his most widely
read book, and makes a strong argument about how the
Church and the individual should react to the modern
world, in the context of a brutal, repressive government. It
centres on Bonhoeffer's extended meditations on the Sermon
on the Mount and his thoughts on what Jesus was really
asking of his followers.

Bonhoeffer, who was born in 1906, became a theologian
and Lutheran pastor and travelled widely as part of his
studies. He returned to Germany in 1931, and became a
founding member of the Confessing Church, a branch of
the Church which opposed the Nazis' ideology and actions.
He was friends with the theologian Karl Barth, and their
conversations in the 1930s centred on the liberal theology of
the Lutheran Church.

Bonhoeffer came to feel that the emphasis on personal
experience and engagement with society was being used
to elevate human society over the teaching of Christ in the
scriptures. Together with Barth he was known as a neo-
orthodox thinker, meaning that they believed that it was

important to go back to the word of God as revealed in the Bible, rather than trust the complex orthodoxies that had built up over the eighteenth and nineteenth centuries within the Protestant tradition.

Bonhoeffer lived in Britain during the mid-1930s, but returned to Germany at a time when his Confessing Church was being suppressed by the SS. His return was in spite of the fact that, in a 1933 radio address, he had denounced Hitler and also the German people for allowing themselves to be led by a corrupt, evil leader and regime, describing Hitler as a false idol. This obviously put him in immediate danger within Germany.

In spite of the bans imposed upon his Church he continued to lead its opposition to the anti-Semitic Nazi drive. The Confessing Church was a reproach to both the official German Church and the Roman Catholic hierarchies, which failed to engage with or oppose Hitler in any meaningful way.

Bonhoeffer was banned from preaching, from teaching and finally from any kind of public speaking whatsoever by the regime. He became involved with opponents of the Nazis and played some part in a plot to assassinate Hitler. He was finally arrested after money that had been used by Jews escaping to Switzerland across the border was traced back to him.

Once the plot to assassinate Hitler failed in 1944 his connections to the conspirators were revealed, and his fate was sealed. He was moved around a succession of prisons and concentration camps before being executed in a brutal hanging at Flossenbürg in April 1945. The end of the war was only a matter of weeks away, but he would not live to see the destruction of the regime he had done so much to oppose.

His writings survived as a record of his beliefs and life. *The Cost of Discipleship* was written in 1937 and takes a look at the meaning of following Jesus. He points out that

Jesus' call is for us to 'come and die'. He is asking us to give up our entire lives for him, not to do things by halves. He is not necessarily asking us to die as martyrs, but to consider our relationship with him deeply, to be sure that we know that we are doing all that we possibly can to follow him.

Bonhoeffer contrasts 'cheap grace' and 'costly grace'. The former is the kind of grace that one bestows on oneself when one imagines one is living a holy life, without truly examining that life or engaging with Christ. The latter is a far more committed form of grace in which we truly ask ourselves if we are living up to the demands that Christ has placed upon us as believers.

For Bonhoeffer, it is not enough to turn up to church on a Sunday and bask in the glory of praying in front of the community. He sees public prayer as a matter of display and argues that only our private prayer and engagement allow us to communicate with God.

Bonhoeffer can sometimes be a harsh writer, especially as he is so insistent on sacrifice, and his theological detail can be intimidating. But his core message is a powerful one. He argues that too many Christians want to know exactly where the path to God will lead them, but instead he urges readers to 'plunge into the deep waters beyond your own comprehension, and I will help you to comprehend even as I do'.

Bonhoeffer's insistence on the pain, suffering and sacrifice we will experience as part of our discipleship has to be placed in the context of the dark times in which he was writing. For him, following his conscience was an intensely dangerous path. He could have stayed away from Germany and preached against Hitler from a distance, but his conscience drove him to re-enter the country at its darkest hour and oppose the man who he recognised as evil.

In the end, this is the knowledge that makes *The Cost of Discipleship* such an empowering and emotive read. Bonhoeffer genuinely did everything he possibly could to fulfil his beliefs in what Jesus would have wanted him to do, so much so that he died a miserable death as a result. So when we read this book we are getting a glimpse into the soul of someone who lived a truly admirable life in the most appalling of circumstances.

We can hope that the cost of our discipleship need not be as great, but at the same time the book forces us to consider what we would have done if we were in Bonhoeffer's place. No one can truly know what they would do in those circumstances, but we can be grateful that there are people who had the courage and resolve to do the right thing in the face of evil.

### The Cost of Discipleship

**THE SPEED READ**

Cheap grace is the characteristic of those who believe that they need not fully engage with Jesus to live a good life. But if we examine Christ's Sermon on the Mount it becomes apparent that he wanted us to commit heart and soul to him. We must experience the pain and suffering of sacrifice to achieve costly grace. We must do whatever it takes to become worthy of being his disciples in the world.

# The Seven Storey Mountain
## Thomas Merton, 1948

'The devil is no fool. He can get people feeling about heaven the way they ought to feel about hell. He can make them fear the means of grace the way they do not fear sin.'

*The Seven Storey Mountain* was written by the Trappist monk Thomas Merton at the age of thirty-one. It is a remarkable account of his life, from an early rejection of religion, through conversion in his twenties, and on to his decision to withdraw into a monastery. The title is a reference to Dante's *Inferno*. The book has sold millions of copies since its publication in 1948. This is largely because of the compelling account it gives of the author's decision to adopt a monastic lifestyle.

Merton was a natural writer. He was well educated and probably could have been successful in an academic career had he chosen to follow that path. His parents died in his youth and he had a complex childhood in which he moved between different homes in France, England and then the US. He had some religious teaching as a young man, but rejected its message declaring that he believed in nothing.

This nihilism led him to lead a relatively licentious life, drinking alcohol and indulging in casual sex. He describes himself at this age in the book as someone who is drifting, failing to find meaning in different areas such as literature and radical politics. Finally, he came back to the Church, converting to Catholicism when he was twenty-three.

He became a monk, living in the Cistercian Order at Gethsemani Abbey in Kentucky. In spite of his confinement, he reported this as a moment when he finally realised his freedom. *The Seven Storey Mountain* gives an appealing picture of the peace and fulfilment that he found as a result of this withdrawal from the world.

The book is well written and compelling, but the scale of its success was something of a surprise to the publishers. We have to bear in mind that the period after the Second World War was a rather strange time, when people were deeply concerned about the threat of nuclear attack, and the world still seemed a rather dangerous place. For many the savagery of the war had left a feeling of angst and pointlessness. *The*

*Seven Storey Mountain* came as a real breath of fresh air into that environment. It described a simpler way of life, and one in which these confusions could be left behind.

It was reportedly an inspiration for many young people who chose to enter the priesthood or holy orders in that period, or at least to turn back to a more contemplative form of religion. The book has been compared to St Augustine's *Confessions*. In both books, a young man turns away from the worldly sins and pleasures of his youth to seek a more spiritual path. Indeed, the Catholic Church was initially rather concerned about Merton's descriptions of his behaviour before he entered holy orders, and some of the passages concerning this period of his life were cut in response to those concerns.

Another concern that some felt about the book was the degree to which it lionised one very specific type of Catholic faith, in the process denigrating other Christian communities and non-Catholic paths. This is probably a valid criticism, although you can also read it as a simple expression of a monk's enthusiasm for the path he has chosen, and take this as something that might inspire anyone, no matter what path they choose to try to find spiritual growth.

Merton himself went on to become a well-known author and thinker, and in some of his later work he did acknowledge that he would have written the book differently if he had written it later in his life. Indeed, his life continued to evolve as he aged – he became interested in leaving the Trappists for a less solitary order. And having hailed the virtues of living a life in pure contemplation, he ended up as a well-known figure, who travelled the world, rather than the silent monk that the book depicts. Merton would become a participant in the peace movement, and his later writing would take a broader view of spirituality than *The Seven Storey Mountain*.

However, none of that detracts from the power of this

book. It is a book that expresses a very particular point of view – that of a man in his thirties who has made a profound decision to turn away from a life of worldly success into private contemplation and prayer. As such it has been an inspiration to many people. So while there may have been more to Thomas Merton, and to his life story, than this single book, *The Seven Storey Mountain* survives as a powerful testament to one part of his journey.

### The Seven Storey Mountain

#### THE SPEED READ

As a young man I was without direction, drifting from licentiousness to radical politics, from literature to academia without finding meaning. Then I converted to the Church and entered the Trappist monastery. There I found peace and fulfilment, and genuine freedom in spite of the four walls that surrounded me.

# The Normal Christian Life
## Watchman Nee, 1957

'God makes it quite clear in His Word that He has only one answer to every human need – His Son, Jesus Christ. In all His dealings with us He works by taking *us* out of the way and substituting Christ in our place.'

Watchman Nee was a church leader who helped to spread Christianity around China in the first half of the twentieth century. He was imprisoned for this activity in 1952 and spent the rest of his life in prison before his death in 1972.

He converted to Christianity in 1920 when he was seventeen years old. He was strongly influenced by the British missionary M. E. Barber who taught him about Christian classics of the past. Most of his learning came from direct study of the Bible and from reading the great books of predecessors who wrote about their spiritual beliefs. For thirty years Watchman Nee travelled around China helping to establish 'local churches', institutions that he saw as indispensable in attempting to support the Christian faith.

He thought it regrettable that people chose to separate the Church of God into different denominations and hierarchies, arguing that the only legitimate way to create a smaller church was on a geographical basis – in other words it was natural for a community to have its own church. The local churches he founded became the bedrock of a Christian Church that was widespread and strong at the time of the communist takeover in 1949.

During 1938 and 1939 Watchman Nee travelled to Europe and gave a series of talks – this was the source material for *The Normal Christian Life*, which would be published in 1957. On the surface, the book is a commentary on the first few chapters of the New Testament book, Romans. The title is a reference to the question that the author starts with: 'What is the normal Christian life?' Watchman Nee's contention is that the average Christian life today is not a normal one, but a subnormal one, which does not come up to the standards that God expects of us.

As a starting point to this question, he returns to the answer given by St Paul in Galatians 2:20 – 'It is no longer I, but Christ.' Watchman Nee argues that this means 'I live no longer, but Christ lives His life in me.' He wants us to live in

Christ, to escape from fear and darkness by recognising the great gift that God has given us, which consists of the forgiveness, absolution from sin and path towards the light which are embodied in Christ.

He is unflinching on the subject of sin: he confronts the problem of why even believers are still tempted by sin, but sees in Christ a way to get beyond this problem. He looks at what it means to live one's life in the Holy Spirit. Even though we should be able to leave sin and the problems of the flesh behind, we struggle to do so. So how can we see ourselves as being liberated in Christ's love?

The problem for Nee is that too many Christians try to live in themselves, in their own strength, and thus in their own feelings. What they need to do is 'take their hands off', and put their faith in Christ. We fail because we do not let Christ into our lives, because we do not understand that God's gift to us was his son, and that the only true path is to live our lives in Christ.

In spite of the communist takeover, after which many of his fellow Christians escaped the country, Watchman Nee felt he had to stay in China and to continue with his work.

His leadership of the local churches inevitably led to him being treated as an enemy of the state. He was arrested in 1952. In 1956 he was finally sentenced to fifteen years of imprisonment. Only his wife was allowed to visit him in this time. His dignity throughout his persecution is one of the reasons that he is remembered as such an inspiration. His very last letter alluded to his suffering, but only in positive terms: 'In my sickness, I still remain joyful at heart.' Since his death in 1972, Watchman Nee's influence has persisted through a wide variety of different spiritual thinkers, and he is remembered for his own words in *The Normal Christian Life* and his many other publications and writings.

*The Normal Christian Life*

#### The Speed Read

The average Christian life is not the normal Christian life, the life that God would want us to live. Rather than trying to live in our own strength, we need to understand the great gift that God gave us in Christ, and live our lives through him. We live in a world of sin and the flesh, but we can escape from temptation by sacrificing ourselves to Christ.

# Community and Growth
## Jean Vanier, 1979

'I know that God has chosen the poor to astound the rich and the strong. I know that he loves me as I am, with my handicaps.'

In the modern world we are often confronted with the opposition between the individual and society. Many political ideas revolve around the question of whether the individual or the state should be the focus of policy and moral agency. Such oppositions miss one of the most fundamental aspects of life, which is that, before we live in a state or society, we live in a community.

In his writings, Jean Vanier treats the idea of community with the seriousness it deserves. This is, after all, a man who has created communities around the world which humble those of us who are too scared or too busy to take responsibility for the weakest members of our communities. Vanier was the founder of the L'Arche movement, an international network of communities in which people from a variety of faith backgrounds live together with people with developmental and learning disabilities. The loving support these communities provide is in stark contrast to the institutions in which people with disabilities often had (and still have) to live in many parts of the world.

L'Arche is French for The Ark, as in the biblical story of Noah. Vanier, who had a background in the navy and in training for the priesthood, created the roots of the organisation in 1964. Inspired by his friendship with the Dominican priest Father Thomas Philippe, and by Val Fleuri, a home and workshop for men with disabilities, Vanier founded a community in a small house in Trosly-Breuil in France. There he would live together with two of the men who he had encountered while they were living in a harsh institution near Paris.

Providing a home for these men was only the start of Vanier's journey: from these small beginnings the organisation grew in size and influence over the years to the international network it has become today.

Vanier has written a number of books on his work and on the ideas that underpin them. One aspect of the L'Arche experience that he focuses on in his writing is the admirable relationship he has with those who live there. Rather than patronising them in any way, Vanier always emphasises the degree to which this is a relationship of friends, not of helper and dependent. Indeed, he stresses how much the more able members of these communities can learn from the 'disabled' members.

He has written that

> the idea of living together was there from day one. The idea of living happily together, of celebrating and laughing a lot, came very quickly and spontaneously. When the idea of the poor educating us came, I don't know exactly. The words of St Vincent de Paul, "The poor are

our masters," were always there, but when they became
a reality is uncertain.

Before L'Arche, Vanier had taken a doctorate in philosophy, where he wrote on the subject of happiness, a term
he defined as 'loving and being loved'. In books such as
*Community and Growth*, it is his ability to describe how
such love and happiness grow from our interactions with
others that shines through. For Vanier, all relationships are
mutual – and all of us suffer from weaknesses – the strength
he describes best is the strength we find in others, and in our
relationships and community.

*Community and Growth* is about more than Vanier's
experiences of L'Arche. It is a book written from deep
Christian beliefs, but one that interests anyone who has pondered the basic moral problems of society. For Vanier, we are
all a mixture of good and bad qualities, strength and weakness, light and dark. When we recognise our own weaknesses
with humility and grace it makes it easier for us to be receptive to the strength and goodness that we find in others.

Some might be inspired by Vanier to think about how they
can help in their community; some might even wish to emulate
the writer and establish a community such as those organised
by L'Arche. But for many readers, the value of his writing is
the light he casts on the idea of living a good life. The modern
catchphrase 'What would Jesus do?' captures an age-old question: how can I live my life in a more Christ-like manner?

Vanier doesn't pretend that this is an easy question, and
he doesn't hide the difficulties of life in a community. He
acknowledges that we are capable of hate as well as love, but
sees forgiveness, humility and a desire to help others as
attributes that are fundamental to a good way of life.

In this respect, *Community and Growth* is relevant to us
all, as we all (with very few exceptions) live in communities.
We all struggle with relationships and friendships on a daily

basis. We can all recognise the difficulties of living up to Christ's admonition to love one's neighbour. That Vanier presents a vivid example of how to do so with the utmost vigour and sincerity can only be an inspiration. *Community and Growth* is a beautiful, gentle book, a meditation on how to live, and a celebration of the things that we all have in common as human beings.

### Community and Growth

#### THE SPEED READ

Jean Vanier is the admirable founder of L'Arche communities, where people of many faiths live together with people who are developmentally disabled. *Community and Growth* is a meditation on the ideas that underpin Vanier's spirituality – the ways humans can live together and support one another, finding love, happiness and mutual support, in the process living in as Christ-like a manner as possible. It offers an inspiration to all, not just to those who might be interested in living in such a community.

# No Greater Love
## Mother Teresa, 1979

'I don't think there is anyone who needs God's help and grace as much as I do. Sometimes I feel so helpless and weak. I think that is why God uses me. Because I cannot depend on my own strength, I rely on Him twenty-four hours a day.'

The public perception of Mother Teresa has been affected by recent revelations that she spent a large part of her life in a depressed condition, and feeling that she had been forsaken by her God. Some see this as undermining her saintliness, but one could equally argue that her continued devotion to the poor and needy in spite of such personal crises makes her achievements all the more remarkable.

Mother Teresa was an Albanian Roman Catholic nun who set up the Missionaries of the Poor in Kolkata (formerly Calcutta) in India. The organisation looked after the poor and the sick, and cared for orphans and the elderly. From its foundation in 1950, this determined, compassionate lady helped literally thousands of people over a period of forty-five years. The Missionaries of the Poor set up missions in more than a hundred countries. She saved lives, gave people hope in dark and difficult times, and fed and cared for those were in the most desperate need. There have inevitably been cavils about some details of her life's work and beliefs, but it is impossible to contemplate her achievements without awe.

*No Greater Love* is a collection of her thoughts, and a glimpse into the mind of someone who put Jesus' admonitions to his followers to exercise charity and to care for the poor at the centre of her life. As a Catholic, she views good works and sacrifice as central parts of the path to salvation, and it has to be acknowledged that we cannot all share her levels of either devotion or self-sacrifice. But this is a deeply inspiring book in spite of this.

In the book she talks of her work as being an attempt to emulate or imitate Jesus, and to act as he would have wanted us to do. At one point she argues that 'if our poor die of hunger, it is not because God does not care for them. Rather, it is because neither you nor I are generous enough.'

Mother Teresa's mission put the care of the needy above the obligation to teach the Christian message. The catechism was taught in the missions, but as she explains, she was impressed by the fact that Jesus chose to feed the crowds before he tried to teach them. She believed that actions speak louder than words, and the example of charity and love that was created by the missions was her legacy.

The book includes anecdotes about some of the people she encountered in the course of her charitable work. She talks with compassion about a woman who gives her crippled son the name of 'Teacher of Love', and of a child who rejected the opportunity to live in one of her homes because he preferred to stay with the mother he loved, and live under a tree. Her conviction that 'we must conquer the world not with bombs but with love' also shines through, and presents us with a wonderful example of someone who was able to improve the world through simple actions.

Some of the posthumously published letters of Mother Teresa made it clear that she had a difficult spiritual life. She felt abandoned by her God, writing in distressing terms of the anguish she felt:

> When I try to raise my thoughts to Heaven – there is such convicting emptiness that those very thoughts return like sharp knives & hurt my very soul. – I am told God loves me – and yet the reality of darkness & coldness & emptiness is so great that nothing touches my soul. Did I make a mistake in surrendering blindly to the Call of the Sacred Heart?

In retrospect it is clear that Mother Teresa suffered from a long 'dark night of the soul'. It was St John of the Cross who gave us this term, which is generally understood to refer to believers who come to doubt their faith and to feel that they have been forsaken by Jesus or God. The truly extraordinary thing in the life of Mother Teresa is that she was able to persist in her charitable actions in spite of this inner turmoil.

It has been observed that those who suffer from such dark nights of the soul can have the greatest spiritual enlightenment. If they are able to continue to live a good life in spite of such doubts, then they have the experience of living life according to religious principle, not for the reward of feeling good because of those actions, but in spite of the emptiness that is engendered. So they are being good for goodness's sake, not for the spiritual rewards that are experienced by others.

The dark night finally lifted late in Mother Teresa's life, and we can only hope that she was then able to look back with joy at her achievements.

This is a beautiful little book, and one that contains gems of real wisdom. It is also a fine way to remember someone who lived out a genuinely Christian life, and was not deflected from the path of goodness by her uncertainties and perceived weaknesses.

## No Greater Love

### THE SPEED READ

God helps me because I am weak, so I rely on him every day. In our missions, we help people because they need to eat before they are able to learn. We should conquer the world with love, not with bombs. By giving people an example of a life that Jesus would commend, we are teaching the world about love. 'Silence of the heart is necessary so you can hear God everywhere – in the closing of the door, in the person who needs you, in the birds that sing, in the flowers, in the animals.'

# 6
# Secular Texts

This section includes titles that are spiritual in themselves but cannot strictly be regarded as religious books. In the case of William Blake (*Songs of Innocence and Experience*) and Fyodor Dostoyevsky (*The Idiot*) the writing is from Christian points of view, but these are such idiosyncratic takes on religion that they seem almost to be an interrogation of spiritual belief rather than a statement of faith.

*The Varieties of Religious Experience* by William James and *Modern Man in Search of a Soul* by Carl Jung each take a psychological approach, attempting to understand our experience of matters of faith and what value spirituality has for us as human beings. Both contain insights into the way our minds work, and both take a mostly sympathetic view of religion.

The last three books in this section are three very different pieces of fiction. On the surface *The Little Prince* by Antoine de Saint-Exupéry and *The Soul Bird* by Michal Snunit are books for children. However, they are both books that have been enjoyed and treasured by adults as well as children and that pack a powerful emotional and spiritual message into a simple format. Neither takes a formal religious point of view, but both are books that can be inspirational for people in need of spiritual refreshment.

Meanwhile *Franny and Zooey* by J. D. Salinger is a more obviously sophisticated book, a story of highly educated New Yorkers and their spiritual fascinations. It is included here for its heady enthusiasm for a wide range of spiritual writing, from the sayings of Jesus and the Upanishads to *The Way of a Pilgrim*, which forms a crucial element of the plot. There are of course many novels that deal with spiritual concerns, so the choice of Dostoevsky and Salinger in this section can only seem arbitrary, but their presence, together with those of the two 'books for children', can act as a reminder that spiritual messages are to be found in a wide variety of sources, some less obvious than others.

## *Songs of Innocence and Experience*
### William Blake, 1789–94

'In every cry of every Man,
In every Infant's cry of fear,
In every voice: in every ban,
The mind-forg'd manacles I hear.'

Sometimes it takes a true maverick to challenge our religious assumptions and make us think about what we truly believe. William Blake was one such maverick thinker. As a radical, mystic, poet and artist, much of his best work has a profoundly spiritual angle to it.

Blake was drawn to Christianity but was strongly opposed to organised religion and to what he saw as the political hypocrisies of his time. His most creative period came in the shadow of the French Revolution – *Songs of Innocence* was published in 1789 as the revolution was underway, while *Songs of Experience* was written five years later when the revolution had clearly turned ugly, and Blake's disillusionment with the cause shows in this more weary set of poems.

He wrote some extraordinary 'prophetic works', using imagery from the Bible and elsewhere to convey his radical ideas. One of the most concentrated explanations of his ideas comes in *The Marriage of Heaven and Hell*. Here he mixes poetry and prose in a story that draws on predecessors such as Dante's *Inferno* and Milton's *Paradise Lost*. He pictures a meeting between a devil and an angel and their visits to each other's realms. Blake's devil is not an evil character, indeed he uses him (and the 'Proverbs of Hell') to make the point that the organised Church has used ideas of religion for its own oppressive purposes.

Blake pictures hell as a place of subversive and creative energy. He describes energy as 'eternal delight' and sees the Dionysian (wild or primal) energy of hell as a challenge to the oppressive system of formal Churches. To a degree this is a political allegory but there is also a theological challenge in Blake's thinking. He acknowledges the degree to which 'Evil' is a construction that can be used to formalise those qualities that the establishment is most uncomfortable with.

He also rejects the mind/body dualism of most philosophy, which has allowed the organised Church to label the natural energy and will of the body as being innately wrong, and to focus on the purity of mind and soul. So for him 'Good' wrongly comes to be identified as passive and obedient to Reason, while Energy is always rejected as being evil.

C. S. Lewis was so appalled by these kinds of ideas that he wrote *The Great Divorce* in response. However, one needn't agree with every aspect of Blake's thought to find his writing on these subjects fascinating and stimulating. And there is also great beauty in his poetry. *Songs of Innocence and Experience* is probably his greatest poetic achievement because it packs such emotion and profundity into such simple verse.

*Songs of Innocence* mostly consists of poems that focus on the simplicity and joy of the natural world: such things as a shepherd's love for his flock, or the beauty of a newborn baby, are Blake's inspirations. In *The Lamb*, he provides a perfectly formed poem introducing us to the creator of the beauty, God, who also called himself a lamb.

*Songs of Experience* followed five years later. It gives a more clouded vision of the human condition. Blake wanders the streets of London, noting the misery and poverty of many of its inhabitants. Many of the poems echo themes from the first volume, but take a darker or at least less innocent view of the same subjects. Blake expresses his anger at the inequalities of his time, through poems on subjects that are universal enough to strike a chord today.

Blake hadn't lost faith in mankind. But the second set of poems did express the idea that innocence and experience are two 'contrary states of the human soul'. For Blake, true innocence depended on the possibility of experience, and vice versa. While raging against a world in which people and children were kept poor and in which religious dogma was rated above simple Christian virtues such as love and mercy, he recognised that we all grow from a state of innocence to a state of experience and that this is a necessary part of life.

Some of Blake's beliefs are specific to his times. But others have been echoed in later strands of thought. One can see elements of psychoanalysis in the way that he believes that energy should not be repressed. And his belief in the importance of creativity and the dangers of oppression from organised religion have been taken on in different ways over the generations.

But the lasting value of *Songs of Innocence and Experience* comes from something far simpler. This is truly beautiful poetry that leads us to contemplate the basic aspects of human existence and what it means to have a soul. In spite of his doubts about the organised Church, Blake conveys some of the basic truths of the Christian message – those of charity, love and mercy in particular.

There may not be a clear message regarding the Christian way of life here, but there is a very clear picture of the complexity of the human soul. Through Blake's poetry we see the world more clearly, and that in itself is a remarkable spiritual achievement.

## Songs of Innocence and Experience

### THE SPEED READ

'Infant Joy' (from *Songs of Innocence*)

> I have no name;
> I am but two days old.
> What shall I call thee?
> I happy am,
> Joy is my name.

'Infant Sorrow' (from *Songs of Experience*)

> My mother groan'd! My father wept.
> Into the dangerous world I leapt.
> Helpless, naked, piping loud;
> Like a fiend hid in a cloud.

# *The Idiot*

## Fyodor Dostoevsky, 1868

'. . . the essence of religious feeling has nothing to do with any reasoning or any crimes and misdemeanours or atheism; it is something entirely different and it will always be so . . .'

Fyodor Dostoevsky always wrote with great intensity and often wrote about faith and reason in his extraordinary novels. He doesn't convey a unified philosophical message in his work: the characters each speak with their own voices and represent different sides of an argument.

Dostoevsky has variously been described as an existentialist, a radical and a pessimist. In fact he is probably best described as a mystical Christian and a Russian nationalist. His life views were partly shaped by two major events. His father died while he was young, probably murdered by his own servants. Later on he came close to being executed for treason. Cruelly he was led to the scaffold, and left blindfolded on the verge of death, before being informed that the sentence had been commuted. Both of these events led him to think deeply about the nature of life and death, crime and punishment, and the condition of his beloved country.

His greatest novel *The Brothers Karamazov* explicitly presents his internal conflict between faith, reason and licentiousness in the characters of the brothers and their father. It also presents us with the parable of the Grand Inquisitor, a tale through which an atheist questions the entire basis of the Church and the degree to which it has sometimes chosen control and eradication of free will over the original teachings of Jesus.

*The Idiot* takes a different approach to spirituality. The main character Prince Myshkin has often been described as Christ-like, because he approaches the obstacles in his life with such purity and innocence. Dostoevsky sets up a complex plot in which the prince is thrown into the Russian society of his day. The prince is an epileptic (like the author), and has been abroad, seeking help with his illness. He therefore comes into this society as an outsider, who takes everyone at face value, as he cannot help but trust in their sincerity and try to act towards them in a goodly manner. He shows a genuine, touching Christian love for many of those whom he encounters, and tries his best to help them, in spite of their deep flaws and problems.

He is often mired in confusion and doubt himself, because he cannot work out how to retain his virtue in the face of such moral complexities. In the end the virtue of the prince is insufficient to overcome the problems he is faced with, but he is nonetheless an inspiring character.

The plot revolves around Prince Myshkin's friendship with Rogozhin, a dark brooding character who is in love with Nastasya Filippovna, a society woman of questionable virtue. Although the prince also comes to love another girl, Aglaya, he is drawn into a love triangle with Rogozhin and Nastasya, as he proposes to the latter in an attempt to save her from herself, out of a Christian sense of duty to help a soul in torment.

As with all Dostoevsky books, this is a long dense read, although there are many hilarious and emotionally involving scenes. From a spiritual viewpoint, the crucial passages come in meditations and conversations on the subject of faith in reason, in particular in some of the exchanges between the licentious Rogozhin and the saintly prince.

At the heart of the novel's religious message is a section in which the prince muses about some recent experiences he has had. First, he talks at length to a well-known atheist on a train. He concludes that while this man was very learned and interesting, he was never truly addressing the issue he believes he was talking about. Something in his approach to atheism prevents him from truly understanding the simple faith of someone like the prince.

Second, he hears an anecdote about two peasants who are old friends. One of the friends covets an expensive watch that the other has obtained, and so cuts his throat to steal it, but he cannot bring himself to do this without first asking the Lord's forgiveness and crossing himself.

Third, he is swindled by a beggar who sells him a cheap cross, pretending it is silver. The prince is perfectly aware that it is tin, but concludes that 'I mustn't be too quick to condemn a man who has sold his Christ. God only knows what is locked away in these weak and drunken hearts.'

Finally he tells the lovely story of a young peasant girl who he saw crossing herself after seeing her baby smile. He asks her why and she responds: 'Well, sir, just as a mother rejoices seeing her baby's first smile, so does God rejoice every time he beholds from above a sinner kneeling down before Him to say his prayers *with all his heart*.' Myshkin comments that this is one of the most beautiful, profound things he has ever heard and that the young peasant girl has expressed the fundamental idea of Christianity. In this short sequence of disparate experiences, Dostoevsky manages to compress some profound thought about the religious experience and the paradoxes it can engender.

It is in passages like this that Dostoevsky's passionate spirituality shines through. He never presents the reader with simple solutions or with a packaged set of opinions. Instead he asks searching questions of his characters, and subjects them to impossible dilemmas as part of his investigation into what faith and reason can achieve in the modern world. In this way he reveals a huge amount about the religious experience, and shows us different ways in which we might choose to lead a spiritual life.

Prince Myshkin is one of the most lovely and tragic figures in literature. His take on Christianity is so simple and open-hearted that, even when he gets himself into irre-deemable tangles and difficulties, we can only love him in spite of everything. Seeing how the author loves his charac-ters in spite of their flaws also leads the reader to see Christian love from new angles, and in the end this is the real subject of this book.

## The Idiot

### THE SPEED READ

Prince Myshkin, a partially healed epileptic, returns from abroad. Befriending Rogozhin, a worldly, difficult man who loves Nastasya Filippovna, he is drawn into a situation of escalating difficulties. He attempts throughout to deal with this with Christian love, curiosity and innocence. Even though he is not able to resolve all the problems he faces, he provides an inspiring and intriguing character, through which we are led to interrogate the nature of faith and reason.

# The Varieties of Religious Experience
## William James, 1902

'Be not afraid of life. Believe that life is worth living and your belief will help create the fact.'

William James was a multi-talented thinker who pub-lished work in many fields other than religion, including physiology, psychology and philosophy. With Charles Sanders he was known as a founder of the philosophical movement, pragmatism. The pragmatists argued that knowledge can only be judged on its practical results in the world – that the usefulness of a belief can be of more significance than whether or not it is possible to prove that belief true beyond all possible doubt. This idea can appeal to someone who believes that their religious faith is an indispensable virtue, whether or not the existence of God can be proven.

James grew up in an intellectual, liberal household. His father was a theologian, and his sister and brother were both skilled writers (his brother Henry was the well-known novelist). In spite of a successful academic career, teaching at Harvard, William had a lifelong tendency to depression and melancholy, which fed into his fascination with spirituality.

James's writing often focused on consciousness and truth. He was unusual among philosophers in that he explicitly recognised the fact that many thinkers, while claiming to search for objective truth, end up producing work that suits their own prejudices and desires rather than being pure reflections of truth.

The idea that writers are often more subjective than they realise was carried into his writing on religious belief. At times he claimed that religion was something that science couldn't penetrate, that it was something that people could only approach on an individual basis. But he wrote elsewhere that it was possible for a study of human nature to help us achieve a more scientific understanding of the religious experience.

In 1890 James published his massive book *Principles of Psychology*, which helped to establish the foundations of psychology as a serious, modern science. He argued that the introspective study of our own minds could help us to comprehend how the mind works. He talked about the 'stream of consciousness' of the human mind, and argued that as well as understanding how the mind works we can perceive how we act with free will.

In *The Will to Believe* (1897) he went on to apply his pragmatic ideas to spirituality. He argued that it is the consequences of believing that are most important in a religious context. He saw belief in terms of individual choices, and defended the idea that we can rationally choose to believe in a proposition, even though we know it lies beyond the realm of provable truth.

Pragmatism was a form of verificationism, in which the meaning of a statement is judged by the consequences of believing it. Later verificationists and pragmatists would use their method to reject all metaphysical beliefs, including those of religion. James was a far more subtle thinker: rather than rejecting metaphysics, he tried to define and understand the way that we choose to believe in metaphysical and religious statements, in spite of our lack of certainty.

It is in *The Varieties of Religious Experience* (1902) that James best sums up his philosophy of religion. Pascal's wager had embodied the idea that you might choose to believe in God in the spirit of a gamble, on the basis that the consequences of being wrong are worse for the person who chooses atheism than for the person who chooses belief. For most believers this is an unsatisfactory compromise, as it implies that you should believe out of fear rather than faith. Up to a point James's writing can be used to justify religious belief in the same way as Pascal's wager did. However, there is more to his view of spiritual experiences. He sees truth as being defined by the personal consequences of belief rather than by how accurately it describes an external reality. So, in his thinking, we can judge how useful (and thus true) a belief in God is by judging its consequences in our life. If we can clearly see that a belief in God leads to better outcomes, then we can judge it to be a useful or true belief.

Of course, one can endlessly debate what a 'better

outcome' is, but on purely ethical grounds, many believers would argue that having God in their lives leads them to live better lives. And James doesn't sneer at this attitude, as many philosophers would.

He also looks at the case of the Quaker religion and its founder George Fox. Many modern observers believe that Fox was schizophrenic. For the scientists and philosophers who were James's primary audience, this would be a reason to reject his beliefs. However, James argues that the origin of a belief is of no consequence when we try to study its value or truth.

He also looks more closely at the idea that religious belief can have real consequences in our lives. He castigates scientists for their tendency to ignore the 'real, physical' consequences of unseen objects and symbols. He talks about how the word 'steak' on a menu or the thought of a lemon can cause us to salivate. In the same way, religious beliefs may have real consequences, so even though traditional science finds it hard to explain those consequences, they shouldn't be ignored.

When James contrasts the healthy mind and the sick soul, modern readers may be uncomfortable with his idea that some people are just 'naturally happy'. However, he does give a convincing picture of different types of people, who we might call optimists and pessimists. The sick souls find it hard to find the good in anything, while the healthy-minded naturally enjoy life and look for the best in any situation.

Possibly thinking of his own depression, James ponders the idea that sick souls can only be cured through a mystical experience. This foreshadowed Jung's later ideas on the same point, ideas that would feed into the founding of Alcoholics Anonymous. For James, 'twice born' souls, those who have been sick but have been cured by a spiritual epiphany, may be the ones who end up most healthy and happy in the end, since they understand life from both perspectives.

You don't read James's writing on religion for spiritual inspiration. But if you approach his writing as an investigation into the psychology of religious belief, you can find many valuable insights. His understanding of the truth and value of spirituality is an unusually sensitive one among scientists and philosophers. By finding ways to justify religion and ethics in a pragmatic, philosophical way, James allows us to see that it is not only possible, but hugely valuable to seek spiritual truth, rather than only accepting that something has value if it is recognised by the pure rationalism of science.

### The Varieties of Religious Experience

#### THE SPEED READ

The truth and usefulness of a statement depends on its consequences in our lives. We cannot reject ideas merely because of their origins, or because they rely on 'unseen factors'. Religious belief can have genuine consequences in life. Healthy souls look for the good in everything, while sick souls suffer from negativity and depression. But a sick soul cured by a spiritual experience can be the healthiest of all souls, as it has been 'born twice'.

# Modern Man in Search of a Soul
## Carl Jung, 1933

'The least of things with a meaning is worth more in life than the greatest of things without it.'

Known primarily as a psychoanalyst, Carl Jung also wrote well on matters of spirituality. *Modern Man in Search of a Soul* is a useful introduction to his writing on this subject. It is a series of essays, written for the layman rather than the expert psychiatrist, which analyse the average person's need to search for their soul.

Jung was a Freudian and a close friend of Sigmund Freud, although their friendship suffered a notorious split in 1913. Jung suffered from some kind of breakdown in the next few years, and a great deal of his subsequent work dealt with his own mental condition during this difficult period.

Jung was also fascinated by a range of subjects that some might regard as somewhat flaky, ranging from myths, Arthurian legend and flying saucers to Eastern philosophy. However, his interest in these areas was often rooted in finding out what drives the human mind to seek meaning in the world around us, and the place of the unconscious in our behaviour.

While Freud saw the unconscious as a place where our primitive self resides, something which we struggle to repress, Jung saw it as a potential source of creativity, and as the source of the friction that leads us towards psychological individuation.

He also wrote about the 'collective unconscious'. This idea shouldn't be understood to mean that people have some kind of shared mind. Instead it means that human beings share so much with one another in terms of experience, understanding, sensory capacity and so on, that we have a similar mental set-up.

At times in Jung's writing he tries to understand how and why we create myths, and in this respect he treats religion as one myth among others. But at the same time, he sometimes spoke of a personal belief in God and religion, and regarded spirituality as being of great importance.

By chance, Jung also inspired the twelve-step programme popularised by Alcoholics Anonymous. He was treating an American patient (known as Rowland H.) who suffered from problems with alcohol. Jung told him of his belief that only a spiritual experience could reform an alcoholic.

Rowland managed to conquer his drinking problem after taking this advice, and returning to America to join an evangelical Christian group. This story came to the attention of Bill Wilson, who in turn managed to conquer his drinking problem and went on to co-found the AA.

The crucial part of Jung's teaching that made its way from a distance into the final twelve-step programme was the idea that a spiritual experience can lead us to transform ourselves. Just as we go through a process of individuation and create a 'self' in which we believe, a spiritual experience can lead us to reform or revise this self at a later date.

In his study of religions ranging from Christianity to Taoism and Gnosticism to Buddhism, Jung saw a common thread in this kind of self-transformation. He saw religion as a journey to find the self and at the same time to search for the divine. He also treated spiritual experience as being essential to our well-being and even sanity.

The essays in *Modern Man in Search of a Soul* lay out an overview of Jung's psychological theories. He writes about dream analysis, symbols, the purpose of psychotherapy, the formation of personality, and life stages. He also contrasts 'modern man' with the 'archaic man'. In his view, the true modern man is one who has taken on board all the modern viewpoints, and who relies on logic and science rather than on unconscious instinct and spirituality. He contrasts this with the relative simplicity of archaic man's lifestyle and belief system.

Jung doesn't claim that either is necessarily better than the other, but he points out that modern man suffers from spiritual unease, possibly because he has become too detached from his unconscious instincts. Jung's time in India had left him fascinated with Eastern religion, and also led him to believe that having a greater appreciation of the unconscious, and integrating spirituality into everyday life, would lead to a healthier mindset. He argues that modern man needs to move back towards values such as faith, love and insight.

In the last essay, Jung makes a comparison between psychotherapists and priests. He says that while priests may not know as much about the scientific study of the mind, they do know a great deal about those values which are necessary for the soul. He believed that many people became psychically unwell, or at least suffered from angst later in middle age and beyond, because they lost their religious outlook, and their modern outlook prevented them from seeking spiritual assistance, whether it be from a priest or other source.

In the end this is possibly the most important message to be taken from this book. Jung believed in the science of psychotherapy and in its ability to comprehend the unconscious mind. But he also recognised the fact that analysis alone was not enough to help with our spiritual unease. We need balance and harmony, and sometimes science and logic are not the solution – instead we need to go back to a more spiritual response to life's challenges.

## Modern Man in Search of a Soul

### THE SPEED READ

Through dreams and symbols, mysticism and myths, we can trace the unconscious need for meaning and purpose in man's life. Religion is a journey of self-transformation, in which we discover ourselves. Deep spiritual experiences can lead us to develop and grow. Modern man has gained much, but he has also lost contact with his instincts and unconscious. As a result he often suffers from spiritual unease, and the modern mindset sometimes prevents him from seeking religious remedies for this. Science and logic teach us a great deal but sometimes they are not enough. Instead we need to return to the simpler values of faith, love and trust in our unconscious.

## The Little Prince
### Antoine de Saint-Exupéry, 1943

'One sees clearly only with the heart. Anything essential is invisible to the eyes.'

*The Little Prince* is a children's book, but it can be a spiritually rewarding read for adults. It is a simple fable about the friendship between a pilot who has crashed in the desert and the little prince he meets there. The author, Antoine de Saint-Exupéry, was himself a keen aviator. He flew airplanes for freight companies in North Africa and South America in the pre-war period. Once he crashed in the Sahara and had to walk for several days to reach safety: this was the inspiration for *The Little Prince*.

The narrator is a pilot who has crash-landed in the desert. We learn that the pilot became disillusioned with the adults in his life while he was a child, as he discusses their failure to realise that a picture he drew of a snake that has eaten an elephant was not just a picture of a hat.

He finds 'serious people' and adults lacking in the

innocence or open-mindedness that comes naturally to children. He is repelled by the inability of adults to approach the world and understand it for its own sake, and to use their imagination and intuition.

Then the pilot encounters a young boy in the desert, who we gradually discover is actually a little prince who has come to earth from a miniature planet far away. The pilot and prince have a series of absorbing and playful conversations. On the prince's planet he has several volcanoes and a single flower, with whom he is in love. He has become sad about this relationship and has run away from home.

He travels to a series of planets where he meets some strange people, including an alcoholic, a businessman who sees the world only in terms of money, a king with no one to rule over, and a lamplighter who keeps lighting and putting out the lights on his planet for no apparent reason.

In each of their ways these characters display a kind of spiritual emptiness. They are obsessed only with one way of valuing the world and fail to see it from a more innocent point of view. From the prince's childish viewpoint they are all equally bizarre.

Finally he reaches our world, where he meets a snake, and visits a garden where he realises that his flower, who he thought so unique, is actually just one of many roses. He also meets a fox, who becomes his pet, but this means that both of them are saddened when they have to part. These encounters feed into the prince's meditations on the strangeness of love, and the way that our attachments to other people are capable of causing us great pain.

However, the prince also learns that his love for the flower is special, even though she is not the unique being he imagined. The bond between them has grown from the reality that he has cared for her and looked after her. The insights into love and the way that love can grow between people are one of the book's most intriguing, if ambiguous elements.

A large part of the appeal of the book lies in the way that it contrasts the adult and child's point of view. At one stage the prince talks about the way that adults perceive a house:

> If you tell grown-ups, 'I saw a beautiful red brick house, with geraniums at the windows and doves on the roof . . .' they won't be able to imagine such a house. You have to tell them, 'I saw a house worth a hundred thousand francs.' Then they exclaim, 'What a pretty house!'

He also argues that people should see with their heart instead of with their minds. The prince is a beautiful character, someone who sees everything in life from a completely fresh point of view. Many of his observations on the strangeness of human and adult behaviour can be applied to all of us. The book reminds us of a simpler time in our life, when we used our childish imaginations to reconstruct the world around us, rather than viewing the world through received ideas.

The emotional nature of the story occasionally means that what appears to be spiritual insight is in fact less profound than a first reading would suggest. But there are some genuine insights in this little book. In the taming of the fox, the prince realises that the important things in our lives develop over long periods through emotional attachments. He also comes to see that love transforms its object – that by loving something or someone, one brings meaning to the world and elevates the existence of both the lover and the loved.

This is something that will strike a chord with anyone who has pondered the nature of love in religious practice, as well as with those who have thought hard about the words of St Paul in 1 Corinthians 13:

> When I was a child, I talked like a child, I thought like a child, I reasoned like a child. When I became a man, I put childish ways behind me. Now we see but a poor

reflection as in a mirror; then we shall see face to face.
Now I know in part; then I shall know fully, even as I am
fully known. And now these three remain: faith, hope
and love. But the greatest of these is love.

Antoine de Saint-Exupéry focuses on the idea that to think
and reason like a child is to return to the innocence we have
lost. Many of the adults in the book are seen as foolish or
pointless, but in the narrator, the pilot, he presents a character who can care for the prince with the same care as that
which a parent might feel for a child, but who is also still in
touch with his own inner child.

The great value of this book is the way that it makes us
think about our own lives and the way that we deal with
being 'grown up'. If we have lost the ability to see the world
as a child, or to love as a child does, then perhaps we are
worse off as a result. But in the end it is more important to
retain some of the aspects of innocence as we grow to be
adults, and to be able to love and understand the world from
an adult point of view as well.

## The Little Prince

### THE SPEED READ

A pilot crashes in the desert. There he meets a little prince, a
beautiful innocent who has travelled across the stars, learning about the foolishness of human nature on his journey.
Through their friendship, both learn more about the nature
of love. To perceive the world only as an adult and to lose
the ability to see the world as a child can rob us of one of the
most important aspects of being a human.

# *Franny and Zooey*

## J. D. Salinger, 1961

'I'm just sick of ego, ego, ego. My own and everybody else's. I'm sick of everybody that wants to get somewhere, do something distinguished and all, be somebody interesting. It's disgusting.'

The writer J. D. Salinger is best known for his hugely successful novel of adolescent angst, *The Catcher in the Rye*. There are elements of spirituality in that book, but he writes more explicitly about mysticism and religious ideas in his books about the Glass family: *Franny and Zooey*, *Raise High the Roof Beam, Carpenters* and *Seymour: An Introduction*. All of these books deal with members of a hyper-intelligent New York clan. The children have all appeared on a radio talk show as precocious youths and, under the influence of their brilliant eldest brother Seymour, are knowledgeable about a wide range of philosophy, theology and spirituality.

The result is a fascinating series of books in which serious ideas about Zen, psychology and the meaning of prayer are casually dropped into the intellectual but entertaining stories. By the last book, *Seymour: An Introduction*, there is barely even a story to break up the spiritual observations, but the earlier *Franny and Zooey*, which introduced the family, has more of a narrative drive.

*Franny* and *Zooey* were originally two separate stories, published in the *New Yorker*. In the shorter *Franny*, the protagonist Franny Glass visits New Haven, meeting up with her student boyfriend Lane, with whom she is to attend the Yale football match and a party. Franny is carrying the Russian book *The Way of a Pilgrim* (see pp. 44–8). In this religious work, an anonymous monk travels across the countryside, studying the *Philokalia* (a collection of Eastern

Orthodox texts) and using a prayer rope as part of his constant practice of the 'Jesus Prayer' ('Lord Jesus Christ, Son of God, have mercy on me, a sinner').

Franny has become fascinated by the suggestion that you should constantly recite the Jesus Prayer, so that it synchronises with your breathing and heartbeat, in order to achieve a state of constant mindfulness. She contrasts this with the shallow self-obsession of college life, personified in Lane's self-absorption and literary pretentiousness. She has become tired of the constant striving for status and self-importance that she perceives around her.

As a result she has quit a play that she was supposed to be acting in, having become distressed by the idea that she has been 'acting fake' all the time. She also seems somewhat disturbed, refusing to eat, becoming faint and retreating to the restroom, where she starts feverishly to read her book. On emerging, she parts company with Lane and it becomes apparent that she has started to recite the prayer under her breath.

*Zooey* picks up the story a couple of days later. Franny's pursuit of the Jesus Prayer has turned into an emotional collapse. She has retreated to her mother's apartment in Manhattan and is refusing to discuss her breakdown with anyone. What she really wants is to speak to the eldest brother Seymour, who killed himself on vacation years before.

Franny is the youngest of the family, and Zooey is her nearest brother in age, a successful actor. The two of them both respect eldest brothers Seymour and Buddy, but feel that they were raised almost as an experiment, with the elder brothers filling them with ideas about their spiritual and philosophical heroes.

The story begins with Zooey taking a long bath, interrupted by his mother, during which he rereads a letter from his brother Buddy, which reveals some of this family history. After rowing with his mother, he attempts to talk to Franny, who is in the living room, refusing to leave the sofa. Zooey interrogates Franny as to what she is trying to achieve by reciting the Jesus Prayer, but she becomes infuriated by what she sees as his presumptuous and condescending approach. He feels he has failed to help her.

He then retreats to the eldest brothers' bedroom, where he spends some time reading a sheet of paper that is tacked to the back of the door, on which the two brothers have noted down some of their favourite quotes from their reading. Salinger's own interests come shining through in the authors referenced, which range from Eastern religious texts such as the Upanishads and the Japanese poet Basho, to less obvious spiritual sources such as Ring Lardner and Franz Kafka.

In some respects this is the spiritual centre of the two stories, as we get a glimpse into a search for meaning that has ranged across such disparate texts in search of an answer to the apparent meaninglessness of modern life.

Franny's breakdown is clearly caused by a kind of existential angst about the inauthenticity of life, and the impossibility of achieving spiritual satisfaction. Her retreat to the Jesus Prayer is both infuriating (in its simplicity) and impressive, in the way that one might be impressed by the life of a genuine monk or nun. There is also a feeling in the book that this is something of a youthful moment of dilettantism, but that it is nonetheless underpinned by powerful feelings of angst.

After reading his brothers' wallchart and reorienting his thoughts, Zooey decides to have one last attempt at talking to his sister. However, having upset her previously, he decides to do this via the persona of their brother Buddy, who has been hard to contact. Impersonating him, he places a call to Franny, who, not knowing that the call is fake and coming from just down the hall, takes it in their parents' bedroom.

'Buddy' starts by listening to her gripes about Zooey, and then they discuss her situation. After a while the mask slips and Franny realises that it is in fact Zooey. She is initially angry but they continue to talk, and this time the conversation goes more deeply into the philosophical and religious underpinning of Franny's angst.

Salinger was fascinated by the Zen idea of 'satori', a mystical moment during which one achieves a new understanding of a spiritual problem. The quotes on the back of the elder brothers' door are an example of the way that he looks for inspiration in both spiritual masters such as Meister Eckhart and more mundane sources. In *Seymour: An Introduction*, he spends several pages elaborating on the idea that you can find a moment of spiritual insight from something as simple as a game of marbles played on the sidewalk.

*Franny and Zooey* is largely about the search for such a moment of spiritual insight. In the end Zooey is able to achieve what he has previously failed to do and communicates something about his understanding of Seymour's thought to Franny. This unlocks her problems and she is able to achieve a peaceful resolution to her breakdown, thanks to Zooey's spiritual assistance.

It is certainly possible to find J. D. Salinger's writing pretentious and self-indulgent. The mystical nature of his later work, combined with his eventual retreat from public life (he refused to publish anything after the combined publication of *Raise High the Roof Beam, Carpenters* and *Seymour: An Introduction* in 1963) gave him the reputation of being a reclusive guru. The 1960s fascination with Eastern religion and existentialism probably helped to create an aura around him as a writer that dissipated only slowly over the years.

However, the books do have an enduring appeal and can be seen as genuinely inspiring from a spiritual point of view. Salinger's fascination with spiritual texts is apparent throughout the stories, and in many cases people have been inspired to investigate the original texts after reading his rather unique take on them. The sheer enthusiasm of the Glass family for books such as *The Way of the Pilgrim* or *The Cloud of Unknowing* makes you want to know more about the original sources.

The Glass family also represent a way of living that might be hyper-intellectual, but nonetheless treats spirituality and mindfulness as central issues. The family have detailed discussions of religion and philosophy on an everyday basis, and the stories show various members in moments of spiritual crisis and resolution. By positing the idea that we should be unembarrassed about spirituality and indeed make it a central part of our lives, Salinger gives us a flawed but inspiring example of a different approach to life.

## *Franny and Zooey*

### THE SPEED READ

Franny, youngest sister in a family of New York child geniuses, doesn't want to be fake any more. She suffers a spiritual breakdown and tries to console herself with constant repetition of the simple Jesus Prayer, following the example of the Russian wanderer in *The Way of a Pilgrim*. Her nearest-in-age brother Zooey contemplates her problem and attempts to help, appealing to spiritual texts of the past and their mutual relationship with their eldest siblings, who tried to teach them to live a life of mindfulness. As a result, Franny finally finds some inner peace in her life.

# The Soul Bird

## Michal Snunit, 1998

'Deep down,
inside our bodies,
lives the soul.
No one has ever seen it,
but we all know it's there.'

A book needn't be a difficult or heavy read to be a spiritual experience. Everyday experiences such as the books we read to our children, the simple prayers we remember from childhood, or the stories we hear on the news can be as inspiring as the most dense religious texts.

One example is *The Soul Bird*, by Michal Snunit. This is a very short, illustrated book that can be enjoyed by children or adults. It contains less than a thousand words, but it can be a source of great wisdom and consolation.

Michal Snunit is an Israeli who was brought up on a kibbutz. She worked within the kibbutz system and also as a journalist, songwriter and magazine editor. Her book is a poetic description of the 'soul bird' who lives inside us all. Starting out by reminding us that we all have a soul, even if we are not in daily contact with it, she goes on to talk about how the soul reacts to our emotional experiences.

One of the powerful aspects of this short book is the way that it honestly faces up to our shortcomings and problems as human beings. Snunit talks about how the soul bird feels when we are angry, jealous or miserable. She also imagines that the soul bird has a series of drawers to which it has the key. These include drawers for our innermost secrets, but also places where we hide away our anger, joy and sorrows.

In conclusion, the book suggests that we don't listen to

our soul bird often enough, that some of us only hear it once in a lifetime. The remedy is that we should try, maybe late at night, or at another time of peace and quiet, to hear the voice of the soul bird, and listen to what it is telling us.

The book has been compared to *The Little Prince*, that other masterpiece of simplicity and emotion, because of the way it manages to wrap a deep emotional punch into its spare and direct language. We all know that we sometimes hide things from ourselves; that we can be subject to self-deceptions and confusions. And we all know that there are moments in life when we feel that we have truly managed to be in touch with our own souls.

By finding a way to express these difficult emotional ideas so beautifully, Michal Snunit clearly struck a chord with many readers. *The Soul Bird* is a hugely popular book, which has been translated into more than twenty-five languages, and sold 400,000 copies in her native Israel alone.

Sometimes in life consolation and encouragement can be found in small, everyday places, and *The Soul Bird* is a lovely book for those moments when you are feeling in need of spiritual refreshment.

### The Soul Bird

#### THE SPEED READ

Deep inside us is our soul bird. We know that it is there but we don't always hear its voice. When someone is unkind to us, our soul bird is in pain. When someone loves or hugs us, our soul bird reacts joyfully. The soul bird has many drawers, and it guards the key to them. Inside are our secret emotions and thoughts. We can't always open the drawers

but the soul bird always has the key. Sometimes when it is
quiet we should try to hear its voice.

## The Five People You Meet in Heaven
### Mitch Alborn, 2003

'It is because the human spirit knows, deep down, that all lives
intersect. That death doesn't just take someone, it misses someone
else, and in the small distance between being taken and being missed,
lives are changed.'

The central ideas of this fascinating popular novel are that
everything happens for a reason, and that all our lives
are interconnected. The main character, Eddie, is an elderly
man working at an amusement park called Ruby's Pier. He
is unhappy in his work, sad when he remembers his wife
who died long ago, and bitter that he hasn't achieved more
in his life. When there is a malfunction on one of the rides,
he is forced to make a sudden decision to try to rescue a girl
who is in the path of an oncoming cart, and in the process he
is struck and loses consciousness.

He awakes, feeling young again, and is met by a man
from his childhood – through their conversation he gradually realises he is dead, and in heaven. He goes on to meet
the five people of the book's title, each of whom is a person
who has played a role at some point in his life: the first is the
'Blue Man' who worked on Ruby's Pier: then he meets the
captain in the army, who shot him in the leg for his own sake
during an escape; Ruby, who the amusement park is named
after; his late wife Marguerite, with whom he shares some

tender moments; and a young girl who also lost her life during the wartime escape. As he talks to each of them, he comes to understand the impact he has had on their lives or the impact they have had on his.

Some of these connections are quite accidental – for instance, the last girl he meets lost her life as a result of the fires he helped to start. There is an odd connection here with a philosophical idea: Nietzsche's idea of eternal recurrence. This is a much misunderstood concept. Some have interpreted it to mean that Nietzsche believed that the universe is actually in some kind of eternal loop. Whereas what Nietzsche is arguing is that imagining this can make you view your actions very differently – instead of treating your actions as being 'light', disposable or forgettable, you are forced to think about what choice you would make if you knew that you had to live your life in an eternal loop and make the same choice over and over. The 'heaviness' that this way of thinking adds to simple choices gives you a clearer understanding of how important each moment of your life might be.

Alborn achieves a similar effect in his book by emphasising how moments in life which might have seemed small at the time can be of huge consequence to others. The 'Blue Man' who Eddie first meets died in a car crash when Eddie was a child, simply because Eddie ran into the road to retrieve a baseball and he swerved to avoid killing him. Ruby is someone who just happens to be able to tell him the true story of his father's death for the first time. And while we won't spoil the end of the story by revealing what happens to the girl that Eddie tried to save, the book's resolution is a satisfying one that brings together the various strands of Eddie's life story.

This is not a facile, sentimental read: Eddie's life has been one full of mistakes and regrets, as well as moments of happiness. The author doesn't give Eddie a simple redemption in which all sins are forgotten, indeed some of the things he discovers are how his actions have harmed others. However, throughout the book we see repeatedly how important Eddie's actions have been and how many people his life has affected, and this forces us to think about the effects our own actions have in our own lives. In this respect it is a book that makes us truly reflect on the morality of our own acts, and the decisions we make on a daily basis. It has had considerable commercial success, and deservedly so because, without taking too narrow a view of religious principles, it asks its readers difficult questions about life, and thus encourages real spiritual reflection.

## The Five People You Meet in Heaven

### THE SPEED READ

Eddie is an unhappy elderly man working at an amusement park. After attempting to save a young girl when one of the rides malfunctions, he wakes up and finds himself in heaven.

He then meets five people who have had a significant connection with him during his life. One of these is his wife, who died a long time ago, with whom he visits some wedding celebrations. However, not all of them are so well known to him: some are strangers whose lives happened to intersect with his at a significant moment. Through his conversations with these people he comes to a deeper understanding of the way that we are all interconnected, and how seemingly tiny moments in our lives may be of supreme importance in the long run.

## *Eat, Pray, Love*
### Elizabeth Gilbert, 2006

'People think a soul mate is your perfect fit, and that's what everyone wants. But a true soul mate is a mirror, the person who shows you everything that is holding you back, the person who brings you to your own attention so you can change your life.'

At the age of thirty-two, Elizabeth Gilbert had what many people would regard as a pretty good life – she had a successful writing career, was married and lived in a nice home in New York City. However, having come to feel spiritually unfulfilled, she started divorce proceedings, became involved in a relationship that only made her unhappier, and ended up alone and wondering what to do next.

She decided to go travelling, and *Eat, Pray, Love* is a memoir of the subsequent year (with the subtitle *One Woman's Search for Everything Across Italy, India and Indonesia*). The first part of the book deals with her time in Italy, where she enjoys the simple things in life, and gastronomic pleasures in particular. Then she moves on to India, where she visits an ashram and learns how the hard work of getting up to clean the temple floor in the middle of the night could be a step towards enlightenment. In Bali she learns even simpler forms of meditation: sitting still and listening to the silence. At this point she starts to look for a balance between the sensual pleasures and the more spiritual paths she has been taking.

Given the title of the book, it is probably not too much of a spoiler to reveal that having gone through this process of self-discovery she eventually goes on to find new love.

It's easy to make fun of this book: many people have

criticised it for the writer's sense of entitlement or for the fact that the choice she made to travel for a year would be beyond the means of many people. However, it is a book that has inspired much admiration and devotion in its readers. Part of the reason for this is that it is a genuinely engaging read. The narrator can be infuriatingly self-absorbed at times, but she is also painfully honest about her own failings, and this helps to make her more likeable. Her introspective investigation into her relationships and the spiritual emptiness of her life also strike a chord with many readers, possibly because so many people find it hard to find spiritual peace in the clamour of modern life. The recent craze for 'mindfulness' is evidence of how many people are looking for ways to find those few moments in the day to become fully absorbed in a simple task, or to reflect on their experiences.

Gilbert ends up arguing that 'happiness is the conse-quence of personal effort', something that you need to strive for and to maintain focus on at all times. But she also recog-nises that spiritual growth is not just a shallow search for happiness: for instance, she also comes to terms with moments of solitude in the book, writing that you need to 'learn your way around loneliness'.

Throughout the book there are many little moments when Gilbert seems to capture a simple truth about the way we understand our own lives, the mistakes we make, and the ways we can slowly overcome our spiritual shortcomings.

If you become impatient with the way she uses a romance plot as a vehicle for these observations, you may find it a dreary read, but millions have enjoyed the book and it would be churlish not to admit that in spite of its shortcom-ings it does offer spiritual solace to many readers.

## *Eat, Pray, Love*

### THE SPEED READ

I had the perfect life, but I felt somehow empty inside. So I threw it all away and tried to find myself. Luckily I had a healthy bank balance, so I was able to take a lovely long holiday. I spent a few months eating lovely food in Italy, a few months learning meditation and spiritual purity in India before going on to find love in Bali.

(Yes, I might sound irritating and fluffy, but every now and then I will say something that catches you off guard by being genuinely quite profound or revealing.)

# 7

# Alternative Approaches

This section can best be seen as an eclectic grab bag of different books that might be of interest to anyone who cares about spiritual matters.

Several of the books included here are fictions that address spiritual matters, including *Siddhartha* by Hermann Hesse and *The Prophet* by Kahlil Gibran. *The Teachings of Don Juan* by Carlos Castaneda claims to be a true story, although some have doubted its veracity; a reminder that not all spiritual gurus are to be trusted.

There are also several primary texts from religious history, including the *Tao Te Ching*, *Letters on the Sufi Path* and *Spiritual Couplets*, while D. T. Suzuki's *Essays in Zen Buddhism* had such a formative impact on the West's view of Zen that it almost deserves to be seen as a religious text in its own right.

Finally, two books from the late twentieth century, *Be Here Now* by Ram Dass and *The Power of Now* by Eckhart Tolle, are representative of the ongoing search for spiritual meaning in the modern age. While some new-age attitudes and self-help manuals can be criticised for their shallow content, there are many thinkers and writers in the modern era who have gone through their own spiritual trials and tribulations and can be acknowledged as having made genuine contributions to the spiritual literature of the world.

## *Tao Te Ching*

### Lao Tzu, Approx. Sixth Century bc

'The Way that can be told of is not an unvarying way;
The names that can be named are not unvarying names.
It was from the Nameless that Heaven and Earth sprang.'

Some ancient religious texts are notably difficult reads for the non-expert. But there are also ancient texts that retain a beauty and fascination even for those who can't follow every turn of the thought presented in the book. The *Tao Te Ching* falls into the latter category. It is over two millennia old, but it is a book of ambiguous and beguiling wisdom that can still be intriguing to a modern Western reader.

It is reputed to be the work of Lao Tzu, although it is uncertain whether he was a real person: the fact that his name can be translated as Old Master or Old Masters casts more doubt on the real source. The name *Tao Te Ching* is also ambiguous, but can be roughly translated as Way-Virtue-Classic Book/Scripture. Essentially this is a book of mystical and everyday wisdom, which centres on the idea of the Tao, or the Path – it was the classic on which Taoism was founded and thus also a major influence on Chinese Buddhism.

It is organised into eighty-one short chapters, in which epigrammatic verses of wisdom are contained. It can be quite laconic, even funny at times, and can also be quite ambiguous. Even scholars of the Tao take different meanings from particular sections, partly because of its terse, poetic nature.

The general framework of the book is based on a kingdom in a state of disorder and a consideration of what action or inaction would be undertaken by a wise ruler to restore harmony. The book considers an age of man prior to civilisation and discusses the way that the Tao has developed and guided man. In its story of the creation, the *Tao Te Ching* describes a genesis in which heaven and earth arise from an eternal, mysterious female. Heaven and earth come from the nameless and 'the named is but the mother that rears the ten thousand creatures, each after its kind'.

The *Tao Te Ching* contains an early version of the Chinese idea of oppositions, yin and yang, male and female. Many of its formulations refer to the rhythm of life, or the river of life which flows through the universe. So the spiritual path is identified as the search for harmony between opposing principles, day and night, mountain and river-valley, hot and cold.

A repeated theme in the book is the idea of returning:

> In Tao the only motion is returning;
> The only useful quality, weakness.
> For though all creatures under heaven are
>     the products of Being,
> Being itself is the product of Not-being.

Life arises from death, but there is a constant return to the eternity of death. This line of thought leads on to a typically oriental fascination with the relationship between form and nothingness. The Tao talks of how the usefulness of a wheel depends on the space in between the spokes. In terms of wisdom, it also talks about the idea that correct decisions arise from forgetting wisdom and trusting to the Tao. In a similar vein the book advises against 'trying too hard', counselling that you can only succeed by setting aside desire and ambition. This relates to the Buddhist aim for a state of emptiness and acceptance of the flow of the world:

> Embracing the Way, you become embraced;
> Breathing gently, you become newborn;
> Clearing your mind, you become clear;
> Nurturing your children, you become impartial;
> Opening your heart, you become accepted;
> Accepting the world, you embrace the Way.

As well as these mystical ideas, the book discusses the value of self-knowledge and deals with ethical issues. Early Christian missionaries to China were attracted to the Tao by some of the surface similarities to Christian ideas – the *Tao Te Ching* advises us to requite injuries with good deeds, which has an obvious resemblance to the teaching of Jesus. The idea of the Tao has also sometimes been compared to the idea of the Word of God, though this may be a case of scholars groping too hard for resemblances between the two religions.

There are more obvious relationships between the Tao and both Buddhism and Confucianism. In many respects, the *Tao Te Ching* expresses the ancient philosophy and wisdom from which those other religions drew breath. When reading the Tao, you cannot always clearly understand the meaning of the text. But there is always the sense that this is a crystallisation of wisdom that has been passed down over the centuries.

It is also interesting to compare this text to the earlier *I Ching* (Book of Changes). While the latter is most often used as a book of divination, it can also be read as a collection of advice on how to live one's life. Both books have a pure simplicity in their expression that reveals greater levels of complexity as you ponder the meaning of the texts – they also both address themselves to the problems of rulers, but can be taken as general advice for any individual. Both books are also subject to extremely variable translations – the lack of exact congruence between the logic of Chinese and English means that translation of such poetic and terse texts is a difficult and creative task.

You can react in a number of different ways to the *Tao Te Ching*. The first is to see this as a historical document, a record of attitudes that developed in an ancient culture and that provide an insight into the mindset of that culture. The second is to take this purely as a book of condensed wisdom, from which we can find advice and guidance today. And finally you can simply read this as a poetic book of spiritual observations which can provoke deep thought on the subjects it discusses.

However you approach it and whatever your religious inclination, this can be a rewarding read, as it addresses some of the most basic ideas of spirituality and morality that life presents us with.

## *The Tao Te Ching*

### THE SPEED READ

The Tao is the river of life that exists before and after mankind. To restore harmony, practise inaction and find tranquillity. The Tao will resolve things naturally and the wise ruler who has refrained from incorrect action will be acclaimed by his people. The river takes the easiest path through the mountains and a valley is created. We come from nothingness and return to nothingness.

# *Letters on the Sufi Path*

## Ibn Abbad of Ronda, 1365–75

'. . . the light of certitude. That is the most sublime thing that can descend from the heavens into the hearts of chosen believers, who comprehend thereby the Mystic Truth of the attributes and names.'

It is beyond the scope of this book to attempt any sort of systematic overview of the complex, wide-ranging tradition of Islamic literature. However, in Rumi's *Spiritual Couplets* (pp. 178–81) and Ibn Abbad's *Letters on the Sufi Path* we see two contrasting examples of literature which are interesting for the light they cast on Islamic thought – Rumi takes an extravagantly poetic approach whereas this book is a more thoughtful, precise meditation.

Both books are also from the tradition of Sufism, a faith which has been popularised in the West but which has been widely misunderstood in the process. For instance, the works of Idries Shah, which were especially popular a few decades ago, presented a rather erratic new-age interpretation of Sufism, describing it as a humanistic, mystical idea that was prior to and separate from Islam.

However, it is also fair to observe that there are wide variations in opinion about Sufism within Islam. It is unfortunate that many in the West tend to perceive Islam as a unitary body of thought, and to see fundamentalists as representative of an entire, living religion that has as many subtle variations as Christianity itself does. In some Islamic states the practices of Sufism have been banned or regarded as inappropriate, whereas other scholars have seen Sufism as an essential part of the tradition.

So what is Sufism? In short it is a body of thought and practice in which the inner, mystical path to God is emphasised more than external acts. This idea can be expressed in differing ways, from the traditional whirling dervishes to more contemplative forms of spirituality. But, in general, Sufism is defined in terms of the believer who seeks to grow closer to God or even, in the more esoteric or mystical strands of Sufism, to become one with him.

Ibn Abbad was an imam who had studied in the madrasahs of Morocco, and who became a member of the Shadhiliyya order of mystics in 1359. At this time the Orthodox religious leaders of Morocco were divided. The Shadhiliyya order represented a moderate form of mysticism within Islam, in which the inner life was emphasised but only within the context of ordinary everyday practice.

The letters included in this collection were written from the small town of Sale to friends of Ibn Abbad's in the main city. They were designed to answer questions about the fundamentals of Sufi spirituality for believers who were troubled or uncertain about their religious practice.

The subjects dealt with are eminently practical ones. For instance one is 'a letter concerning the actions and spiritual states required of a penitent if he is to be confirmed in the station of repentance' while another addresses 'the question of Pilgrimage and its legal requirements in relation to individuals and circumstances'. Thus they provide an insight into the practices of Islam and Sufism in this period, and into the root ideas that underpin this tradition.

This is not a poetic *tour de force* like the work of Rumi, nor is it the mystical pantheism that you might expect from Sufism if you relied on Idries Shah as your guide. Instead it is an example of Sufism as a simple everyday religious practice in which you approach godliness by focusing on practical matters and the spiritual well-being that you can achieve in everyday life.

Ibn Abbad has been compared to St John of the Cross. While there are many differences between the two, they do share an emphasis on the ways in which everyday virtue and practice can move us closer to God in our hearts. It is this focus that makes this an enlightening book to read, regardless of your religious background, as well as being a useful insight into the Islamic tradition of which the West knows so little.

### Letters on the Sufi Path

#### THE SPEED READ

Fifty-four letters from Ibn Abbad of Ronda to his followers regarding their spiritual problems and practical religious thoughts. A tantalising glimpse into Sufism as a mystical part of the Islamic culture of the past and present.

## *Spiritual Couplets*
### Rumi, Thirteenth Century

'When you do things from your soul, you feel a river moving in you, a joy.'

Rumi was a thirteenth-century Persian Muslim poet and theologian. His full name, Jalal ad-Din Muhammad Rumi, roughly translates as 'Majesty of Religion'. He was born in present-day Afghanistan and died in Turkey, in areas that were at the time both part of Persia, in the Seljuk Empire, and he wrote in the Persian language. He is regarded as a classic spiritual writer within the overlapping traditions of Islam and Sufism, and is widely read today in Iran, Afghanistan and other areas that retain a Persian influence. He is also remembered as the inspiration behind the Mevlevi Order, better known to the West as the whirling dervishes, who express their religious worship through a musical and dance ceremony known as the *sema*.

His major work is the *Masnavi* or *Masnavi-I Ma'navi*. The title means 'Rhyming Couplets of Profound Spiritual Meaning' but it is often published under the title *Spiritual Couplets*. This is a vast work that includes elements of fable, everyday anecdotes, scriptural reference to the Qur'an, and metaphysical speculation. It has been described as the Persian Qur'an, but it is more accurate to describe it as a poetical work rather than a piece of scripture. While Rumi is writing within the Islamic tradition, his thoughts have a universal appeal. He saw religion as an intensely personal experience and focused on the role of the soul, the act of creative love, and our desire to be reunited with God.

He writes about the concept of Tawhid (unity), a common theme in Sufism, which centres on the idea that we have been cut off from union with the beloved, the divinity, and spend our lives trying to seek union. He saw creative acts such as music, dancing and poetry as expressions of the soul's love for God: this was the inspiration behind his development of ideas that would influence the whirling dervishes.

Within the Mevlevi tradition, the ceremony of *sema* represents an attempt to seek truth and perfection by abandoning the ego and loving all creation. This idea of spiritual growth through creativity and transcendence of the self is something that goes beyond specific religions – Rumi is often quoted by thinkers as varied as Zen masters, Christian theologians and modern Islamic scholars.

In the theology of Rumi, man is separated from the divine ego, and is then compelled to follow an evolutionary journey back towards union with the divine. The fall of Adam is interpreted within this context as man's initial separation from God. Through an evolutionary and creative process, we then seek to return to God, meaning that God is the goal of all existence.

The universal, yet personal nature of Rumi's thought can be illustrated with a quote from his work:

> I searched for God among the Christians and on
>     the Cross and therein I found Him not.
> I went into the ancient temples of idolatry; no trace
>     of Him was there.
> I entered the mountain cave of Hira and then went
>     as far as Qandhar but God I found not.
> With set purpose I fared to the summit of Mount
>     Caucasus and found there only 'anqa's habitation.

The verse continues in this vein until Rumi writes that he finally looked into his own heart and found God there. In passages such as this he neither rejects nor accepts traditional religions, and his writing has to be understood in the context of the Islamic tradition. However, his focus on the personal nature of the search for God gives his writing a universal appeal. In the end, his message is that God is located in our hearts and only by exploring our hearts will we be reunited with him.

Rumi also represents an example of the great Persian tradition of thought. Modern-day Iranians are as familiar with Rumi's work as many Westerners are with Shakespeare or Milton. However, the vexed relationship which Iran has had with other countries in the region as well as with the West probably means that we have less understanding of Persian traditions than we do (for instance) of the religious texts of Japan, India and China. Rumi provides a glimpse into those traditions, as well as being the ideal introduction to the beautiful poetic literature of the region.

*Spiritual Couplets*

### THE SPEED READ

This thirteenth-century poetic Persian classic tells us that we are separated from God and spend our lives seeking to be reunited with him. We can be helped in this quest by religious scripture but in the end the search must begin in our own hearts. Through music, poetry and dance, we can overcome our ego and start the search for God from within our souls.

# Siddhartha

## Hermann Hesse, 1922

'Wisdom is not communicable. The wisdom which a wise man tries to communicate always sounds foolish . . . Knowledge can be communicated but not wisdom. One can find it, live it, be fortified by it, do wonders through it, but one cannot communicate and teach it.'

Hermann Hesse is a German writer whose books were first successful in the early part of the twentieth century: he went on to attain a trendy reputation in the post-war period, partly as a result of the hallucinatory imagery of his 1927 novel *Steppenwolf*, and partly because of his dabbling with Eastern spirituality.

Since then he has been subjected to a critical re-evaluation and many feel that his work was somewhat over-rated. However, there is still much to admire in his writing.

*Siddhartha*, one of his most explicitly spiritual books, grew out of Hesse's fascination with Indian religion. It deals with themes from both the Hindu and Buddhist traditions, and while Hesse pursues his own ideas, sometimes at the cost of accuracy to the source religions, he manages to give a reasonably accurate impression of some aspects of those traditions.

Siddhartha is the book's hero. In a plot that skips to and fro in time, we encounter him as an old ferryman, who spends his time observing and listening to the river. He was once a wandering wise man, and a follower of Gotama the Buddha. (The Buddha was actually called Siddhartha Gautama, and many people have taken the book to be an allegory of his life, although Hesse's actual intentions are clearly to set Siddhartha up as a separate figure in his own right – the fact that Gotama appears as a character in the book makes this clear.)

Siddhartha is the son of a Brahmin, a handsome, wise, charismatic man who becomes a religious adept at an early age. In spite of the worldly opportunities open to him, he leaves home in the company of his close friend Govinda to pursue a life of asceticism. They are in search of enlightenment.

The two friends encounter Gotama, the Buddha, and spend time with him. Govinda vows to stay with him, but Siddhartha believes that his enlightenment must be something he achieves alone, so the two friends part.

Siddhartha then plunges back into the world of earthly wealth and pleasures, after meeting the courtesan Kamala, with whom he fathers a son. She introduces him to a merchant who is her friend, and Siddhartha makes his fortune. He takes his place among the 'child people', who are not interested in enlightenment, only in worldly things.

Throughout this process Hesse discusses the concept of samsara. The river, which is a recurring metaphor in the book, is a metaphor for the Indian concept of the flow of life

– samsara refers to the constant flow of the world into which we may be reincarnated, and in which we experience suffering and evil – it is a version of the 'circle of life'. By plunging himself into the world of pleasure and money, Siddhartha is pursuing a different approach to knowledge, but one that means nothing to him until he realises the worthlessness of this life.

It is once he starts to suffer from the sickness of the soul, which Hesse describes as being the characteristic feature of the wealthy, that Siddhartha leaves all that he has attained behind. He meets with the ferryman, who helps him across the river for free, and eventually Siddhartha will himself come to tend the riverboat.

Late in the book, Siddhartha encounters the son that he didn't know he had, after the death of Kamala, who was on a pilgrimage to meet the Buddha. Here we encounter a different version of the circle of life, as Siddhartha's son turns out to be ungrateful and difficult, while Siddhartha himself discovers that he doesn't know how to deal with this young man. Just as the young Siddhartha was self-willed enough to leave home in search of enlightenment, he discovers that his own son is also unwilling to learn from his elders.

From these disparate experiences together Siddhartha finally attains a kind of wisdom. Finding that he is in rhythm with the spirit of the passing river, Siddhartha reaches his own epiphany and overcomes the spiritual problems of his own life.

There are some failings in Hesse's interpretation of Hindu and Buddhist thought. While he gives reasonable explanations of ideas such as samsara and nirvana, Siddhartha's journey is clearly not in tune with Buddhist exhortations to escape from the self. Instead he is trying to discover the self – and his final epiphany continues this self-centred approach, which may explain why its greatest popularity came in the West in the 1950s and 60s.

However, while one can find faults in it, this is still a rewarding read. At the very least Hesse provokes you to think about the concepts that he is discussing and, perhaps, to go and discover more about Eastern religion, from less maverick sources.

## Siddhartha

### The Speed Read

Siddhartha sat by the river, contemplating the flow of life. As a child he had run away from a life of privilege to seek enlightenment. After his friend Govinda stayed with Gotama the Buddha, someone that Siddhartha admired but would not join as a follower, Siddhartha plunged into a decadent world of wealth and pleasure. When his soul sickened as a result, he left it all behind and ended up back by the river. Then his son came to visit him, and it all went badly wrong, but it all helps to show how that old river keeps on flowing by.

# The Prophet

## Kahlil Gibran, 1923

'Life is indeed darkness save when there is urge, And all urge is blind save when there is knowledge, And all knowledge is vain save when there is work, And all work is empty save when there is love.'

*T*he Prophet is the best-known book of Kahlil Gibran, who was born Lebanese, but whose family moved to

America in 1895. Gibran studied in Boston and New York, and became well known as an artist, but it was his writing that would bring him the most lasting success.

Written in 1923, *The Prophet* is a collection of poetic essays which centre on a fictional prophet called Almustafa. The prophet has been away from his home in the city Orphalese for a long time, but now chooses to return home. On his journey he discusses his ideas with a group of acquaintances.

Religion and spirituality were natural subjects for Gibran. He was fascinated by theological subjects such as the schism that had occurred between the Orthodox and Catholic traditions, and also by the similarities that can be found across all religions in spite of the enmities that often exist between them.

The prophet teaches his companions about a range of subjects, including world religion and the state of being a human. He also talks about more everyday subjects such as love, work, learning and marriage. His thoughts are simple but often inspiring. And the language used by Gibran to express the prophet's thoughts is beautifully poetic.

Gibran often strives to find common ground among religions and to interpret the thinking of Jesus in the light of this. He concurs with Jesus' reaction to the harsher forms of Old Testament scripture, arguing that 'an eye for an eye, and the whole world would be blind'. He also follows Jesus in emphasising the importance of love, for instance writing:

Love gives naught but itself and takes naught but from itself.
Love possesses not nor would it be possessed;
For love is sufficient unto love.

When he is searching for ecumenical common ground, Gibran's writing can become rather vague. For instance, he writes, 'I love you when you bow in your mosque, kneel in your temple, pray in your church. For you and I are sons of one religion, and it is the spirit.' At times you feel that he is over-reaching, attempting to create a new scripture to unite different religions, without truly comprehending the elements that separate them.

Gibran was intrigued by the Bahá'í faith and its emphasis on the spiritual unity of mankind. It has been claimed that he modelled the prophet on Abdul-Bahá, the founder of the faith: this would help to explain the book's emphasis on the unity and similarity of different kinds of faith around the world.

Gibran also emphasises a sensual understanding of the world. At one point he writes that we should 'forget not that the earth delights to feel your bare feet and the winds long to play with your hair'. This is reminiscent of a very different thinker, William Blake, who argued that the organised Church had turned against the energy and will of the body and decreed that all sensual enjoyment was evil. Gibran would side with Blake at least in arguing that sensual feelings could be a positive force.

*The Prophet* suffers from a tendency to woolly vagueness and a poetic approach that dresses up indeterminate ideas in beautiful language. It can be unclear as a result whether the ideas being expressed are profound or shallow. On the other hand Gibran himself argues that perplexity is the first step towards knowledge. He suggests that our confusion about the world is actually a positive thing as it forces us to try to understand the world in all its complexity.

He is also a powerful advocate for the idea that love and beauty can be important aims of human endeavour as well as simple truth. It at least has to be admitted that in *The Prophet* the author succeeds in creating a genuine work of beauty.

## The Prophet

### THE SPEED READ

On the way home, the prophet Almustafa stopped to share his great wisdom. He told us to believe in truth and beauty, and that all of mankind seeks God, even if we do so through different faiths and methods. Above all he told us many beautiful things about love, some of which are a bit hard to remember in retrospect, but they seemed lovely at the time.

# Essays in Zen Buddhism
## D. T. Suzuki, 1927–34

'The truth of Zen, just a little bit of it, is what turns one's humdrum life, a life of monotonous, uninspiring commonplaceness, into one of art, full of genuine inner creativity.'

Zen Buddhism acquired considerable popularity in the West during the twentieth century. However, in the process it was misrepresented by sources as varied as Robert M. Pirsig's *Zen and the Art of Motorcycle Maintenance* and Jack Kerouac's *Satori in Paris*.

As a result it is hard to write clearly about Zen – there is so much baggage attached to its Western interpretation that it can be hard to set that aside. One remedy for this might be found in the work of D. T. Suzuki, the first great champion of Zen in the West. While his own work can be accused of containing certain distortions, it is at least a serious exploration of the religion written by an author with direct experience of the real thing.

Zen is a branch of Mahayana Buddhism which grew (as *Chan*) in China in the seventh century and spread throughout the region, reaching Japan, where it was called Zen. While it is a part of traditional Buddhist tradition and shares much with other branches of the religion, it places more emphasis on dharma practice and the wisdom of experience than it does on scriptural sources and teachers. The form of meditation know as *zazen* is directed towards awakening, through meditation and contemplation.

Suzuki (1870–1966) grew up in a Japanese family that practised Jodo Shinshu Buddhism, but went on to study a wide variety of strands of Buddhism in his youth. Although he was not a fully ordained Zen monk, he spent four years studying under the Zen master Shaku Soen, who was unusual among his contemporaries for having travelled to Theravada and Pali Buddhist schools in India.

In the 1890s, Shaku Soen travelled to a religious conference in the US. When he was asked to help a local academic with translations of Eastern religious texts, he recommended Suzuki for the task, and this was the start of a long and illustrious career for Suzuki during which he translated many Eastern titles for the Western market, and also wrote erudite explanations of Eastern ways of thought.

Suzuki wrote the *Essays on Zen Buddhism* in the 1920s and 30s. Some of his shorter works address the same material but there is a rich diversity of material in these volumes that conveys the full range of his thinking. It is interesting to note that Suzuki personally retained a fascination with Jodo Shinshu Buddhism, but for the most part focused intentionally on Zen in his Western writings.

This was partly because he believed that Zen was better suited to the West. The fact that Zen is less reliant on knowledge of past masters and scriptures certainly gives it an appeal to the impatient Western mind, and the many amusing tales of Zen masters and their relations with pupils also make it a memorable religion to study.

It is also interesting to note a difference of opinion between Suzuki and his Zen master Shaku Soen, whose writings emphasised the fact that Zen was essentially a branch of Mahayana Buddhism. By contrast Suzuki believed that Zen had absorbed a great deal from Taoism in China. He also liked to draw parallels with Western thinkers such as Meister Eckhart.

This element of his thinking was influential in the 1950s and 60s: as Zen became more popular, it was often interpreted as though it was a solitary outpost of Buddhism – with more in common with other mystical religious practices – rather than as part of a living religion.

Suzuki also focused on the idea of *satori* (awakening) as the goal of Zen training, and he wrote a great deal about the way that this had developed in Japanese and Chinese culture within the everyday routines of monastic routine – so that *satori* might arise from mundane tasks such as gardening or carpentry, or even housekeeping. This element of his thought was a clear influence on those Western thinkers who tried to reinterpret Zen through a variety of everyday practices from archery to motorcycle maintenance.

D. T. Suzuki was a wise scholar who brought a wide variety of Eastern sources to Western attention through his writings and translations. He was also a brilliant writer, and anyone interested in Buddhism or Zen would be well advised to start from his essays, as they are an excellent source.

It is also important to understand that because his writing was so influential, much of the Western idea of Zen is in fact an interpretation of one man's views on the subject, and that he came at the subject from a specific angle, one that emphasised certain aspects of the 'Eastern mind', and that brought a uniquely Japanese viewpoint to the study of a religion that actually originated in China.

For those who wish to truly understand Zen, it is worth bearing in mind that this is a tradition that goes far beyond the Western version of it, and that a wider variety of sources would need to be studied to achieve a deeper understanding of its real meaning. But Suzuki's writing remains invaluable both as an introduction to Zen and as a way to understand the path Zen took into Western culture in his wake.

## Essays in Zen Buddhism

### THE SPEED READ

A scholarly, brilliant exposition of Zen Buddhism as D. T. Suzuki understood it. The ideal starting point for anyone interested in Zen, and an antidote to the bowdlerisations that have followed in popular culture. But remember that this is only one source among many and even this wise master can't tell us everything about Zen.

# The Teachings of Don Juan:
# A Yaqui Way of Knowledge
## Carlos Castaneda, 1968

'Look at every path closely and deliberately, then ask ourselves this crucial question: Does this path have a heart? If it does, then the path is good. If it doesn't, it is of no use.'

It seems almost too obvious to mention, but not all spiritual books are to be trusted, even when they have the reputation of being classics. The mystical works of Carlos Castaneda have sold millions of copies and were extremely popular in the later 1960s and 70s. However, later researchers have created serious doubt as to whether his work was fact or fiction.

His first book, *The Teachings of Don Juan*, was published in 1968, and a series of sequels followed over subsequent years. The books outline Castaneda's knowledge of shamanic practices, which he claimed to have acquired from a traditional wise man, Don Juan Matus, a Yaqui Indian from the north of Mexico. Don Juan was supposed to have identified Castaneda as having the energy of a 'nagual', and thus able to be chosen by the spirit to become a leader of seers. He wrote often of the way that shamanic practice could allow one to expand one's perception to realms that are usually unknown to humans. He spoke of this 'nonordinary' realm as something that was real but only obtainable to those who could learn new ways of perceiving.

Strange experiences abound in the books, from Castaneda's transformations into animals such as crows, to his travels to alternate dimensions and meetings with spirits and witches. At times the books recommend using psychotropic drugs to achieve an understanding of this nonordinary realm: Castaneda describes the use of peyote and other natural drugs to achieve altered states of consciousness.

Castaneda's work includes a good deal of authentic detail about shamanic practices. He was awarded academic qualifications on the basis of his research, and many anthropologists accepted his work as authentic in the years after publication. However, in 1976 Richard de Mille and Daniel Noel published sceptical investigations, and from then onwards a stream of scholars who analysed the books started to point out inconsistencies and problems.

The books seem to contain discrepancies in terms of time and narrative, and there are alternative published sources for everything that Castaneda wrote (critics particularly point to the degree to which his writing appears to draw on Barbara Myerhoff's work). Also, no one was able to locate any likely suspect for the figure of Don Juan himself.

The most damning evidence of all was probably the work de Mille did on Castaneda's library requests, which show that at times when he claimed to have been present at peyote ceremonies, he was actually in the library of the University of California reading books that described such ceremonies. More and more critics started to view Castaneda as a mere charlatan who piggybacked on the work of others to create a fraudulent body of work.

His life gradually became more outlandish: he founded the Tensegrity movement to promote shamanic practices, and apparently lived with a gaggle of 'witches', who proved very difficult to trace after his death. None of this has prevented his books from continuing to sell. Some modern readers enjoy them on the basis that they are fiction, but enjoyable and fascinating to read. Others accept that his accounts are questionable but see the books as powerful works of philosophy and spirituality in spite of that.

Can you find enlightenment in work that has a dubious provenance? Some people certainly think so, and Castaneda's work has inspired devotion and fascination in many readers over the years. In his own lifetime Castaneda convinced many to trust him on the basis of his charisma and evident powers of persuasion. The 1960s and 70s are remembered as times of new ideas and experimentation but it was inevitable that some would take opportunistic advantage of the credulity that was engendered.

If you read Castaneda today it is perhaps best to view the books as charming, intriguing journeys into one man's dreams and imagination rather than as genuine accounts of shamanism. On this basis they can be entertaining reads, but rather than being guides to authentic spirituality they become relics of a strange period of history, when people wanted to believe in something new and exciting, no matter how ludicrous it might be.

### The Teachings of Don Juan

#### THE SPEED READ

I travelled to Mexico and met Don Juan, a Yaqui Indian man of knowledge. He taught me many amazing things, such as becoming a crow, seeing spirits, taking copious amounts of peyote and other feats of spiritual wonder. Trust me, this is all true . . .

# Be Here Now
## Ram Dass, 1971

'It is important to expect nothing, to take every experience, including the negative ones, as merely steps on the path, and to proceed.'

R am Dass is now known as a teacher of spiritual ideas, in particular those of Eastern religion. However, he started out as a successful psychologist in the Western tradition. He was called Richard Alpert, born 1931, and was teaching at Harvard in the early 1960s when he became fascinated by hallucinogenic drugs and their effects on the mind.

Of his own use of the drugs, he later wrote: 'Psychedelics helped me to escape . . . albeit momentarily . . . from the prison of my mind. It over-rode the habit patterns of thought and I was able to taste innocence again. Looking at sensations freshly without the conceptual overlay was very profound.'

This was in the early days of LSD when it was quite common for intellectuals to become interested in the ways in which the drug altered consciousness and what that might teach us about how the mind worked. Alpert was in esteemed company – he worked with Allen Ginsberg, Aldous Huxley and Timothy Leary, among others. It was Leary that introduced Alpert to teonanácatl, the Mexican psychoactive mushroom, after Alpert flew them to Mexico in his private plane.

However, the Harvard establishment was less open to the idea of drug-induced enlightenment, and Alpert was dismissed from his post as a result of his work. He went on to study yoga, meditation and other spiritual practices. He became an environmental and political campaigner and also a devotee of the Indian guru Neem Karoli Baba, a Hindu adept of bhakti yoga who regarded service to others (*seva*) as the ultimate form of unconditional love for God.

After Alpert changed his name to Ram Dass, he would help found the Seva Foundation, which aimed to abolish world poverty. Neem Karoli also practised an inclusive form of teaching: in spite of India's caste system and natural tendency to hierarchical social practices, he preferred to make his students feel like part of the process, and to believe that their contributions were as valid as anyone else's. This is an attitude that Dass took into his own teaching.

In some ways Ram Dass seems like a typical exponent of the mystical, optimistic ideas that were in fashion in the 1960s. But you shouldn't underestimate the subtlety of his thinking. His writing has developed over the years and he has the wisdom to be able to acknowledge how much of his early work was influenced by the zeitgeist than by genuine revelation. One of his late books, *One-Liners*, brings his story up to date and shows a funny, likeable man who can understand his own failings, but who still has a real message of love.

However, it was *Be Here Now*, published in 1971, that initially made Dass's reputation. The book has sold over a million copies, but was originally distributed as a pamphlet by the Lama Foundation, a commune in New Mexico whose founders were friends with Dass. The Lama Foundation later gave the copyright and an equal share of the proceeds to the Hanuman Foundation, another of Dass's ventures which worked to advance his spiritual aims.

The book is divided into four parts. The first tells the story of Richard Alpert's journey to becoming Baba Ram Dass. He is open about his use of psychedelic drugs and the revelations he felt he experienced while under their influence, but he focuses more on other alternative paths. The second part is a series of charming aphorisms on the spiritual life, together with his own illustrations. In the third part Dass examines practices, including yoga and meditation, through which you might make spiritual progress. Finally, in the last section Dass recommends writings and texts that might help the reader to discover their own spiritual path.

Dass is never prescriptive in his teaching. He puts his own life forward as an example, but allows us to see his faults as well as his achievements. And he understands that his path may not work for everyone. This aspect of his writing gives it a particular charm, and is arguably the most important thing he learned from his own guru, Neem Karoli Baba. Part of the book deals explicitly with the ways a student–teacher relationship can both help and hinder spiritual growth.

*Be Here Now* continues to sell to this day. Ram Dass has continued to write over the years, but this is the book that most clearly encapsulates his early espousal of Eastern religious techniques as a path to a more enlightened life. It was also a book that had some positive influence at the time, as the theory that drugs could lead to enlightenment became more and more obviously a dangerous idea that had led many into addiction or psychosis.

By putting himself forward as someone who had learned from drugs but who had moved on to a yogic lifestyle, Dass was sending an important message to the post-hippy community. He showed that it was possible to come from a drug-influenced background, to learn from that background and then move on to safer, more positive ways of 'freeing one's mind'. Now that most people recognise the dangers of drugs more clearly, *Be Here Now* works both as a testament to the mood of its times, and as a lesson in alternative routes to enlightenment.

Ram Dass's legacy is not restricted to his writings. He also has a powerful record of trying to effect positive change in the world through the various foundations with which he is associated. If you can judge a man on the life he has lived, then Ram Dass is someone who deserves great respect.

## *Be Here Now*

### THE SPEED READ

I am just a beginner on the path to enlightenment, but I am here to share the little I have learned with you. I took a lot of acid and drew these crazy pictures, but now I continue my journey through yoga and meditation, as I learned to do from my Hindu guru. Each of us finds their own way, and their own way of sharing what little wisdom we might acquire. 'Our rational minds can never understand what has happened, but our hearts . . . if we can keep them open to God, will find their own intuitive way.'

# The Power of Now

## Eckhart Tolle, 1999

'Being is the eternal, ever-present One Life beyond the myriad forms
of life that are subject to birth and death. However, Being is not only
beyond but also deep within every form as its innermost invisible
and indestructible essence. This means that it is accessible to you
now as your own deepest self, your true nature.'

*The Power of Now* is an interesting book because it is a self-
help manual, and thus part of a genre that contains many
rather shallow books (and Tolle's books are lauded by the
likes of Oprah Winfrey): however, this is a book that tran-
scends its genre and that does address real spiritual concerns.

Tolle was born in Germany and lived in Spain and
England as a young man, before moving to Canada. He had
a rather solitary childhood and suffered from depression in
his twenties before undergoing what he refers to as an 'inner
transformation' at the age of twenty-nine.

*The Power of Now* begins with an account of this moment
and how it saved him from a period of suicidal anxiety. The
book teaches that we are too absorbed in 'doing' rather than
'being' and that we become too absorbed by the past and the
future, so much so that we lose sight of the importance of
the Now.

Tolle talks about the ego, but uses this term differently to
Freudian analysis. For Tolle, the ego is our construction of
what we believe our self to be. So the past is the story we
base our idea of self on, while the future rules us because
we are always driven by our ego to seek future resolution of
problems. He sees all problems as illusions caused by our
perception of time and ego.

So we reject the present to dwell on the past, whether it is
a sad or happy past, because that is the story we allow to

define us. And we reject the present to dwell on the future, which merely adds to our anxieties because, no matter what schemes and ambitions we have for the future, we know it will end in our deaths.

Tolle argues that the way to escape these traps is to live more fully in the Now. Rather than believing in the ego we have constructed, we need to react directly to the world as we see it, and to transcend the ego. The emotional 'pain body' we have built is also a function of time and our inability to free ourselves from attachments.

This is comparable to the Buddhist concept of detachment. Tolle doesn't advocate any specific religious path, as his focus is on the individual's place in the world, but readers familiar with Buddhist literature will see the parallels. However, for Tolle, the goal isn't extinction of the self in nirvana. Instead he argues that we have an underlying identity, an 'I Am' which is simply the part of us that perceives the now in stillness and without interpreting it through the ego.

Analysts might argue that the id he seems to be referring to is not a reliable thing to regress to in our search for spiritual peace. Buddhists might object that he retains too much sense of self. But his argument is persuasive, and appeals to influences as varied as Krishnamurti, Meister Eckhart and the *Tao Te Ching*. He also respects the teaching of the New Testament but believes that Jesus' teaching is often misunderstood. He sees love as something that can only arise from a true recognition of one's underlying self rather than from reliance on the ego.

In Tolle's other books, such as *Stillness Speaks* and *A New Earth*, he develops his ideas further, but *The Power of Now* remains the best introduction to his work, as it expresses his most basic ideas in a powerful way. The book will appeal most to those who are suffering from depression or other crises, as it promises a way to solve such problems, and it is this that leads to it being categorised as a self-help book.

However, the way that Tolle speaks of the construction of the ego is also interesting for anyone interested in spirituality. In the end many religious and spiritual teachers show us that either introspection or a retreat from the world can bring us a deeper understanding of ourselves and our relationship with the world. Such ideas can encourage unhealthy levels of self-absorption, but so long as you are aware of this danger, they can also lead to a genuine breakthrough in understanding how we perceive ourselves.

In *Walden*, Thoreau suggested setting aside material things in order to find a simpler way of life, and the eremitic tradition suggests that solitude is the path that will lead us to God. Tolle's teaching is related to these ideas, but he offers a framework within which we can examine the way we think about the world, and the degree to which our thoughts of the past and future define our ego. Understanding this can potentially help us to focus more on the present moment and to react more authentically to the world around us.

## The Power of Now

### THE SPEED READ

People allow themselves to be distracted by thinking about time – the past creates a story upon which we base our ego creation. The future calls to us as we create desires and ambitions for our ego. All of this creates pain and emotion in the present and prevents us from appreciating and understanding the present as it happens. We need to transcend the ego to find our real selves and to engage with the world in a purer, simpler way.

# Index